Shorewood – Troy Library
650 Deerwood Drive
Shorewood, IL 60404
815-725-1715

ART IN WORLD HISTORY

Mary Hollingsworth
Art in World History
(Original title: *Wealth and Ideas:
A History of World Art*)

From a project by Francesco Papafava
Iconographic Research by Scala Archives,
Florence

Graphics
Carlo Savona

Drawings
Paolo Capecchi

Maps
Rosanna Rea

Managing editor and art consultant
Gloria Fossi

Italian staff editors for the English edition
*Sara Bettinelli, Franco Barbini,
Lucrezia Galleschi*

Page format
Studio Scriba, Bologna

Editing of the original English text
Emily Ligniti

English translation of original Italian maps,
timelines, and glossary
Julia Weiss

The author wishes to thank many friends
and colleagues, above all John Onians
and Daniele Casalino,
and dedicates the book to the memory
of her grandmother.

Library of Congress Cataloging-in-Publication Data

Hollingsworth, Mary.
Art in world history / Mary Hollingsworth.
p. cm.
Includes index.
ISBN 0-7656-8069-6 (set : alk. paper)
1. Art--History. I. Title.
N5300 .H674 2004
709--dc22   2003015510

ISBN 0-7656-8069-6

Printed and bound in Italy – Giunti Industrie Grafiche S.p.A. (Prato)

The paper used in this publication meets the minimum requirements of
American National Standard for Information Sciences--Permanence
of Paper for Printed Library Materials, ANSI Z 39.48.1984.

(G) (c) 10 9 8 7 6 5 4 3 2 1

ART IN WORLD HISTORY

MARY HOLLINGSWORTH

VOLUME 2

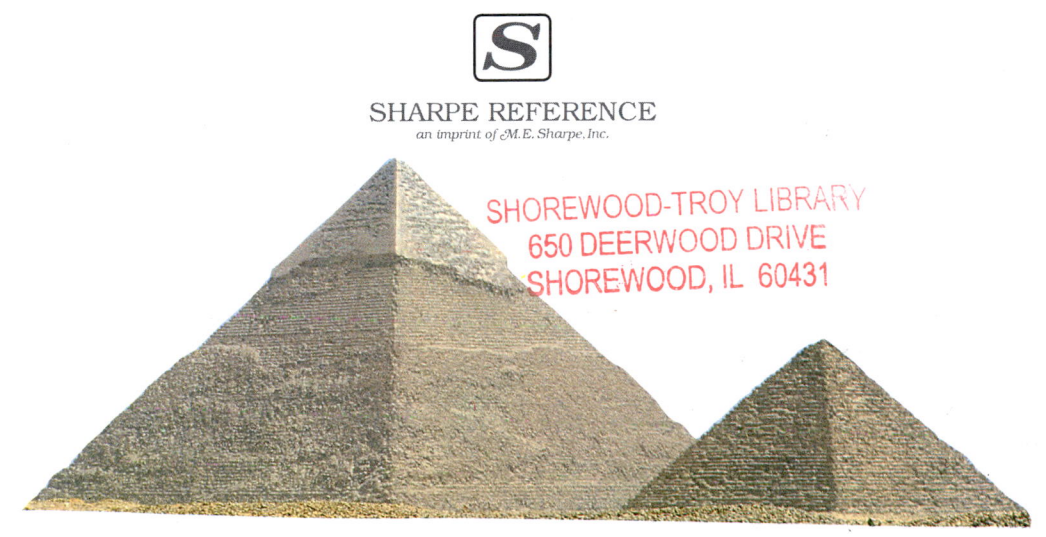

S

SHARPE REFERENCE

an imprint of M.E. Sharpe, Inc.

CONTENTS

● Greece and Rome

**● Religions and Conquests
Between East and West**

18. THE REVIVAL OF THE PAPACY
Art in Medieval Italy
171

● **The Middle Ages: New Horizons**

19. MEDIEVAL REFORM MOVEMENTS
Franciscan and Dominican Art
179

20. ROYAL AND PAPAL COURTS
Gothic as a Decorative Style
189

21. THE RISE OF CIVIC POWER
Art in the Italian City-States
197

22. PERCEPTION AND REALITY
Italian Art in the Fourteenth Century
205

● **The Fifteenth Century**

23. GUILDS AND MERCHANTS IN FLORENCE
The Early Renaissance
213

● The Sixteenth Century

● **The Eighteenth Century**

II.

FROM THE SIXTEENTH
TO THE TWENTIETH CENTURY

THE IMMINENT ARRIVAL OF A NEW
century has often provoked
irrational fears of world destruction.
In late fifteenth-century Christian Europe,
this fear produced a substantial crop
of apocalyptic images. The Bible
provided no few examples of how God
punished materialism, extravagance,
and moral corruption. The preachers
of the time found a ready audience for
their message. In Florence the Dominican
friar Girolamo Savonarola urged people
to burn portraits of finely dressed young
girls, deeming them a contradiction
of the chastity and simplicity of the Virgin.

CHAPTER 30

REFORMATION AND COUNTER-REFORMATION

Religious Images, 1500–1600

Other critics directed their anger at the
proliferation of pagan images in a Christian
context. The works of artists in northern
Europe, especially Germany, expressed
the growing intensity of religious feeling.
In his *Altarpiece* of Isenheim, Mathias
Grünewald emphasized the horrors
of Christ's suffering by the use of color
and through the tortured figure of Christ,
disproportionately larger than the other
figures in the scene. By taking up a practice
that had been common in medieval
art, these artists showed an instinctive
rejection of the rational world of the
Renaissance.

58

1

The Protestant Reformation

The attack on the secularization of religious art was part of a wider condemnation of corruption within the Church. The criticism was not new but gained a special intensity at the beginning of the sixteenth century, particularly in northern Europe, where humanism was used to further theological debate. Among those who took critical positions with respect to the Church hierarchy were Erasmus of Rotterdam (1466–1536), who used his knowledge of Latin and Greek to correct the Latin translation of the Bible (the Vulgate) that had been used throughout the Middle Ages. He also wrote a stinging satire on the extravagances of Julius II and urged reform of abuses within the Church. But it was the practice of selling indulgences to finance the rebuilding of St. Peter's that finally provoked the storm. Indulgences were an established way of obtaining remission of sins through pious acts, such as taking part in the celebrations in Rome during the Holy Year (1450). By 1500, however, it was possible to buy an indulgence for a tiny fraction of the cost of a trip to Rome. When Martin Luther (1483–1546) attacked this and other practices in a list nailed to the church door in Wittenberg (1517), he was expressing a general discontent with the Church establishment that ultimately led to the Protestant Reformation. His list was immediately printed and distributed throughout Europe. The printing press was a powerful tool in the hands of Protestant reformers, giving voice all at once to the movement for institutional reform, the growing intensity of religious feeling, and the desire for a more personal religion without the mediation of priests. Luther's preaching gained him a considerable following and proved enormously fortuitous; Pope Leo X,

2. Luca Signorelli, The Deeds of the Anti-Christ. *Duomo, Orvieto. Fresco. 1500. According to Apocalyptic literature, the coming of the Anti-Christ would be foretold by miracles, atrocities, the appearance of a false prophet, and the desecration of the Temple at the hands of soldiers—all combined in this fresco by the Cortona painter Luca Signorelli (ca. 1445–1523).*

3. Albrecht Dürer, The Four Horsemen of the Apocalypse. *Uffizi, Gabinetto dei Disegni e delle Stampe, Florence. Woodcut. 1498. Albrecht Dürer (1471–1528) wrote that he was "inwardly filled with awful images." His fears are reflected in his series of Apocalyptic prints.*

1. Girolamo da Treviso, Four Evangelists Stoning the Pope. *Royal Collection, Windsor. Panel. Ca. 1536. Presenting Protestant imagery of a powerful kind, this grisaille painting by Girolamo da Treviso (1497–1544) depicts the wrath of the Four Evangelists at the behavior of the pope, shown on the ground with personifications of Greed and Hypocrisy.*

by excommunicating him as a heretic in 1520, formalized the rift in the Catholic Church.

New Attitudes Toward Religious Art

Other reformers like Zwingli and Calvin followed Luther's example, rejecting papal supremacy and responding to the growing desire for a personal religion based on the authority of the Bible. New forms of worship demystified traditional Catholic dogma. Religious reform was extended to politics. Calvin's theocratic government in Geneva, based on civic responsibility and moral rectitude, rigidly suppressed any form of moral laxity, including dancing, theater, and taverns. Following the biblical proscription of idolatry, many Protestants questioned the validity of religious art. Iconoclasts stripped church walls of their medieval decoration and smashed sculptures. As the demand for religious art declined in Protestant countries, many painters sought employment abroad. Patronage concentrated on secular imagery. Portraiture flourished, and other secular themes were developed. Among these were scenes of peasant life, which reflected a growing interest in local traditions in preference to the Italian styles adopted at the Catholic courts of northern Europe (see chapter 31).

Political Upheaval in Italy

The precarious balance of power in fifteenth-century Italy among Milan, Naples, Florence, Venice, and the Papal States fell apart under the onslaught of confident and powerful monarchies in northern Europe, which looked on the small Italian states with greed. For the entire first half of the sixteenth century, Italy was the battleground of Europe, as the rulers of France, Spain, and the Holy Roman Empire fought out

5

7

4. *Mathias Grünewald, Isenheim Altarpiece. Musée d'Unterlinden, Colmar. Panel. Ca. 1510–1515. Intended to inspire inner strength, this altarpiece by the German painter Grünewald (ca. 1480–1528) was painted for a hospital, where the image of Christ's suffering would have had an obvious meaning.*

5. *Lucas Cranach, Martin Luther. Uffizi, Florence. Panel. 1543. A friend of Luther, Lucas Cranach (1472–1553) was court painter to the elector of Saxony.*

6. *Pieter Brueghel the Elder, Peasant Wedding. Kunsthistorisches Museum, Vienna. Panel. 1565. Pieter Brueghel the Elder (ca. 1530–1569) painted many scenes of peasant life, emphasizing the ordinary pleasures of drinking and brawling.*

6

7. *Hieronymous Bosch, The Garden of Earthly Delights. Prado, Madrid. Panel. Ca. 1485. The minutely detailed pictures of Hieronymous Bosch (ca. 1450–1516) were meticulously painted and filled with complex and often hidden images of sin, death, and decay. Although they may look chaotic, they were in fact very carefully worked out.*

The term "Mannerism" generally refers to the styles of architecture, sculpture, and painting that emerged in the 1520s and dominated sixteenth-century European art before the development of the Baroque in the 1590s. The term specifically refers to Italian art of the period. Far from being a homogeneous movement, however, Mannerism reflects a wide variety of styles and attitudes.

The term emerged in the eighteenth century to describe what was seen as the overly stylized, artificial, non-classical art that had replaced the pure classicism of the High Renaissance. But the designation has not always been applied critically. For Vasari, writing in the mid-sixteenth century, *maniera*, or style, was one of the key features that distinguished his contemporaries from earlier artists and that made their art greater. Similarly, modern art historians such as John Shearman (1967) have taken their cue from Vasari and emphasized the "poise, refinement, and sophistication" of the period. Stylistic differences between the High Renaissance and Mannerism are easily recognized. Whereas High Renaissance artists aimed at harmonious and balanced compositions, Mannerist painters and sculptors developed elaborate and contorted poses in asymmetrical compositions. In architecture, the Mannerist style is characterized by the use of classical features assembled in a non-classical way.

Nevertheless, Mannerism today is often understood as a logical extension of the innovations of the Renaissance rather than a rejection of them. Among the many artists, sculptors, and architects associated with the movement are Pontormo, Perino del Vaga, Ammannati, Benvenuto Cellini, Bronzino, Daniele da Volterra, Parmigianino, Giulio Romano, Salviati, and Vasari.

8

8. Pontormo, Joseph in Egypt. National Gallery, London. Panel. 1515–1518. Paintings of the High Renaissance, such as those by Raphael, reflected a tendency toward increased complexity. By contrast, Pontormo (1494–1556) evolved a more contorted style, expressed in the curved staircase and the contrived poses of his figures.

10. Rosso, Deposition. Museo, Volterra. Canvas. 1521. Somber and contorted, this painting by the Florentine artist Rosso (1495–1540) was typical of the new approach to composition and figures developed during the 1520s.

9

9. Giulio Romano, Fall of the Giants. Palazzo Te, Mantua. Fresco. 1530–1532. Trained in High Renaissance Rome, Giulio Romano (ca. 1499–1546) moved to the Gonzaga court at Mantua (1524) to work for Federico II. His designs for both the building and the decoration of Federico's villa, the Palazzo Te, contained many images of the collapse of the old order.

10

their rivalries on its soil. In 1527, Rome was sacked by imperial troops. Political upheaval, the devastation of war, and general instability were all reflected in art. Images such as Giulio Romano's *Fall of Giants* at the Palazzo Te in Mantua made specific references to the physical collapse of the old order. At a stylistic level, harmony and balance were replaced by disorder and complication. Attitudes to antiquity changed as designers rejected the simple straight lines of the Renaissance and found inspiration in different classical models that encouraged novelty and intricacy as an expression of the virtuosity, skill, and imagination of the artist.

Pictorial composition and figural poses became more complex. Increasingly somber and contorted styles reflected the instability of the period. Painters like Correggio explored the potential of illusion for dramatic effect. Others exploited the dramatic contrasts between light and shade. These changes were far from uniform. Modern art critics, in an effort to impart coherence to the diverse aspects of sixteenth-century figurative style, coined the term "Mannerism" as a generic designation. This expression, however, like others devised after the fact to define varied and complex trends in narrow terms, is inherently limited and

has created more problems of interpretation than it has solved. In any event, it is difficult to avoid the conclusion that developments in sixteenth-century European art were a reflection of the radical political and social instability of the times.

Pope Paul III

The election of Paul III (1534–1549) marked the beginning of a major campaign to reassert papal authority and the supremacy of the Catholic faith. The sack of Rome (1527) had left its mark on the city. Paul III began an ambitious program of urban

11

13

12. Correggio, Assumption of the Virgin. *Duomo, Parma. Fresco. Ca. 1525. The use of* sotto in su *perspective, developed by Mantegna in Mantua, was further exploited by Correggio (1498–1534) to give heightened drama to a traditional subject.*

11. Salviati, Visitation. *San Giovanni Decollato, Rome. Fresco. 1538. Elaborate compositions and variety of poses were essential features of the Mannerist style, and Francesco Salviati (1510–1563) exploited them to dramatic effect.*

13. Titian, Paul III. *Museo di Capodimonte, Naples. Canvas. 1543. Arguably the leading portrait painter in sixteenth-century Italy, the Venetian artist Titian (ca. 1490–1576) created a powerful image for this leading figure of the Counter-Reformation.*

renewal, building new streets and replanning the city's defenses. He also restored the dilapidated Roman Capitol. The equestrian statue of Marcus Aurelius was moved from its medieval site outside San Giovanni Laterano, and Michelangelo was commissioned to redesign the square around it. The site of medieval communal government and, more importantly, the religious center of Ancient Rome, the Capitol was converted into an image of papal power. The religious art and architecture commissioned by Paul III and his successors provided further images of that power. Paul III replaced the fifteenth-century fresco of the *Assumption of the Virgin* on the altar wall of the Sistine Chapel with an image more appropriate to the time, the *Last Judgment*. Michelangelo's interpretation of this theme emphasized the emotional anguish of the event rather than the physical horrors highlighted by earlier artists; its somber mood contrasted with the confidence of the ceiling he painted thirty years before. The same emotional intensity characterized his frescoes in Paul III's new chapel, the Cappella Paolina.

The major project undertaken by Paul III and finished by his successors was St. Peter's. Started by Julius II (see chapter 28), this prime image of papal power was still far from completion. Paul III's appointment of Michelangelo as the architect (1546) was a decisive attempt to reverse this situation. Michelangelo's major contribution to St. Peter's was the dome, as he provided solutions to the structural problems that had frustrated his predecessors.

Michelangelo was also responsible for a radical alteration of the ground plan, with a design based on a Greek Cross that revived many elements of Bramante's original project. But centralized plans were impractical for Christian worship.

14

14. Michelangelo, The Conversion of St. Paul. *Cappella Paolina, Vatican. Fresco. 1545–1550. The commission to decorate Paul III's chapel gave Michelangelo (1475– 1564) the opportunity to exploit his talent for dramatic interpretation. In this scene he captures Saul at the moment he realized he was blind.*

15. Michelangelo, Last Judgment. *Sistine Chapel, Vatican. Fresco. 1536–1541. Painted on the altar wall of the prime image of papal authority, Michelangelo's fresco reasserted the awesome power of the Roman Catholic Church.*

15

The religious center of Ancient Rome, the Capitol became the site of Roman government during the Middle Ages and a symbol of its political independence. Pope Paul III and civic representatives made the decision to restore the dilapidated square in 1537, and the ancient equestrian monument of Marcus Aurelius was moved there from its site outside San Giovanni Laterano the following year.

Michelangelo's initial involvement with the project included a new pedestal for the statue and a new ceremonial staircase to provide a triumphal approach to the square. Work stopped during the pontificate of Paul IV (1555–1559) but was restarted by the Medici pope, Pius IV (1559–1565). Michelangelo's plans for the square as a whole were thereby realized. Its unusual trapezium design had precedents in Venice (St. Mark's Square) and Pienza but was determined, ultimately, by the relationship between two existing medieval buildings, the Palazzo Senatorio at the back and the Palazzo dei Conservatori on the right. Michelangelo's design for the latter provided the model for the Palazzo Nuovo on the left (begun ca. 1650). His use of the giant order with distinctive Ionic capitals was an important influence on Baroque architects of the seventeenth century. The square was further embellished by colossal statues of Castor and Pollux (the so-called *Dioscuri*, excavated around 1560) at the top of the staircase and by an elaborate inlaid pattern of travertine marble whose oval form was designed to give unity to the whole. The renovated Capitol reinforced the link between the papacy and the old empire, providing an image of power that has inspired modern architects in their design of monumental urban spaces.

16

17

18

16. *Michelangelo,* Piazza del Campidoglio. *Rome. 1538–1564.*

17. *Michelangelo,* Dome of St. Peter's. *Rome. 1546–1564. Vast and imposing, the dome was a monumental image of papal power as well as a structural and stylistic tour de force.*

18. *Giorgio Vasari,* Side altars in Santa Croce. *Florence. 1565–1571. Uniformity and regularity gave visual expression to the Church's desire to impose order on chaos. Duke Cosimo de' Medici commissioned Vasari (1511–1574) to design these new altars to replace the old medieval ones.*

The axiality embodied in a Latin Cross was considered essential by the more traditional and conservative elements in the Church. Just as Bramante's Greek Cross plan had been altered by his successors, so Michelangelo's plan was adapted to include a proper nave. Once again artistic ideals were compromised to take into account the ideas of the patron.

The Council of Trent

Paul III was the main force behind the Council of Trent (1545–1563), a major turning point in the efforts of the Catholic Church to respond to the Reformation.

To confront the Protestant heresy, he also reorganized the tribunal of Sant'Uffizio, on which the Inquisition depended. In short, the call for reform that had triggered the Protestant Reformation was finally answered. The Council of Trent redefined Church dogma and instituted long-overdue clerical reforms. In response to the Protestant condemnation of religious images as idolatrous, the Council also attempted to redefine the boundaries between sacred and profane images, which had become blurred in the religious art of the fifteenth century. Recognizing the power of art to influence the human spirit, the Council laid down

strict guidelines for both the style and content of religious art. Nudity was banned not only for its pagan overtones but also because it was inappropriate and potentially lascivious. Paul IV (1555–1559), who had been appointed the first Inquisitor General by Paul III, had fig leaves added to the Vatican collection of antique sculpture. Daniele da Volterra was commissioned to paint draperies on Michelangelo's nudes in the *Last Judgment*. Spirituality replaced secularization. Veronese was called before the Inquisition (1573) to explain the inclusion of soldiers, servants, dwarfs, and drunkards in his *Last Supper*, and

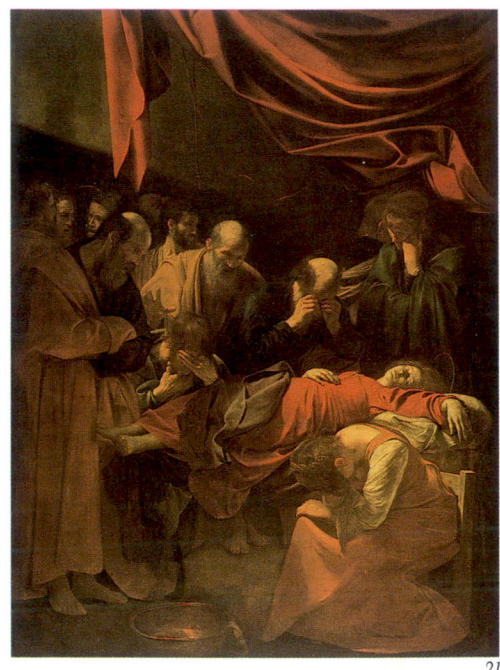

19

21

19. *Veronese,* Feast in the House of Levi. *Accademia, Venice. Canvas. 1573. It was the incidental details in this painting that caused so much trouble with the Inquisition, determined to reinforce strict control over religious images.*

20. *Bronzino,* Martyrdom of St. Lawrence. *St. Lawrence's, Florence. Fresco. 1565–1569. Complicated poses reinforce the drama of this scene of martyrdom by Bronzino (1503–1572), painted for Cosimo de' Medici.*

20

21. *Caravaggio,* Death of the Virgin. *Louvre, Paris. Canvas. 1605–1606. Apparently based on the body of a woman drowned in the Tiber, this interpretation of the Virgin by Caravaggio (1571–1610) was criticized as inappropriate by its patrons, the monks of Santa Maria della Scala in Rome, and they rejected it.*

the work was renamed *Feast in the House of Levi*. Caravaggio was later criticized for his excessively realistic portrayal of the dead Virgin.

Clerical reform was also reinforced by new rules for church design. Centralized planning was rejected in favor of axial plans. This undoubtedly influenced the changes to Michelangelo's designs for St. Peter's. It also contributed to the introduction of oval plans in preference to circular forms, which had been traditional in the Middle Ages for martyria and adopted by Renaissance architects because of their use in the pagan temples of antiquity.

Rood screens across church naves, which had separated the clergy from the laity, were removed to allow closer contact between the priest and his congregation. Private chapels and altars, the traditional arena for the expression of personal wealth, were now to be made uniform and anonymous.

The cleansing of artistic images was echoed in other repressive measures. Pius V (1566–1572) sought to make adultery punishable by death. Indexes of forbidden books were published beginning in 1554, other texts were purged of offensive material, and criticism of the Church was declared heresy.

New Images for the Counter-Reformation

New images developed to reinforce the new Catholic dogma. Martyrs were a particularly popular way of reasserting the power of Christian faith. Earlier images of St. Lawrence had emphasized his role in donating the wealth of the Church to the poor. Bronzino's *Martyrdom of St. Lawrence* gave prominence to the strength of his belief. New images of the Virgin were developed to replace the homely types common in the fourteenth and fifteenth centuries, like the Madonna feeding her child that had been banned by the Council of Trent. New images

24. Giorgio Vasari, St. Bartholomew's Day Massacre. Sala Regia, Vatican. Fresco. 1570s. The triumph of Catholicism over Protestant heresy was a central theme in the decoration of the Sala Regia at the Vatican palace.

23

22. El Greco, Resurrection. Prado, Madrid. Canvas. 1605–1610. Born in Crete, El Greco (1541–1614) earned his nickname after moving to Spain. His highly personalized style reinforced spiritual fervor through elongated figures and dramatic contrasts of light and shade.

23. Federico Barocci, Madonna del Popolo. Uffizi, Florence. Canvas. 1575–1579. Portraying the Virgin as protectress and intercessor, Federico Barocci (ca. 1530–1612) emphasized her heavenly associations.

22

24

reinforced her role as intercessor and protectress; representations of the Immaculate Conception became much more common, although the cult remained controversial. Catholic supremacy was reinforced by anti-Protestant propaganda. The Sala Regia, the audience chamber where the pope received official visitors, was decorated with scenes of temporal rulers submitting to the superior authority of the papacy. And Pius V commissioned paintings of two important Catholic victories, the Battle of Lepanto against the Turks (1571) and the Massacre of the Protestant Huguenots in Paris on St. Bartholomew's Day (August 23–24, 1572).

The Jesuits

The desire for reform within the Church also encouraged the foundation of new religious orders. Foremost among these were St. Ignatius Loyola's Jesuits, approved by Paul III in 1540. Strenuous defenders of the Catholic faith and unquestioning in their obedience to the pope, the Jesuits were a vital instrument in the diffusion of Counter-Reformation ideals. Their new church in Rome, the Gesù—whose construction was paid for by Cardinal Alessandro Farnese, the grandson of Paul III —reflected the reforms in church design

instituted by the Council of Trent. Its huge open interior was undivided by either rood screen or aisles. The idea of a single nave with side chapels was imposed on Vignola, the architect responsible for the project, by its patrons, Cardinal Farnese and the Jesuits themselves. The Gesù established a formula for church design that was to be of central importance to religious architecture in the seventeenth and eighteenth centuries.

25. *Vignola, Gesù. Rome. Begun 1568. Opulent, grand, and spacious, the interior of the prime Jesuit church owed its form to the Counter-Reformation and its decoration to the triumph of Catholicism in the seventeenth century.*

25

26. *Map of Protestant and Catholic Europe:*
a) Catholic;
b) Lutheran;
c) Calvinist;
d) Anglican.

26

BY ABOUT 1500 IT WAS CLEAR THAT THE small independent states of the Italian peninsula were no match for the increasingly powerful monarchies of Europe: France, Spain, the Holy Roman Empire, and England. During the course of the sixteenth century, Italy was invaded repeatedly. Although the Italian states retained varying degrees of independence, political power in Europe now rested north of the Alps. Descending into Italy, the European monarchs came into direct contact with the classical culture of the Italian Renaissance courts. Profoundly affected by what they saw, they adopted these

CHAPTER 31

POWER AND IMAGE

European Courts, 1500–1600

images to express their own power and growing sense of national identity.

Francis I and Italian Culture in France

Under Charles VIII (r. 1483–1498), Louis XII (r. 1498–1515), and Francis I (r. 1515–1547), France saw the consolidation of a powerful centralized monarchy and developed a growing passion for Italian culture. The fashion received a particular boost from Francis I, who adopted it to create an image for his absolute authority. Royal wealth and power were expressed in an ambitious program of art and architecture. Like the

lords of the Italian Renaissance, Francis I added classical and humanist texts to the royal library. He brought some of the leading Italian artists to his court, notably the Florentines Leonardo da Vinci, Andrea del Sarto, Rosso Fiorentino, and Primaticcio; Michelangelo and Titian both declined his invitation. Francis I also bought numerous works by Italian painters, including Leonardo's *Mona Lisa*, and commissioned copies of Michelangelo's sculptures. His collection of statuary included bronze copies cast from molds of famous antique sculptures, such as the *Apollo Belvedere* and the *Laocoön*, brought to France by Primaticcio

at Francis's request. The interior of his new palace at Fontainebleau, near Paris, was decorated with stucco and painted panels in contemporary Italian style. The iconographic program, conceived by Rosso and Primaticcio, was based on historical, mythological, and Christian images intended to reinforce the authority of the French king; among them were various representations of Francis dressed as a Roman emperor, elegantly expressing his conception of power.

The invitation extended by Francis I to another Italian, Sebastiano Serlio (ca. 1540),

had important repercussions in the development of French architecture. Serlio's theories on the classical orders had already had a major effect on building design in Venice (see chapter 29). Now they were an important influence on the design of new royal buildings on the site of the medieval palace of the Louvre. The most decorative of the classical orders, the Corinthian and Composite, were combined with elaborate ornamentation as an expression of French royal wealth and power. But despite its use of Italianate detail, the Louvre was unmistakably French. Images such as Jean Goujon's sculpture of the *Caryatids* were uncommon

3

1. *Rosso Fiorentino,* Galerie de François I. *Fontainebleau. 1533–1540. Designed to house the copies of antique sculptures commissioned by Francis I, this gallery followed the precedents established by collections at the courts of Ferrara, Mantua, and elsewhere in Italy.*

2. *Leonardo da Vinci,* Mona Lisa. Louvre, *Paris. Panel. 1503. Leonardo (1452–1519) spent the last two years of his life in France, where Francis I had assembled a major collection of Italian paintings, including this famous portrait.*

2

3. *Pierre Lescot,* Square Court. Louvre, *Paris. Begun 1546. Classical, elaborate, and decorative, the new royal buildings at the Louvre were strongly influenced by Italian styles of the age.*

4

4. *Andrea del Sarto,* Holy Family. Louvre, *Paris. Canvas. 1515. Sarto (1468–1530) was one of the leading Italian artists attracted to the French court who gave visual expression to Francis I's new power and prestige.*

in Italy and demonstrated the increasing independence from Italian influence. French writers and artists also created a distinctive French culture by imitating the Italian example and using classical models. The great French Renaissance poet Pierre de Ronsard, for example, borrowed his style and ideas from the literature of antiquity to promote the power of the French monarchy. Serlio designed castles in either the French manner or the Italian manner; he was well aware of the existence of a distinctively French style, derived from classical prototypes but characterized by more decorative and complex forms, especially a high-pitched roof. The growing sense of national identity was reflected in Philibert de l'Orme's treatise on architecture (1567), which included designs for a "French order."

Restoration of the Medici

The French invasion of Italy by Charles VIII forced Piero de' Medici to flee from Florence (1494). Thus ended 60 years of de facto control of the city by the Medici family through the manipulation of elected government representatives. In 1530, however, the family was effectively reestablished as the ruling power of Florence through the efforts of two Medici popes, Leo X (1513–1521) and Clement VII (1523–1534), and the support of Holy Roman Emperor Charles V. Medici wealth in the fifteenth century had financed the patronage of art and architecture on an unprecedented scale, creating an image of power that was fully exploited by the second Medici duke, Cosimo I (r. 1537–1574). Like his ancestors, Cosimo was a prolific patron and fully aware of the power of art as propaganda. A series of family portraits by Bronzino established his new status. In the religious realm, in an effort to improve his relationship with the papacy, Cosimo spared no means to institute many

5. *Jean Goujon*, Caryatids. *Louvre, Paris. Ca. 1550. Described by Vitruvius in his treatise* De architectura, *these female figures embodied the new classical image at the French court.*

5

6. *Michelangelo*, Tomb of Giuliano de' Medici, Duke of Nemours. *St. Lawrence's, New Sacristy, Florence. Marble. 1520–1534. Designed by Michelangelo (1475–1564) to complement Brunelleschi's Old Sacristy, the project allowed the designer considerable freedom in his development of unorthodox solutions for architectural and sculptural detail.*

6

7

7. *Bronzino*, Eleonora of Toledo and Her Son. *Uffizi, Florence. Canvas. Ca. 1550. Stylized and austere, the distinctive style of Bronzino (1503–1572) provided an image of wealth and prestige for the wife of Duke Cosimo I.*

Cosimo I de' Medici (1519–1574) came to power in 1537, after the assassination of the first duke, Alessandro. His diplomatic and political skills led to stability at home, and his marriage to Eleonora of Toledo (1539), the daughter of the viceroy of Naples, produced enough children to guarantee succession.

Made grand duke in 1569, Cosimo succeeded in strengthening ties between Florence and the major European rulers by arranging for one of his sons, Francesco I, to marry Joanna, the daughter of Ferdinand I of Hapsburg, and for another, Ferdinando, to be made a cardinal (1565).

Under his leadership, Florence was transformed into a spectacular setting for the new status of the Medici. Its squares were enriched with statues, fountains, triumphal columns, and other trappings of imperial power inspired by Ancient Rome.

In 1565, the Piazza Santa Trinita was decorated with a giant antique granite column taken from the Baths of Caracalla in Rome and given to Cosimo by Pope Pius IV. A new inscription commemorated Cosimo's famous victory over the Sienese at Montemurlo (1538). Above all, the renovation of the Piazza della Signoria gave visual expression to Cosimo's prestige.

This old symbol of Republican power now took on a new meaning. Cosimo commissioned Giorgio Vasari to design a block of government offices (the Uffizi) that effectively extended the square down to the river. One of the many sculptural monuments commissioned for the square, Bartolomeo Ammannati's *Neptune Fountain* alluded to the naval power of the new state. This was also given visual expression in the reconstruction of the port of Portoferraio, renamed Cosmopolis.

8

8. Giorgio Vasari, Uffizi. *Florence. Begun 1560. Linked to the new Medici palace (the old Palazzo Pitti) by a private corridor over the river, these government offices were designed by Giorgio Vasari (1511–1574), who combined classical architectural details in a distinctly nonclassical manner.*

9. Vasari, Brunelleschi Presenting St. Lawrence's to Cosimo il Vecchio. *Palazzo Vecchio, Florence. Fresco. Ca. 1565. Less concerned with historical authenticity, Vasari was intent on promoting the Medici as patrons of the arts and as discerning judges of talent.*

9

10

of the reforms called for by the Council of Trent (see chapter 30). He embarked as well on an ambitious program of public and private works that included fortifications, roads, and government offices on a scale that gave visual emphasis to his new position as the undisputed ruler of Florence. This was reinforced by the transfer of his residence from the old Palazzo Medici to the Palazzo della Signoria (1540), the traditional seat of Florentine government, and his restoration of the surrounding area. The great Giorgio Vasari was commissioned to design an office block to house Cosimo's administration. The square in front of the Palazzo della Signoria, which already contained such monuments of republican Florence as Michelangelo's *David* (1501), was now embellished with more sculpture, including Benvenuto Cellini's *Perseus* and Bartolomeo Ammannati's *Neptune Fountain*. These classically inspired works deliberately reinforced the cultural image of the new regime.

The Medici Legend

The same image was promoted in the redecoration of the interior of the Palazzo della Signoria. Here Cosimo I established the Medici legend. Playing down the family's past as bankers, he celebrated his ancestors as statesmen and, above all, as patrons of the arts. Images like Vasari's *Brunelleschi Presenting St. Lawrence's to Cosimo il Vecchio* were a far cry from the medieval and Renaissance tradition of depicting a patron in the act of dedicating his building to the Virgin. The role played by the early Medici in the development of the Renaissance was also promoted by Vasari's *Lives*, biographies of the most outstanding architects, painters, and sculptors of Italy. Appropriately, Vasari dedicated the work to Cosimo (first edition in 1550, second in 1568). In his eagerness to emphasize the contributions of Florence, Vasari sometimes

10. Benvenuto Cellini, Perseus. *Loggia dei Lanzi, Florence. Bronze. 1545–1554. This work by Cellini (1500–1571) reflected Vasari's emphasis on the importance of style, embodied in effortless elegance, inventiveness, sophistication, and refinement.*

12. Giuseppe Arcimboldi, Summer. *Louvre, Paris. Canvas. 1573. Employed by Ferdinand I at the Hapsburg court in Vienna, and by his successors Maximilian II and Rudolph II, the Italian painter Giuseppe Arcimboldi (1527–1593) developed a talent for creating bizarre portraits composed of fruits, vegetables, and fish; he even depicted the court librarian made out of books. In this work, Arcimboldi used the fruits, flowers, leaves, and vegetables of summer to compose a "portrait" of the season.*

12

11. Bartolomeo Ammannati, The Neptune Fountain. *Piazza della Signoria, Florence. Bronze and marble. 1563–1575. Elaborate and expensive, these classical figures also provided allegorical support for the new Medici regime.*

11

took liberties with the truth, but the image of cultural achievement presented in the *Lives* was so convincingly presented that many of its conclusions have yet to be challenged. The way in which Vasari presented his contemporaries—especially his hero, Michelangelo—reflected current thinking on the supreme importance of style, understood as a combination of inventiveness, sophistication, refinement, and elegance. The very fact of writing the biographies reflected the immense changes that had taken place in the status of the artist throughout Italy since 1500. To safeguard their new prestige, artists joined together in associations modeled after earlier literary academies founded to promote classical learning. One of the first was the Accademia del Disegno in Florence, founded by Vasari and counting among its members Bronzino, Cellini, and Ammannati. These artists remained well aware of the importance of patronage, however, so much so that they invited Cosimo himself to assume the presidency of the academy (1563).

Charles V

When Charles V was elected Holy Roman emperor (1519), he found himself ruler of the largest European empire since the time of Charlemagne. The sole heir to both his grandfathers, King Ferdinand of Spain and the Holy Roman Emperor Maximilian I, Charles also inherited the Netherlands from his father. His dream of a united Christian Europe defeating the Turks was wrecked by the reality of political and religious dissension ravaging Europe. His empire found room to expand west, to America, following the routes discovered by Columbus (1492). The conquest of Mexico by Hernán Cortés (1521) and of the Incas by Francisco Pizarro (1534) brought immense wealth to the Spanish crown (1534). Charles's visit

13

14

13. Titian, Federico Gonzaga. Prado, Madrid. Canvas. Ca. 1525. Titian's reputation as a portrait painter was established throughout Europe, and he obtained commissions from many foreign heads of state.

14. Titian, Charles V. Prado, Madrid. Canvas. 1532. One of a number of portraits of Charles V painted by Titian, this imperial image was the least formal.

15. Palace of Charles V, courtyard. *Granada. Begun 1527. The use of the classical orders, Doric and Ionic, was inspired by High Renaissance architecture in Italy and chosen deliberately to promote the power and prestige of Holy Roman Emperor Charles V.*

15

to the highly cultured Mantuan court of Federico Gonzaga (1532) led directly to his appointment of Titian as his court painter (1533). Titian's portrait of Federico Gonzaga provided the model for the first of a series of imperial portraits. No doubt influenced by Federico, Charles recognized that hiring an artist of high standing itself enhanced the reputation of the patron, who thereby demonstrated that he possessed the wealth to pay for exceptional talent as well as the ability to recognize it. The prestige of Italian art and architecture was already reflected in Charles's palace at Granada, where the use of the classical language of architecture, an entirely new style for Spain, became a prominent symbol of the king's enormous power. Finally worn out by his endeavors, Charles abdicated in 1556, dividing the empire between his brother, Ferdinand I, who succeeded him as Holy Roman emperor, and his son Philip, who inherited Spain and the Netherlands.

Philip II

Philip II (r. 1556–1598), a zealous supporter of the Counter-Reformation, engaged in a strenuous defense of the "true faith" within an empire that he wanted to remain uniformly Catholic; his repressive anti-Protestant policies led to open rebellion in the Netherlands. Philip married Queen Mary of England, who sought to impose Catholicism on her subjects, and he was largely responsible for the first major Christian victory against the Turks at the Battle of Lepanto (1571). But his attempt to mount a Catholic crusade against the Protestant regime of Mary's successor, Elizabeth I, met with disaster (1588). His patronage of the arts focused on the building and decoration of his palace, the Escorial near Madrid, the supreme image of his power and wealth. The Escorial was not simply a palace. Centered on a church filled with relics

16. Juan Battista de Toledo and Juan de Herrera, The Escorial. 1563–1584. Begun by Juan Battista de Toledo (died 1567) and completed by Juan de Herrera (ca. 1530–1597), this monastery-palace was dedicated to St. Lawrence. Its plainness and austerity gave visual expression to Philip II's attitude toward power. He insisted that even his visitors wear black.

17. El Greco, Adoration of the Name of Jesus (the Dream of Philip II). Escorial, Madrid. Canvas. 1579. Giving visual expression to the religious devotion of Philip II, this painting by the Cretan artist El Greco (1541–1614) was done soon after the artist moved to Spain (1575), where his mature, visionary style developed.

16

17

personally acquired by Philip, the complex included a monastery, mausoleum, library, and administrative offices, as well as his private apartments. The project was largely designed by the humanist and mathematician Juan Battista de Toledo and completed by Juan de Herrera. Its classical architectural features created an austere image that reflected the defense of religious and political traditions with which Philip II was by now identified. The interior decoration of the palace reflected his literary and intellectual interests. Although he never visited Italy, his marked preference for Italian artists reflected the high status of Italian art at the courts of

TITIAN'S *POÉSIE*

Perhaps the best-known works of the Venetian painter Titian (ca. 1490–1576) are his mythological paintings, which he called *poésie.* These consist of a "translation" into images of celebrated excerpts from Greco-Roman mythology.

Not popular with patrons in his native city, Titian's *poésie* were essentially painted primarily for two wealthy collectors—Alfonso d'Este, duke of Ferrara (r. 1505–1534), and King Philip II of Spain (r. 1556–1598). It is believed that Philip II commissioned Titian to paint an entire series of paintings inspired by Ovid's *Metamporphoses* just after seeing the Venetian's *Danae* (1553–1554), today housed in the Prado, Madrid.

According to mythology, Danae was one of the many mortals loved by Jupiter. The god visited her in the form of a shower of gold, and the child of their union was Perseus. Titian's nude figure of Danae, idly plucking at the bedsheets, illustrates the artist's skill at rendering the human form and the textures of flesh and velvet, as well as his ability to capture the spirit of the story.

Subtle, harmonious, and poetic, Titian's innovative use of color was a great inspiration to many later artists.

18. *Titian,* Danae and the Shower of Gold. *Prado, Madrid. Canvas. 1553.*

18

19

19. *Titian,* Spain Coming to the Aid of Religion. *Prado, Madrid. Canvas. 1571. The use of classical figures to convey an allegorical meaning was well established in Italy. This particular image gave visual expression to Philip II's role in the Christian victory over the Turks at the Battle of Lepanto (1571).*

Europe. Philip's personal agents toured Italy in search of artists suitable for the decoration of the Escorial. Inside the palace hung his remarkable collection of paintings by old masters, especially the Dutch artist Hieronymus Bosch (see chapter 30). Philip had inherited several of the works, purchased others, and acquired still others through confiscation. He was also an important patron of contemporary painters. Foremost among these was Titian, who, after the death of Charles V, continued to work for the Spanish court. His works included portraits and mythological *poésie* based on stories from Ovid's *Metamorphoses*, allegories of the Catholic victory at Lepanto, and such religious subjects as the *Martyrdom of St. Lawrence*, intended for the high altar of the church in the Escorial. Philip's choice of a scene of martyrdom and Titian's emotional interpretation of it reflected the new subjects and styles inspired by the Counter-Reformation.

England and Religion

Religious issues had a profound effect on patronage by the English monarchy. Henry VIII (r. 1509–1547) wrote a pamphlet that violently attacked the ideas of Luther and was rewarded by the pope with the title "defender of the faith." But when the pope refused to grant him a divorce from Catherine of Aragon, Henry repudiated papal authority and declared himself supreme head of the Church of England. The act not only allowed him to remarry and produce an heir, but it also allowed him to confiscate property of the Catholic Church. The Dissolution of the Monasteries (1536–1539) generated substantial funds, which financed the repair of Henry's palaces and the construction of eight new royal residences, including the ostentatious Nonesuch (now destroyed). Construction of Hampton Court was begun

20

20. *Titian*, Philip II in Armor. *Prado, Madrid. Canvas. 1551. Titian's attention to the effects of light reflected on metal conveyed a sense of dignity despite the nonmilitary bearing of his sitter.*

21. *Titian*, Christ on the Cross. *Escorial, Madrid. Canvas. Before 1574. Bought by Philip II and installed in his private chapel, this awesome image of the crucified Christ emphasized the physical reality of his suffering.*

21

under the guidance of Cardinal Wolsey, who gave the palace to Henry to earn his favor. The gesture did not bring Wolsey the desired results, but the king kept the palace and had it enlarged. Like Francis I, Henry commissioned works that adopted classical and Italianate details, applying them as a decorative veneer to more traditional structures.

Henry VIII was succeeded by his son, Edward VI (r. 1547–1553) and two daughters, Mary (r. 1553–1558) and Elizabeth I (r. 1558–1603). England became Protestant under Edward, only to revert to Catholicism under Mary. Elizabeth, in turn, restored

Protestantism but followed a policy of religious tolerance until Catholics became identified with attempts on her life. Staunchly opposed to European interference in English affairs, Elizabeth rejected every European-inspired image for her court. It is noteworthy as well that her name was not tied to a single work of architectural patronage. She preferred to celebrate the new national festivals she had instituted—especially her Accession Day—with tournaments and theatrical masques. Official portraits of Elizabeth presented an entirely different image from those of the other European monarchs. The atmosphere was formal,

the representation stylized, and her minutely detailed costumes and jewels included symbols and emblems of royal power and prestige. If Elizabeth was not a patron of architecture, however, some of her courtiers built on a grand scale. These were generally men of the middle class who owed their standing at court to Elizabeth's desire to undermine the traditional power of the English nobility. The wealth and prestige acquired by the representatives of this new class of high officials found expression in the construction of splendid residences intended to rival those of the old aristocracy.

22

24. Burghley House. *Northants. 1575 onward. Commissioned by Queen's Chancellor William Cecil, this grandiose expression of power and prestige was typical of the nouveau-riche administrators of Elizabeth's reign.*

24

22. Hampton Court, Base Court. *1531–1536. Decorative and fortified, the building includes only a single reference to the interest in classical culture developing elsewhere in Europe: a set of roundels of Roman emperors on the gateways.*

23. (attrib.) George Gower, Elizabeth I, the Armada Portrait. *Woburn Abbey, Bedford. Panel. Ca. 1588. As in many other official portraits of Queen Elizabeth, this work features a sharp contrast between her highly stylized facial features and the carefully painted details of her clothes and jewels. Its marked divergence from Italian and French styles reinforced her staunchly anti-European policies.*

23

THE ISLAMIC WORLD IN 1200 HAD expanded far beyond its foundation in seventh-century Arabia. The majority of Muslims were now of non-Arab origin, and regional differences were expressed in profound religious and political divisions. The increasing power of the Shi'ite sect, which emphasized devotion to the twelve *imams*, or teachers of Islam, was opposed by the Sunnis, who supported the spiritual descent of the caliphs in Baghdad from the early followers of Mohammed. Local rulers asserted their independence from the caliphs, and the old Arab Empire broke apart. While retaining spiritual authority over all Sunnis, the caliphs

CHAPTER 32

TURKS, MONGOLS, AND ISLAM

Art at the Muslim Courts

in 1055 were forced to cede political supremacy to the Seljuks, descendants of central Asian Turks who had settled in Iran. Within the context of Islam, national cultures thus began to emerge. In Iran, a wealthy and civilized court encouraged scientific and literary talents, such as the astronomer-poet Omar Khayyam. Iran's new power was reflected in the development of Persian as a literary language, epitomized by Firdawsi's *Shah-nama*, an epic history of Iranian heroes. Persian influence spread throughout the Seljuk Empire. The growth of secular culture was expressed in architectural types new to Islam, including the mausoleum, a personal

1

memorial of temporal power. The presence of religious dissension was reflected in the appearance of the *madrasa*, a school for teaching Sunni orthodoxy, which soon became an integral part of Seljuk mosque complexes. The Seljuk Empire was weakened by Crusader conquests in the Near East (see chapter 16) and was dealt a decisive blow by the invasion of the Mongols and their capture of Baghdad (1258).

The Mongols

The Mongol migration from Central Asia under Genghis Khan (ca. 1167–1227) was dramatic. After conquering China, where they ruled as the Yan Dynasty (see chapter 14), the Mongols moved into Russia, Europe, and then the Islamic world. Defeated by the Mamluks (1260), they retreated into Iran, where they established the Il-Khan Dynasty (1256–1370). The Mongols were hardly the destructive savages commonly depicted in Western culture. With no native tradition of monumental architecture, they nevertheless recognized its value as propaganda, and in both China and Iran they promptly adopted indigenous cultural traditions. After their conversion to Islam (1295), the Il-Khans became active architectural patrons, building mosques, *madrasas*, and tombs on a scale that reflected their new power. Through contact with China, a new series of motifs, including lotus flowers, dragons, and birds, began to appear in Islamic decoration.

Mamluk Art and Architecture

The Mamluks took control of Egypt and Syria after halting the Christian invasion of Egypt by King Louis XI of France (1250) and defeating the Mongol armies (1260). As slaves who had obtained their freedom through

1. Carpet. Museo Poldi-Pezzoli, Milan. Sixteenth century. Woven in state factories, the elaborate patterns of Persian carpets were an important element in the decoration of both religious and secular buildings.

2. The Tomb of Zubayda. Baghdad. Ca. 1152. Under Seljuk influence, the mausoleum developed from a square body crowned by a dome to more elaborate forms.

3. Mosque of Sultan Hasan. Cairo. Begun 1356. Combining elements of the Fatimid tradition in Egypt with Seljuk influence from the East, the Mamluks developed a distinctive architectural style.

4. Minaret, Suq al-Ghaz. Baghdad. Twelfth century. The tradition of ornamental brickwork spread from Iran under Seljuk influence throughout their empire.

military service, the Mamluks remained true to their origins in running the empire, rejecting hereditary succession and restricting high military and civilian offices to an elite of specially trained slaves. The remarkable system survived until the Ottoman conquest (1517). Mamluk wealth was based on trade; this was reflected in the extravagance of their metalware, inlaid with silver calligraphy and enameled glass. Noted for their cultural conservatism, the Mamluks continued the traditions established by the Seljuks. Their rulers commissioned mosques, *madrasas*, and tombs. Their refusal to use firearms was the principal cause of their downfall against the superior fighting power of the Ottomans.

The Rise of the Ottomans

The Mongol retreat into Iran had left a vacuum in Anatolia. The Byzantine Empire was too weak to seize the opportunity for expansion, and the area became populated by various Turkish tribes. By the fourteenth century, the Ottomans had emerged as leaders and proceeded to conquer both the Byzantine and the Mamluk Empires before moving into Eastern Europe. By establishing their capital at Constantinople (captured 1453) and renaming it Istanbul, the Ottomans reinforced their conquest of Byzantium and new position as the dominant power in the eastern Mediterranean.

In the highly centralized Ottoman state, standards in art and architecture were established by the imperial court. Before the conquest of Constantinople, Ottoman architecture had generally followed the Seljuk example. The prestige of the new Islamic regime now was expressed in the adoption of old Christian architecture. Justinian's Hagia Sophia (532 C.E.; see chapter 9) was converted into a mosque by the simple expedients of replacing

5

6

5. Mosque lamp. *Victoria & Albert Museum, London. Enamel on glass. 1356–1363. Made for the Mamluk Sultan Baybars II, this lamp features elaborate calligraphic renderings of passages from the Koran as well as a dedication.*

6. Suleyman Besieging Belgrade (1543). *Topkapi Museum, Istanbul. TKS.H.1517, from the manuscript* The Name of Suleyman, *by Ali Amir Bea Sirvani. 1558. Minute attention to detail and the use of rich colors recorded Suleyman's invasions of Christian Europe.*

Christian imagery with Islamic decoration and adding minarets.

Suleyman the Great

The Ottoman Empire nearly doubled in size under the rule of Suleyman (r. 1520–1566), who was able to exploit the political and religious divisions in Europe. Suleyman was an important patron of the arts, and his court at Istanbul outclassed those of his European contemporaries in refinement, scale, and magnificence. European ambassadors were duly impressed by the show of wealth and power at his palaces. Suleyman's major architectural projects were designed by his court architect, Sinan, who was appointed (1539) after a brilliant military career in the imperial army. The Suleymaniye Mosque (1550–1557), the preeminent image of Suleyman's power, was a direct imitation of the Hagia Sofia, the architectural symbol of the old Christian Empire, and established a model that was copied in cities throughout his empire. As befitted an Islamic ruler, Suleyman's mosque was part of a larger complex that included a school, hospitals for both teaching and treatment, and a soup kitchen. Conquest had stimulated trade and a taste for luxury, and Suleyman amassed a vast collection of Renaissance statuary, manuscripts, and clocks. Under imperial patronage, factories produced fine silks, brocades, and ceramics; the use of tile to decorate the interiors of mosques and palaces stimulated their manufacture at Iznik. Under Suleyman, the prevailing taste for blue and white gave way to a preference for multicolored wares, reflecting the increasing extravagance of the court. Although the Ottoman Empire began to decline in the seventeenth century, it survived until the aftermath of World War I, when it was formally dismantled.

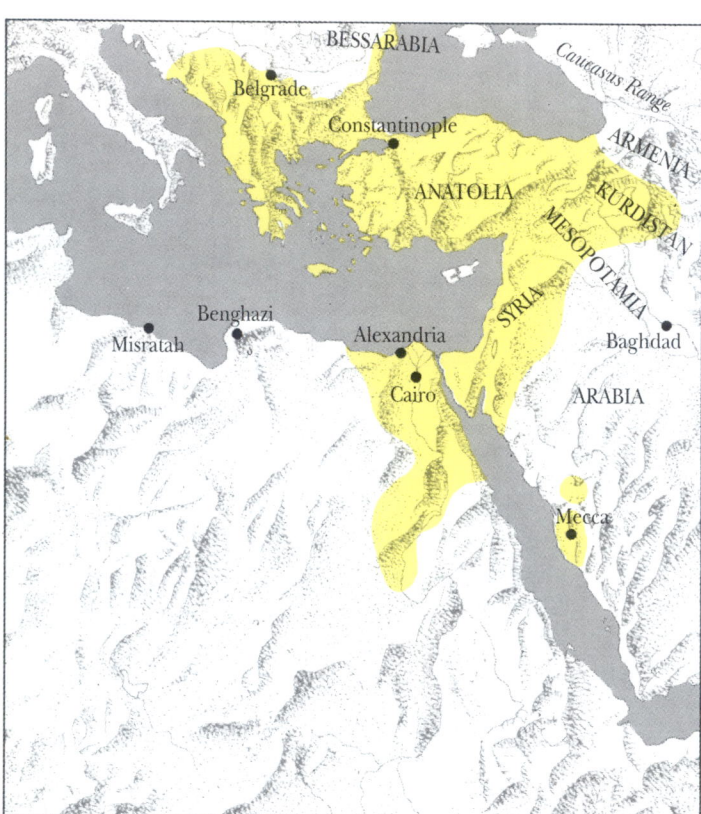

7. *Map of the Ottoman Empire.*

8. *Sinan,* Mosque of Sultan Selim II. *Edirne. 1570–1574. Built for Suleyman's son and successor, this mosque followed the pattern established by his father in Istanbul.*

Tamerlane and the Timurid Empire

In the East, the Mongol Il-Khans were conquered by another Turkish tribe, led by Tamerlane, who established the Timurid Empire in Central Asia. His military conquest (1370–1405) was followed by an extensive building program to reinforce the new regime. Tamerlane concentrated his efforts on the capital of Samarkand; his successors embellished other cities in the empire, building mosques, palaces, and tombs on a grand scale. The wealth and power of the new rulers were also expressed by the extension of tile decoration,

Herat became the capital of the Timurid Empire after Tamerlane's death. His son and successor, Shah Rukh (r. 1405–1447), moved the court there and established a manuscript workshop attached to his palace.

The distinctive Herat style of illumination emerged in the late fifteenth century, above all in the works of Bihzad of Herat. Developing an interest in the pictorial representation of space, the artists

THE HERAT SCHOOL OF MINIATURES

used horizontal divisions to establish a series of receding planes that culminated in a high horizon. Figures, architecture, and especially landscape were used to reinforce the spatial progression.

Despite the stylization of facial features, the human figure was presented in a variety of poses and minutely detailed clothing. Build-

ings, trees, flowers, and birds painted in rich colors emphasized the reality of the scenes. After the capture of the city by Shah Isma'il, many of the Herat painters were forced to move to the Safavid capital, Tabriz.

Bihzad was made director of the new manuscript workshop, and the increasing elaboration, detail, and richness of the Herat style provided images of prestige for the new dynasty.

11. *Sinan,* Suleymaniye Mosque. *Istanbul. 1550–1557. As court architect to Suleyman, Sinan (1489–1578/1588) developed a new format for the Islamic mosque based on the Christian architecture of buildings like Justinian's Hagia Sophia.*

12. Mausoleum of Timur (the Gur Emir). *Samarkand. 1403–1405. Immense brick structures decorated with ceramic tiles reinforced the power and prestige of the Timurid Empire.*

13. Miniature. *Topkapi Museum, Istanbul. Album 2160. Late fifteenth or early sixteenth century.*

9. Penbox. *Topkapi Museum, Istanbul. Sixteenth century. The use of porcelain, gold, rubies, and other precious stones reflected the immense wealth of the Ottoman court.*

10. Astrolabe. *Victoria and Albert Museum, London. Brass. 1666. Elaborately decorated, these scientific instruments were developed to show planetary movements and establish the correct hours for prayer.*

13

12

14

14. Blue Mosque. *Tabriz. Begun 1465. Adopting the brick construction techniques of central Asia, Timurid architects exploited the potential of pointed arches, squinches, and pendentives to create monumental scale.*

which now completely covered the brick structures. As in the case of other Islamic cultures, the decorative arts produced for the Timurid rulers responded to a desire for the opulent display of wealth. Textiles were woven with gold and silver thread; ceramic factories attempted to reproduce the traditional blue-and-white porcelain of China. Figurative art, banned in religious buildings and books, flourished in a secular context. The miniaturists of the period, among them Bihzad of Herat, continued the Persian tradition of recording and illustrating the deeds of their rulers in highly detailed paintings that reflected the love of luxury at the Timurid courts.

The Safavid Dynasty in Iran

The conquests of Shah Isma'il Safavi established the Safavid Dynasty as rulers of Iran (1502–1730). This Shi'ite Empire, which blocked the eastward expansion of the Ottomans, promoted an image of nationalist revival. The works of the old Persian poets were extensively copied, which stimulated the development of modern religious and secular literature. The royal library at Tabriz hired miniaturist painters for the lavish illustration of these manuscripts. State factories produced traditional Persian carpets on a grand scale. Jugs and ewers, an essential feature of the interior decoration of royal palaces, imitated Chinese blue-and-white porcelain.

The reorganization of the state under Shah Abbas I (r. 1587–1629) was reinforced by the construction of his new capital at Isfahan, centered on a huge square, the Maidan. The square was surrounded by several buildings, including the royal palaces, but its axis focused on the enormous Masjid-i-Shah Mosque. The importance of the mosque was further expressed in its elaborate and extensive tile decoration.

15. Page from the *Baburnama. Museum, New Delhi. Late sixteenth century. Importing Persian manuscript illuminators to their Mughal Empire, Babur and Akbar were responsible for new stylistic influences on local Hindu artists.*

16. Maidan-i-Shah. *Isfahan. Begun ca. 1600. This enormous square, designed as an image of power for the Safavid emperor Shah Abbas, covered more than 20 acres.*

17. Ali Kapu Palace. *Isfahan. Ca. 1598. Designed as part of the Maidan-i-Shah complex, this royal pavilion was located opposite the smaller of two mosques that dominated the enormous square.*

15

18. Fatehpur Sikri, *entrance gateway. Begun 1571. Laid out informally with none of the grand vistas and rigid organization of Islamic cities like Isfahan, Akbar's Fatehpur Sikri reflected his pragmatic attitude to government. But the project was too ambitious. Residents had to carry water into the city, and the project was abandoned after his death.*

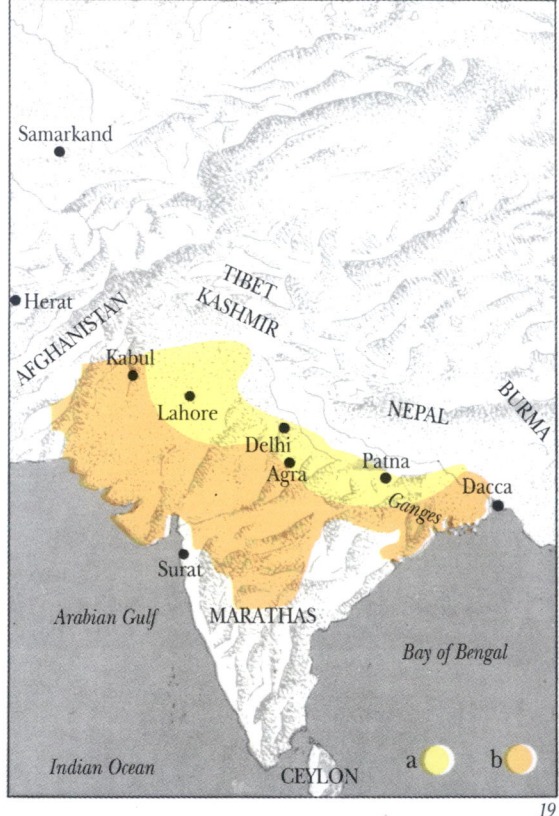

19

16

17

18

Mughal Rulers in India

Arab merchants had long been aware of the wealth to be acquired in India, and successive Muslim invasions finally established an Islamic kingdom in northern India during the thirteenth century. Muslim rulers imposed their own culture, building mosques, palaces, and tombs in the style of Islamic countries that had little in common with local traditions. The foundation of the Mughal Empire by Babur (r. 1526–1530) and its expansion under his grandson, Akbar (r. 1556–1605), began a new phase in the development of an Indo-Islamic culture. Babur and Akbar introduced the luxury and refinement of the Persian court to India. But far from imposing Muslim culture on his Hindu subjects, Akbar showed unusual interest in their traditions, so much so that one of his closest friends was a Hindu musician. Akbar commissioned manuscripts of Indian literature and established a painting school where Hindu artists were taught by Persian masters. The pointed arches and domes of the buildings in his new capital, Fatehpur Sikri, were recognizably Persian, but tile decoration on important buildings was replaced by local sandstone and marble inlay. Akbar's successors continued this pattern of tolerance. A portrait of his son, Jahangir (r. 1605–1627), emphasized the latter's Islamic faith but also included distinctly European motifs, such as *putti*, and even a portrait of James I of England. Jahangir recognized the value of trade links with Europe and signed an agreement with the English East India Company (1618). His son, Shah Jahan (1628–1658), was responsible for building the Taj Mahal. A mausoleum for his wife, Mumtaz Mahal, the monument was built of rubble and completely faced with marble, inlaid with a wealth of decorative detail and inscriptions. Scale, craftsmanship, and materials were combined to create one of the most enduring images of Mughal rule.

20

21

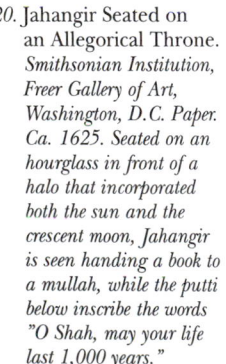

22

19. *Map of the Moghul Empire in India:*
   a) *under Babur (r. 1526–1530);*
   b) *expansion under Akbar (r. 1556–1605).*

20. Jahangir Seated on an Allegorical Throne. *Smithsonian Institution, Freer Gallery of Art, Washington, D.C. Paper. Ca. 1625. Seated on an hourglass in front of a halo that incorporated both the sun and the crescent moon, Jahangir is seen handing a book to a mullah, while the putti below inscribe the words "O Shah, may your life last 1,000 years."*

21. and 22. Taj Mahal. *Agra. Completed 1653. Elegant and extravagant, the polygonal plan and dome of this mausoleum derived from earlier Islamic tradition. Black stone inlay in the pure white marble included decorative patterns as well as Koranic inscriptions.*

THE SEVENTEENTH CENTURY

Various trends characterized art in seventeenth-century Europe, which is considered the Baroque era (and that even spread to the Spanish colonies in the New World).

In Italy, key figures at the dawn of the century were Carracci and Guido Reni from Emilia and Caravaggio, who was trained in Lombardy and then moved to Rome. A tormented soul, Caravaggio moved around various cities in central-southern Italy and was the protagonist in a shift that would even influence foreign artists (which today are grouped under the label "Caravaggesque"), who to varying degrees were aware of a new luminosity in painting. In architecture and sculpture the dominant figures of the Roman Baroque were Aderno, Borromini, and Bernini. In addition to his wealthy private clients, Bernini worked primarily for the Popes Urban VIII, Innocent X, and Alexander VII. Even the new religious orders, established in the wake of the Counter-Reformation, played a fundamental role in the development of Baroque art. As different ways of interpreting the landscape (classic, such as the style of Poussin, or sensitive to weather and light, like Rubens) were evolving throughout Europe, in Holland, Spain, France, Italy, and in the German states, a new style developed in portraiture. The great artists were traveling more frequently and working at various European courts. This era was characterized by artworks created for the wealthy bourgeois classes, as well as for the lavish and aristocratic circles such as the Stuarts in England and Louis XIV in France.

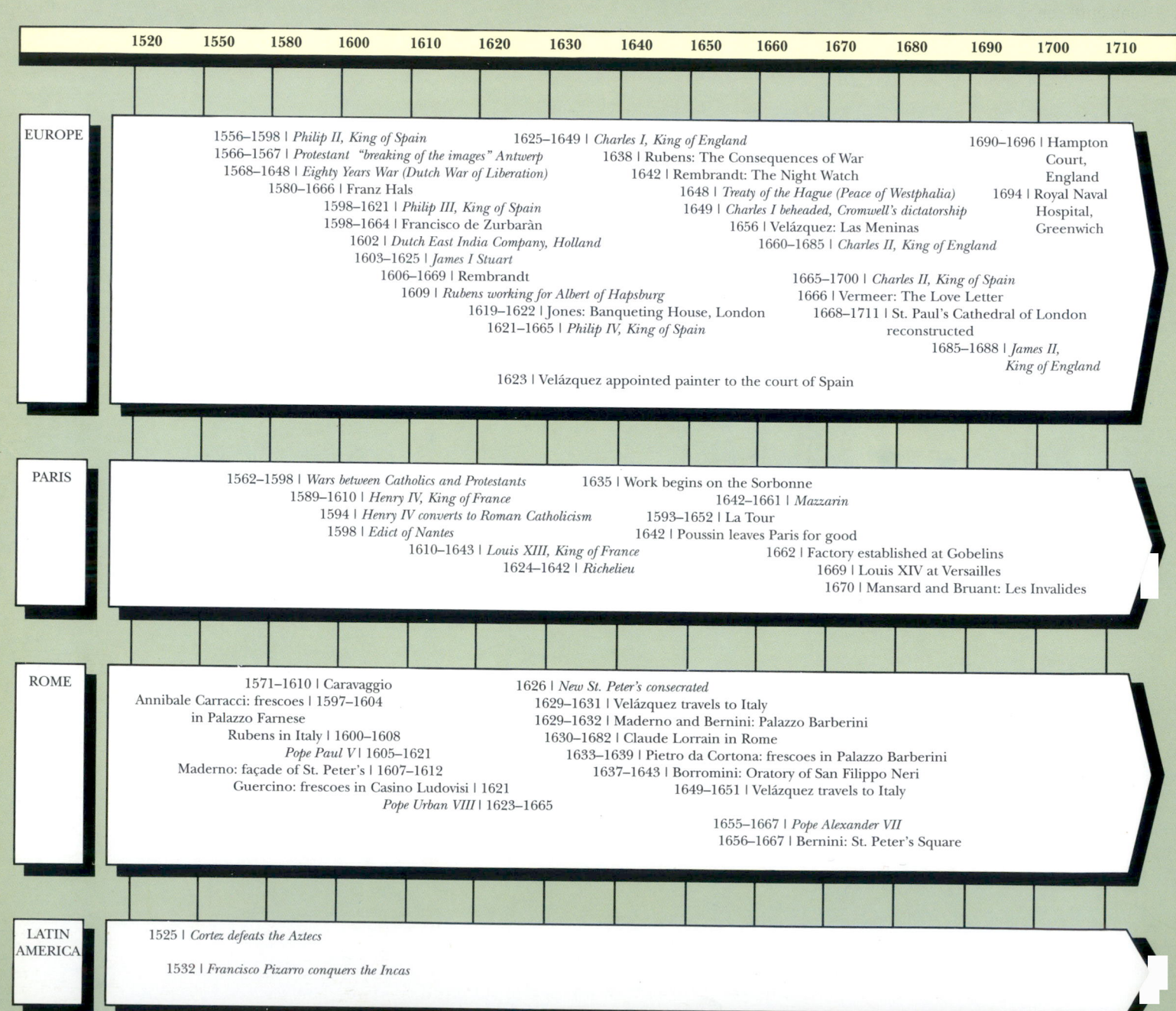

	1520	1550	1580	1600	1610	1620	1630	1640	1650	1660	1670	1680	1690	1700	1710

EUROPE

1556–1598 | *Philip II, King of Spain*
1566–1567 | *Protestant "breaking of the images" Antwerp*
1568–1648 | *Eighty Years War (Dutch War of Liberation)*
1580–1666 | Franz Hals
1598–1621 | *Philip III, King of Spain*
1598–1664 | Francisco de Zurbaràn
1602 | *Dutch East India Company, Holland*
1603–1625 | *James I Stuart*
1606–1669 | Rembrandt
1609 | *Rubens working for Albert of Hapsburg*
1619–1622 | Jones: Banqueting House, London
1621–1665 | *Philip IV, King of Spain*

1625–1649 | *Charles I, King of England*
1638 | Rubens: The Consequences of War
1642 | Rembrandt: The Night Watch
1648 | *Treaty of the Hague (Peace of Westphalia)*
1649 | *Charles I beheaded, Cromwell's dictatorship*
1656 | Velázquez: Las Meninas
1660–1685 | *Charles II, King of England*
1665–1700 | *Charles II, King of Spain*
1666 | Vermeer: The Love Letter
1668–1711 | St. Paul's Cathedral of London reconstructed
1685–1688 | *James II, King of England*

1690–1696 | Hampton Court, England
1694 | Royal Naval Hospital, Greenwich

1623 | Velázquez appointed painter to the court of Spain

PARIS

1562–1598 | *Wars between Catholics and Protestants*
1589–1610 | *Henry IV, King of France*
1594 | *Henry IV converts to Roman Catholicism*
1598 | *Edict of Nantes*
1610–1643 | *Louis XIII, King of France*
1624–1642 | *Richelieu*

1635 | Work begins on the Sorbonne
1642–1661 | *Mazzarin*
1593–1652 | La Tour
1642 | Poussin leaves Paris for good
1662 | Factory established at Gobelins
1669 | Louis XIV at Versailles
1670 | Mansard and Bruant: Les Invalides

ROME

1571–1610 | Caravaggio
Annibale Carracci: frescoes | 1597–1604 in Palazzo Farnese
Rubens in Italy | 1600–1608
Pope Paul V | 1605–1621
Maderno: façade of St. Peter's | 1607–1612
Guercino: frescoes in Casino Ludovisi | 1621
Pope Urban VIII | 1623–1665

1626 | *New St. Peter's consecrated*
1629–1631 | Velázquez travels to Italy
1629–1632 | Maderno and Bernini: Palazzo Barberini
1630–1682 | Claude Lorrain in Rome
1633–1639 | Pietro da Cortona: frescoes in Palazzo Barberini
1637–1643 | Borromini: Oratory of San Filippo Neri
1649–1651 | Velázquez travels to Italy
1655–1667 | *Pope Alexander VII*
1656–1667 | Bernini: St. Peter's Square

LATIN AMERICA

1525 | *Cortez defeats the Aztecs*
1532 | *Francisco Pizarro conquers the Incas*

THE CATHOLIC CHURCH HAD SURVIVED the religious upheaval and insecurity of the sixteenth century, and by the year 1600 the austerity of the Counter-Reformation had given way to a new spirit of confidence. Ostentatious display proclaimed the revived power of Rome, as the patronage of seventeenth-century popes and cardinals reached unprecedented heights. Visually dramatic and often described as anticlassical, Baroque art and architecture in fact owed much to the luxury and opulence of Imperial Rome. Wealth and power were expressed in excess and extravagance. The style created in seventeenth-century Rome was a vehicle

CHAPTER 33

THE TRIUMPH OF CATHOLICISM

Rome and Baroque Art

for spreading the word of religious faith and the temporal power of the Church. The Baroque was deliberately overwhelming in its scale, combination of materials, and use of illusion and drama.

St. Peter's: Urban VIII and Bernini

The new St. Peter's was finally consecrated in 1626. The intermittent progress of construction, begun under Pope Julius II (1503–1513), reflected the changes in fortune and ideas that took place during the course of the sixteenth century (see chapters 28 and 30). The façade and nave had been

1

completed by Pope Paul V (1605–1621), whose name was prominently inscribed in the frieze. The election of the Florentine Maffeo Barberini as Pope Urban VIII (1623–1644) and his patronage of Gian Lorenzo Bernini opened a new era of papal extravagance. One of Bernini's first projects was the vast *baldacchino* over the supposed tomb of St. Peter, the focal point of the basilica's interior. Reinterpreting the form of a medieval *ciborium*, Bernini supported his canopy on twisted columns inspired by descriptions of Solomon's temple in Jerusalem. The decoration, however, was dominated by references to Urban VIII himself. The leaves, for example, were not

of the vine—a traditional symbol of Christ— but of laurel, an emblem of the Barberini family, like the ubiquitous bees. Bernini was also put in charge of the design of altars placed in each of the four giant piers supporting the dome and that would house the church's most important relics: the lance of Longinus, the veil of Veronica, the head of St. Andrew, and a fragment of the True Cross. But the greatest expression of Urban's desire for self-glorification was his tomb, commissioned from Bernini and placed in a prominent position as part the pope's decorative scheme. The grandiose scale of the tomb and the opulence of its materials

reinforced both Urban's prestige and that of the papacy. Here the Baroque tendency to catch the moment of drama was given a macabre twist: Death, flanked by Justice and Charity, has just finished writing Urban's name on his scroll.

St. Peter's: Alexander VII and Bernini

Urban's successor, Innocent X (1644–1655), concentrated his energies elsewhere (see below). The next pope, Alexander VII (1655–1667), continued the embellishment of St. Peter's as well as the employment of Bernini. Bernini's *Cathedra Petri* (Throne of Peter)

1. *Andrea Pozzo,* Triumph of St. Ignatius of Loyola. *St. Ignatius's, Rome. Fresco. 1691–1694. Drama and illusion in a religious context reinforced the spiritual power of the founder of the Jesuit Order in this fresco by Andrea Pozzo (1642–1709).*

4. *Bernini,* Baldacchino. *St. Peter's, Vatican. Bronze. 1624–1633. The bronze for this monument was taken from the Pantheon and inspired the epigram* "Quod non fecerunt barbari, fecerunt Barberini" *("What the barbarians did not do, was done by the Barberini").*

2. *Carlo Maderno,* St. Peter's, façade. *Rome. 1607–1612. The giant Corinthian order reinforced the impression of scale, essential to this prime image of the Roman Catholic faith.*

3. *Bernini,* St. Peter's Square. *Rome. Begun 1656. The arms of the Mother Church were given visual expression in Bernini's giant curved colonnades embracing the square in front of St. Peter's.*

is arguably the ultimate expression of the triumph of Catholicism. In this elaborate monument, located in a dominant position at the center of the apse, bronze, marble, gilt, stucco, and light join together in a dramatic statement of the Petrine tradition. Its centerpiece is St. Peter's modest wooden seat, encased in bronze and supported by four doctors of the Church. On the chair, Christ hands St. Peter the keys of the Church, as the *putti* above carry the papal tiara and key. The effect was overwhelming, its message of papal primacy impossible to misunderstand.

Alexander VII also commissioned Bernini to give visual unity to the area in front of

St. Peter's. Typically Baroque, the piazza was likewise designed for maximum visual and symbolic effect. Bounded by two sweeping semicircular colonnades, representing the open arms of the Church, the square was perfectly suited for the throngs of pilgrims that gathered on Easter and other occasions for the traditional papal blessing. The scale of the piazza is fully appreciated in the context of seventeenth-century Rome: the original

contrast between the narrow streets and the huge square was lost with the building of the Via della Conciliazione.

Innocent X and the Piazza Navona

The election to the papacy of Giambattista Pamphili, who took the name Innocent X, was a deliberate reaction to the extravagances of Urban VIII; this was reflected in his patronage. Instead of continuing the embellishment of St. Peter's, Innocent chose to concentrate on San Giovanni Laterano, the traditional seat of the pope in his role as bishop of Rome. At first he avoided hiring

5. Bernini, Cathedra Petri. St. Peter's, Vatican. Bronze, marble, and stucco. 1656–1666. Three-dimensional figures on Earth and a carved relief in heaven reinforced the difference between the two states; the oval window emphasized direction.

6. Bernini, St. Longinus. St. Peter's, Vatican. Marble. 1629–1640. Gian Lorenzo Bernini (1598–1680) established his reputation as a sculptor through his work for Urban VIII at St. Peter's.

7. Bernini, Tomb of Urban VIII. St. Peter's, Vatican. Bronze and marble. 1628–1647. Extravagant and dramatic, Bernini's inclusion of the Barberini bees—as if wandering over the monument— reinforced the identity of the patron.

6

7

5

Bernini, commissioning another architect, Borromini, to remodel the church's interior (1647–1649); the medieval frescoes were stripped away and replaced with more up-to-date decoration. Innocent's major project was the renovation of the Piazza Navona. The site of his family palace and the ancient Stadium of Domitian, the square held great potential for an image of Pamphili power. In addition to enlarging the palace, Innocent commissioned a new church, St. Agnes's. Borromini's façade, with its complex interplay of convex and concave forms, was typical of the Baroque desire to overwhelm. Bernini was finally hired to sculpt the square's two large fountains.

The Cornaro Chapel

Urban VIII's patronage had made Bernini the leading artistic figure in Rome, but Innocent X's desire to avoid every association with the Barberini left the architect and sculptor free to accept private commissions. The Cornaro Chapel in Rome's Santa Maria della Vittoria was designed for the Venetian Cardinal Federico Cornaro as his burial place and dedicated to St. Teresa, one of the new Counter-Reformation saints. Architecture, sculpture, and painting fused into a unified whole. The combination of gilt, stucco, and multicolored marbles was overwhelmingly

extravagant. On the walls of the chapel, Bernini painted illusionary balconies on which were found depictions of Federico and other members of the Cornaro family who had achieved greatness: Federico's father, who had been doge of Venice, and six cardinals. The central element of the pictorial decoration, however, was the sculpted figure of St. Teresa (with an angel), depicted at the moment so vividly described in her writings when an arrow seemed to pierce her heart and fill her with the intense pain and pleasure of the love of God. The combination of rich and varied materials, movement, drama, illusion, and skill made this one of the outstanding

9. *Francesco Borromini,* St. Agnes's in Piazza Navona, façade. *Rome. 1653–1657. The exploitation by Borromini (1599–1667) of the expressive potential of concave and convex curves over the façade of this church was typically Baroque.*

8. *Diego Velázquez,* Pope Innocent X. *Galleria Doria-Pamphili, Rome. Canvas. 1650. The Spanish court painter Velázquez (1599–1660) traveled to Italy on official business for the king, taking up the commission to paint Innocent X's portrait and using the opportunity to study Italian painting.*

10. *Bernini,* Four Rivers Fountain. *Piazza Navona, Rome. Marble. 1648–1651. Despite Innocent X's earlier opposition to Bernini, he commissioned two fountains from the sculptor for his renewal of the Piazza Navona. This one included personifications of the rivers of four continents: the Nile, Ganges, Danube, and Rio de la Plata.*

Bernini's marble statue of the vision of St. Teresa (1645–1652) remains one of the most powerful evocations of triumphant Catholicism and Baroque Rome.

A great mystic and strict disciplinarian who instituted rigorous monastic reforms in the Carmelite order to which she belonged, St. Teresa (1515–1582) founded the Discalced, or barefoot, Carmelite order in Spain. She recorded her spiritual experiences, including the occasion when her heart was pierced by the arrow of divine love, made famous by Bernini's statue.

The sculptor displays his exceptional talent by idealizing the beauty of the saint in ecstasy while, at the same time, conveying the reality of the religious experience. It is difficult to believe that the fluttering draperies of the angel or the rumpled clothes of the saint are made of stone. Exquisitely carved and highly finished, the expressions on their faces clearly describe the emotions and feelings of both figures, above all the physical pain and spiritual joy of the saint. Bernini created a dramatic environment for this heavenly vision, deliberately contrasting the white marble of the sculpted figures with red and green porphyry of its architectural setting and the gilded bronze rays and stucco clouds above. Like the sets he designed for the theatrical spectaculars that were such an important element in the entertainment devised for the papal court, its illusionism was dramatic. In typical Baroque fashion, Bernini depicted the event at the moment of maximum intensity and encouraged observers to participate in its reality. His fusion of sculpture and architecture and his extraordinary ability in re-creating magnificent effects with light is quite evident in this particular masterpiece.

THE TRIUMPH OF CATHOLICISM

11

11. *Bernini,* Cornaro Chapel. *Santa Maria della Vittoria, Rome. 1645–1652.*

12. *Bernini,* Ecstasy of St. Teresa. *Santa Maria della Vittoria, Cornaro Chapel, Rome. Marble. 1645–1652.*

12

examples of Baroque art. Bernini's ability to make an extraordinary spiritual experience wholly plausible reflected not only his own devout Catholicism but the religious fervor that swept Rome in the seventeenth century.

The Baroque in Secular Art

Baroque art was not restricted to religious projects. Bernini's talent for verisimilitude was exploited in portraiture as well. His bust of Cardinal Scipione Borghese, the nephew of Paul V, showed the sitter with his mouth slightly open as if caught in conversation. Bernini also became

known for his superb antique forgeries. Classical models inspired a series of statues commissioned by Scipione Borghese to add to the outstanding collection of old masters and antique statues that decorated his villa. Palace decoration continued to be dominated by mythological themes, as it had during the sixteenth century, but the more sensuous classicism of Annibale Carracci now heralded stylistic changes. His *Triumph of Bacchus and Ariadne* was one of a series of panels presented separately within a fictive architectural framework, or *quadratura*. Soon, however, this device was exploited for even greater dramatic effect. Guercino's

Aurora eliminated the subdivisions and used both real and fictive architecture to create an illusion of soaring space.

Pietro da Cortona's *Glorification of the Reign of Urban VIII*

The most effective use of quadratura was Pietro da Cortona's fresco in the main reception room of the Palazzo Barberini (1633–1639). The iconographic program, devised by Urban VIII's favorite poet, Francesco Bracciolini, took the pope's achievements as its central theme. The ceiling shows Divine Providence in the act

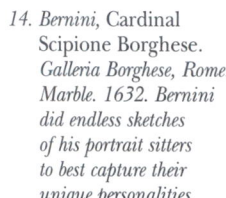

13. *Bernini*, Pluto and Persephone. *Galleria Borghese, Rome. Marble. 1621–1622. Deliberately choosing a moment of high drama, Bernini brought immediacy to the physical struggle by showing Pluto's fingers pressed into Persephone's flesh.*

14. *Bernini*, Cardinal Scipione Borghese. *Galleria Borghese, Rome. Marble. 1632. Bernini did endless sketches of his portrait sitters to best capture their unique personalities.*

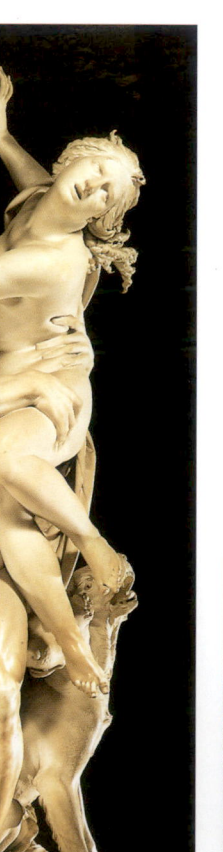

14

15. *Maderno and Bernini*, Palazzo Barberini. *Rome. 1629–1632. Commissioned by Cardinal Francesco Barberini, this was the largest private palace in Rome at the time. With no courtyard, its style recalled the villas of Ancient Rome and Nero's* Domus Aurea *(see chapter 8).*

13

15

of commanding Immortality to crown Urban VIII. Part of a deliberate campaign to consolidate the power of the Barberini dynasty, the message was a clear statement of power and prestige. Urban's election was presented as a family achievement, as indeed it was: it had, in effect, made the fortunes of three nephews, two of whom were made cardinals and one of whom was given charge of the papal armies—all positions with substantial financial advantages. And lest the visitor needed reminding, the ceiling was covered with bees and laurels, the Barberini family emblems.

New Religious Orders

The vital role played by Church reformers and the founders of new religious orders in the success of the Counter-Reformation soon gained recognition by the Church. The reformer St. Charles Borromeo was canonized in 1610, and the founders of the Jesuits and the Oratorians, St. Ignatius Loyola and San Filippo Neri, respectively, were canonized in 1622, along with St. Teresa, the founder of the Discalced Carmelites. The new orders were prolific patrons of Baroque art and architecture. Borromini was commissioned by the Oratorians to design

a small oratory next to their main church, Santa Maria in Vallicella. The classical details of its façade, which doubled as the monastery entrance, were a study in contrast: concave and convex, angular and rounded. A hallmark of Baroque architecture, the sculpted curvilinear façade was designed deliberately for effect. Borromini's interest in complexity was also reflected in his church plans, which were remarkable for their originality. Decorative schemes reinforced and celebrated Catholic dogma. Gilt, stucco, marbles, and other materials emphasized the wealth and power of the Church. And traditional themes were revived. Lanfranco's *Assumption*

16

18

17

16. *Guercino,* Aurora. *Casino Ludovisi, Rome. Fresco. 1621–1623. Guercino (1591–1666) combined fictive architecture and painting to create a dramatic illusion of the arrival of Aurora, the goddess of dawn.*

17. *Annibale Carracci,* The Triumph of Bacchus and Ariadne. *Palazzo Farnese, Rome. Fresco. Begun 1597. The style of the Bolognese painter Annibale Carracci (1560–1609) was very different from the complexities of Mannerism and deliberately recalled the ideals of the High Renaissance.*

18. *Pietro da Cortona,* Glorification of the Reign of Urban VIII. *Palazzo Barberini, Rome. Fresco. 1633–1639. Promoting an image of power and prestige for the Barberini family, Pietro da Cortona (1596–1669) included allegories of learning, abundance, and morality—along with the ubiquitous Barberini bees—in one of the most dramatic Baroque frescoes.*

of the Virgin created a vision of heaven that was deliberately overwhelming. In their own writings, the saints of the Counter-Reformation provided a new figurative language for the exaltation of Catholic faith. The *Spiritual Exercises* of St. Ignatius Loyola specifically encouraged the visualization of religious events as part of a program of meditation. The spiritual fervor generated by these exercises was reflected in Baroque art. The same decorative devices that were used to promote secular wealth and power were also used to propagate the Catholic faith. The quadratura, which had produced illusions of mythological heavens in a secular context, was now used to create spectacular visions of Christian paradise. Drama and illusion convinced the spectator of direct participation in the event being depicted.

19. Baciccia, Adoration of the Name of Jesus. Gesù, Rome. Fresco. 1674–1676. Giovanni Gaulli, known as Baciccia (1639–1709), gave visual expression to the religious fervor of Baroque Rome.

19

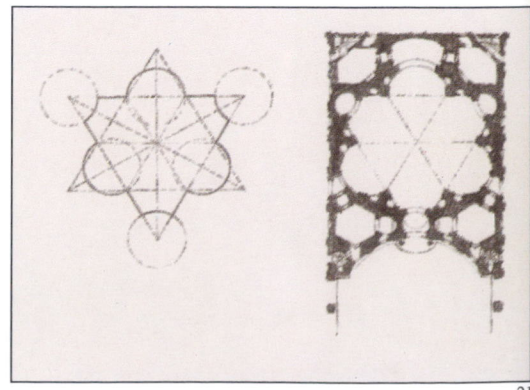

20

20. Francesco Borromini, Oratory of San Filippo Neri. Rome. Begun 1637. Variety and contrast—between convex and concave curves, elaborate pediments and window shapes—created an impressive façade design.

21. Sant'Ivo alla Sapienza, plan. Rome. 1642–1650. Borromini experimented with complexity in plans as well as elevations.

21

PROTESTANTISM HAD BEGUN AS AN ATTACK on traditional religious dogma, but it soon became the focus of political dissent that questioned established concepts of authority in the temporal arena. In France and England, where sovereign powers attempted to extend their authority and impose absolute rule over their subjects, the nature of monarchic rule became a particularly pressing issue. Art and architecture remained important tools for propagating the image of power. Works of this period, along with those produced contemporaneously in Rome, are generally grouped under the heading of "Baroque."

IMAGE AND RELIGIOUS CONFLICT

France and England, 1600–1700

In fact, royal patrons in France and England attempted to assert their independence, supporting the politics of power with their own interpretations of classical themes.

Henri IV and Marie de' Medici

In France, Catholics and Protestants fought at length for supremacy (1562–1598). The political nature of these so-called religious wars became clear when the Protestant King Henri IV (r. 1589–1610) recognized that his desire for power was greater than his religious convictions. Henri became a Catholic to gain control of Paris

(1594) but remained tolerant of Protestant countrymen, passing the Edict of Nantes four years later. Henri's determination to revive monarchic authority led to administrative reforms and policy measures to improve trade and agriculture. Peace, prosperity, and reform were given visual expression in Paris with a program of urban renewal. Symmetrical and regular, the new streets and squares imposed formal solutions on public spaces, reflecting the new order imposed in Henri's kingdom. The Place de France, with its radiating streets named after French provinces, reinforced national pride. The idea of regularized town planning

was based on the Italian model, and ultimately that of imperial Rome. As an image for his regime, Henri opted for simple classical buildings made of common, inexpensive materials. After his assassination by a Catholic fanatic, Henri's wife, Marie de' Medici, became regent for their son, Louis XIII (r. 1610–1643). In that capacity, she promoted a very different image of royal power. Her two galleries at the Luxembourg Palace (1615) were decorated with paintings by Peter Paul Rubens, court artist to the Spanish rulers in the Netherlands (see chapter 36). One depicted events from her own life, the other episodes from her

husband's life. In these cycles, religious and mythological allegories were combined to reinforce Marie's rights as regent, which were increasingly undermined by the rise to power of Cardinal Richelieu.

Richelieu and Mazarin

For nearly half a century, France was dominated by ministers to the crown appointed by Louis XIII: Cardinal Richelieu, who ruled as first minister (1624–1642), and his successor, Cardinal Mazarin (1642–1660), who guided the nation through the minority of Louis XIV (r. 1643–1715), the son

1. *Rubens,* Henri IV's Triumphant Reentry into Paris. *Uffizi, Florence. Canvas. 1628–1631. This triumphal image by Rubens (1577–1640) celebrated the political advantages that accrued to Henri IV after his conversion to Catholicism. "Paris," he is believed to have said, "was worth a mass."*

2. *Rubens,* The Apotheosis of Henri IV and the Proclamation of the Regency of Marie de' Medici. *Louvre, Paris. Canvas. 1622–1625. Rubens's powerful composition gave dramatic expression to the divine rule of the French monarchy.*

2

3. *Philippe de Champaigne,* Cardinal Richelieu. *Louvre, Paris. Canvas. Ca. 1635. A leading artist at the French court, Philippe de Champaigne (1602–1674) painted a number of portraits of the great cardinal; his careful attention to style, pose, and detail gave visual expression to the sitter's prestige.*

4. *Louis Le Vau,* Vaux-le-Vicomte. *Melun. 1657–1661. Grand and imposing, the extravagance of this building contributed to the downfall of its patron, Finance Minister Nicolas Fouquet.*

4

5. *Nicolle,* View of the Sorbonne. *Château Malmaisons, Musée, Paris. Watercolor. Late eighteenth century. Designed by Jacques Lemercier for Cardinal Richelieu, the church of the Sorbonne (begun 1635) introduced a new type of façade into French architecture, inspired by developments in Rome.*

3

5

of Louis XIII. Richelieu's policies, continued by Mazarin, sought to establish the king as the focal point of national unity and to undermine the traditional influence of nobles. Determined to eradicate any and all opposition, Richelieu rescinded the political rights of Protestants, leaving them only their religious freedom (itself lost when the Edict of Nantes was revoked in 1689). In foreign affairs, the judicious support of Spain's opponents by Richelieu and Mazarin helped established France as the leading power in Europe.

Both Richelieu and Mazarin were great patrons of art and architecture. Richelieu built palaces and châteaus that rivaled royal projects in scale and expense, and he built a town that he graced with his own name. The church of the Sorbonne, which he commissioned, introduced several elements characteristic of contemporary Roman architecture: a two-story façade and volutes linking the central unit with the lower side sections, following the pattern established by the church of Gesù in Rome (see chapter 30). Preferring a more restrained and classical style to the opulence of Roman Baroque, Richelieu commissioned works from Roman-trained French painters such as Poussin (see chapter 38) and Simon Vouet. Cardinal Mazarin, for his part, amassed an impressive collection of extravagant inlaid cabinets and vases made of jade, rock crystal, and other precious gems. His finance minister, Fouquet, built a château of unprecedented splendor at Vaux-le-Vicomte. Louis XIV had him arrested for embezzlement (1661) and used Fouquet's workers for the construction of his own projects.

Louis XIV, The Sun King

After Mazarin's death, Louis XIV decided to rule alone, appointing Colbert (1619–1683)

6. *Bernini,* Model for Equestrian Monument of Louis XIV. *Galleria Borghese, Rome. Terracotta. Ca. 1678. The enormous number and variety of portraits of Louis XIV testified to his belief in the power of the arts as propaganda.*

6

7. *Pierre Mignard,* Louis XIV. *Galleria Sabauda, Turin. Canvas. 1673. Roman imperial costume and the scale of Louis XIV's charger gave classical authority to this image of power.*

8. *Hyacinthe Rigaud,* Louis XIV. *Louvre, Paris. Canvas. 1701. One of the many artists employed at court, Hyacinthe Rigaud (1659–1743) contrasted the varying textures of ermine, velvet, and silk in this extravagant statement of the power and prestige of the French monarchy.*

7

8

as his chief advisor. In a letter to the king, Colbert pointed out two ways of reinforcing royal power and prestige: warfare and building. With the help of Colbert, Louis did both in grand style, establishing France as the preeminent power in Europe and creating an image of absolute authority that inspired royal courts throughout Europe. In addition to the administration and the army, Colbert succeeded in reorganizing the French arts as well.

As a vehicle of state propaganda, the arts needed to be both effective and efficient. Under Colbert, the attitude of institutions toward art and art production changed appreciably. To maintain literary standards, Richelieu had set up the Académie Française (1635). This was soon followed by an academy for the figurative arts (1648), which Colbert made part of the state apparatus (1663) under the direction of Charles Le Brun. The founding of the French Academy in Rome (1666) reflected the importance of Italy and the classical tradition. Academy professors taught a set of rules deemed essential for the production of quality art. Le Brun wrote a treatise on the expression of emotion. Artists were exhorted to imitate the masters, especially the ancients, Raphael, and Poussin. Venetian artists were to be avoided because their use of color defied rule or rationale. The new independence in French art was reflected in the rejection of Bernini's plans for the Louvre (1665) by Louis XIV. Royal patronage dominated the art market, and art production was centered on the Gobelins factory. Under Le Brun, the facility's director and chief designer, an army of painters, goldsmiths, sculptors, and cabinetmakers produced quantities of items that were destined fill the royal palaces with paintings, tapestries, silverware, and furniture.

9. Jules Hardouin Mansart and Liberal Bruant, Les Invalides. *Paris. Begun 1670. Plain and austere, this royal hospital for soldiers was a considerable contrast to the opulence of Louis XIV's projects at Versailles.*

9

Versailles

Louis XIV commissioned countless royal portraits in which he was portrayed in state robes, much as a Roman emperor, or together with his family, in images that commemorated his military achievements, reinforced his royal power, and emphasized dynastic continuity. But the greatest expression of the power and prestige of Louis XIV was undoubtedly his palace at Versailles. Following his decision to move the royal court from Paris to a former hunting lodge outside the city, Louis created a palace complex of unprecedented scale and grandeur whose name would become synonymous with monarchic excess.

The palace itself was set in an artificial landscape designed by André Le Nôtre. Its plan reflected the extreme formality of court life, the strict rules of etiquette, and the widening gulf between the king and his subjects. The succession of rooms that formed the king's apartments (there was a separate set for the queen) was decorated with mythological allegories of Louis XIV's achievements; the decorative program culminated in the fresco of the Room of Apollo, in which the monarch was depicted in his favorite attire, that of the Sun King. A statue of Apollo on his sun chariot also graced the lake outside. The most eloquent image of wealth and power, however, was the Galerie des Glaces, or Hall of Mirrors, designed by Le Brun. The ceiling was decorated with scenes commemorating the king's military victories, in which he is depicted in the robes of a Roman emperor. Even if his kingdom was undoubtedly smaller than that of Ancient Rome, Louis had succeeded in reviving the scale and grandeur of the latter. The Galerie des Glaces soon lost much of its opulence, however, as a financial crisis forced the silver furniture to be melted down (1698). In this case, palace decor

10

12

11

10. Mansart and Le Vau, Versailles, garden façade. 1669 onward. Ornamental richness and variety, projection and recession, and, above all, monumental scale were combined by the architects Louis Le Vau (1612–1670) and Jules Hardouin Mansart (1646–1708) in this prime image of French monarchic power.

11. Salon de Diane. *Versailles. 1670s. Part of the lavishly decorated suite of rooms that formed the king's apartments, the salon now contains Bernini's bust of Louis XIV (1665).*

12. Le Brun, Galerie des Glaces. Versailles. Begun 1678. The prime statement of royal power at Versailles, the decoration of this room uses a combination of mirrors, marble, gilt, and allegorical paintings to dramatic effect.

The *Manufacture royale des meubles de la Couronne*, commonly known as the Gobelins factory, was established in France (1667) by King Louis XIV and his finance minister, Colbert, for the manufacture of furnishings for royal palaces (1667).

The state-controlled organization was of enormous importance in the development of a distinctive French style in the fine and decorative arts. Under the directorship of Charles Le Brun (1619–1690), the factory trained ap-prentices and employed a workforce of about 250 artists—painters, embroiderers, goldsmiths and silversmiths, engravers of precious stones, experts in mosaic and marquetry, cabinetmakers, and tapestry weavers. Stimulated by the heavy demand for luxury furnishings required for the decoration of Louis XIV's palace at Versailles, the factory flourished.

Initially, many of its craftsmen were of Italian and Dutch origin, called to France by Cardinal Mazarin and Fouquet. By the end of the seventeenth century, however, the workforce was largely French and produced luxury goods at a standard unparalleled elsewhere in Europe. Particularly important were the specialized techniques for which the Gobelins became famous. Among these was the tortoiseshell and brass inlay known as Boulle marquetry. The factory also produced the extravagant silver furniture used to decorate Louis XIV's Galerie des Glaces and the Salon de la Guerre at Versailles.

Although much of the work produced by the Gobelins has now disappeared, some idea of its scope can be seen in the tapestry, designed by Le Brun (who was director of the Gobelins during its golden age), illustrating a visit made by the king on October 15, 1667.

13. *Le Brun*, Louis XIV Visiting the Gobelins. *Gobelins Museum, Paris. Tapestry. 1663–1675. The efficient reorganization of the arts under the state control of Louis XIV's minister, Colbert, had important ramifications for the official domination of the arts in France in later centuries.*

13

expressed the wealth of the crown in a very real sense.

The Stuarts and Innovation in England

In England, meanwhile, the death of Elizabeth I (1603) marked the end of the Tudor Dynasty. Whereas Elizabeth had been staunchly anti-Europe, her Stuart successor, James I (r. 1603–1625), reinforced his links abroad. James's son, Charles I (r. 1625–1649), was married to Henrietta Maria, the daughter of Henri IV of France. Although neither one was Catholic, James and Charles both believed that their power was ordained by God and absolute. The Divine Right of Kings was a fundamental aspect of the new image promoted at the Stuart court. Art and architecture, which Elizabeth had largely ignored, gave visual expression to their prestige.

While the Office of Works under Elizabeth had an annual budget of about £4,000, James I spent £73,000 on building in three years (1607–1610). The contrast was reinforced by a revolutionary change in style, as the Stuarts adopted classical architecture as the preferred model for their projects. Inigo Jones, who had been to Italy and is known to have owned a copy of Palladio's treatise, was appointed court architect (1615). His Banqueting Hall for James I was part of a plan for enlarging London's Whitehall Palace on a scale that would have competed with the courts of continental Europe as an expression of wealth and power. Following precedents set abroad, Charles I commissioned Peter Paul Rubens to paint the *Apotheosis of James I* for its ceiling. The importance of the new style was underlined when Charles insisted that the Earl of Bedford include Jones in the design of his commercial center at Covent Garden. Symmetrical and regular, the square imposed formal solutions on what

14

15

14. Rubens, Apotheosis of James I. *Banqueting Hall, London. Canvas. 1634. Imitating the precedents established by other European monarchs, the Stuart Dynasty introduced not only classical architectural style but different pictorial types to give visual expression to their own power.*

15. Anthony van Dyck, Charles I. *Louvre, Paris. Canvas. Ca. 1635. The Flemish painter Anthony van Dyck (1599–1641) was appointed court artist by England's Charles I (1632). His distinctive style emphasized elegance and informality.*

INIGO JONES

As architect to the Stuart kings James I and Charles I, Inigo Jones (1573–1652) was responsible for the realization of his patrons' desire to introduce classical architecture, common elsewhere in Europe, into Britain. The leading theater designer at court, Jones earned his reputation with settings for court masques by Ben Jonson. He traveled to Italy (1613–1614) with Lord Arundel, a leading connoisseur of classical art, where he developed an interest in the architecture of Andrea Palladio (1508–1580); he also met Vincenzo Scamozzi (1552–1616), who was responsible for the completion of many of Palladio's unfinished buildings. Appointed court architect after his return (1615), Jones adapted Palladio's style to his royal commissions, most notably the Queen's House in Greenwich (1616) and the Banqueting Hall in London. Part of a much larger project for Whitehall Palace, the Banqueting Hall illustrated Jones's debt to Palladio in his use of classically inspired rustication, columns, and capitals with alternating triangular and segmental pediments over the windows. Jones's ideas and designs were of fundamental importance to the development of the eighteenth-century Palladian movement in Britain (see chapter 42).

previously had been left to chance, introducing the classical and Italian ideas of town planning used by Henri IV in Paris. Contact with European courts gave Charles I a taste for connoisseurship, and he amassed a spectacular collection of antique casts and old masters, including the inevitable Titians as well as works by Leonardo da Vinci, Mantegna, and Correggio. Charles appointed Anthony van Dyck, a pupil of Rubens, as his court painter. Van Dyck painted more than twenty portraits of his royal patron, promoting an image of elegance and refinement rather than any overt display of military prowess.

16

16. *Inigo Jones,* Banqueting Hall. *London. 1619–1622.*

17. *John Michael Wright,* Charles II. *National Portrait Gallery, London. Panel. Ca. 1660. John Michael Wright (ca. 1617–1700) trained in Rome before being appointed court painter to Charles II. His minute attention to the details of the king's garter robes reinforced the royal image.*

17

Parliament and Civil War

The ideal of absolute power as promoted by Charles I took no account of the role of Parliament, whose Puritan members objected to the Catholic influence at court and to his belief in the Divine Right of Kings. The English Civil War broke out in 1642, and Charles was beheaded seven years later outside the lavish monument of Stuart power, the Banqueting Hall. Under the leadership of Oliver Cromwell, the arts suffered. The Puritans condemned mythology as pagan, religious painting as idolatrous, and nudity as indecent. Charles's great collection was sold to eager monarchs on the European continent, and waves of iconoclasts swept through churches to strip away their decorations. The English predilection for monarchy finally prevailed and, shortly after Cromwell's death (1658), the son of Charles I—Charles II (r. 1660–1685)—was restored to the throne. Nevertheless, religious conflict and parliamentary power limited the exercise of royal authority. Charles was succeeded by his brother, James II (r. 1685–1688), who was forced to abdicate because of his Catholic faith. Parliament invited his daughter, Mary, and her Dutch husband, Prince William of Orange, to rule (1680–1702), effecting a bloodless revolution that established the position of Parliament within a constitutional monarchy.

The Restoration

The fire that destroyed the City of London (1666) provided a major stimulus to public and private patronage. Charles II appointed the architect Christopher Wren to take charge of the rebuilding of numerous city churches and its cathedral, St. Paul's (1666–1711). The new St. Paul's would be the first major Protestant church built in England since the

18

18. Christopher Wren, Great Model. St. Paul's Cathedral, crypt, London. Wood. 1673. A scientist by training, Sir Christopher Wren (1632–1723) was aware of contemporary Baroque architecture in France, reflected in the curved walls of his original plan for the rebuilding of St. Paul's.

19. Christopher Wren, St. Paul's Cathedral. London. 1675–1709. The final design of St. Paul's was a compromise between Wren's artistic ideals and the dictates of the clergy. Construction was paid for by taxes on coal.

19

Reformation, and its design was keenly anticipated. But Wren's initial plan, represented by his *Great Model* (1673), combined features that the Protestant clergy found hard to accept: a pagan classical temple front, an impractical central plan, and a dome reminiscent of the prime image of Catholicism, St. Peter's in Rome. Wren was forced to compromise. Like Bramante and Michelangelo in Rome before him (see chapter 30), he transformed his centralized plan to one based on the Latin Cross.

As patrons of the arts, the later Stuarts were careful to avoid the ostentation that James I and Charles I had promoted as the image of royal power. Displays of wealth were limited to public and charitable projects. The Royal Naval Hospital at Greenwich, built by William and Mary, was considerably grander than their extension to the royal palace at Hampton Court, designed by Wren. Its succession of staterooms may have been reminiscent of Versailles, but the comparison ends there; this modest brick building made no pretense of absolute power. Private patrons, meanwhile, were less restricted. The Baroque grandeur of Blenheim Palace, designed by John Vanbrugh for the duke of Marlborough and paid for by Queen Anne (r. 1712–1714), made it an ideal royal gift for the duke's role in the wars against France. The decoration of the palace celebrated the revival of English military power with overt symbolism, including a depiction of the British lion crushing the French cock above the arches on either side of the courtyard.

20

21

20. Christopher Wren and others, Royal Naval Hospital. *Greenwich. Begun 1694. Institutions for the soldiers and sailors who had fought for their country were important expressions of both charitable intent and national prestige.*

21. John Vanbrugh and Nicholas Hawksmoor, Blenheim Palace. *Woodstock. 1705–1720. "A Gift from a Grateful Nation," Blenheim Palace was named for one of the duke of Marlborough's military victories. It was one of the few buildings in England to compete with continental Baroque in variety, drama, and grandeur.*

22

22. Christopher Wren, Hampton Court Palace, garden façade. *1690–1696. Contemporary with Versailles, this English royal palace was remarkably modest by comparison. It reflected the Baroque style of the age in its contrasting use of materials and variety of window shapes.*

AMERICA MAY HAVE BEEN KNOWN TO the Vikings, but it was only after Christopher Columbus's epic voyage across the Atlantic (1492–1493) that Europe became aware of the existence of this vast continent. Discovery was followed by invasion. The Spanish conquistador Hernán Cortés arrived at the Aztec capital of Tenochtitlán with 600 soldiers in 1519, and by 1600 the ancient civilizations of Central and South America had been conquered. Determined to impose their own Christian culture on the continent, the invaders systematically pillaged cities, temples, and palaces. Fortune hunters removed

CHAPTER 35

AMERICA BEFORE THE CONQUEST

Pre-Columbian Art

masks, trinkets, helmets, sacrificial knives, and statuettes made of gold, silver, turquoise, and other precious stones. It was not until the nineteenth century that serious efforts were made to discover more about the cultures of the people who had inhabited America before the Spanish conquest.

The ancestors of the indigenous tribes of America are generally believed to have migrated from Asia across the Bering Strait, a land bridge between the two continents that disappeared at the end of the Ice Age (ca. 15,000 B.C.E.). Cut off from the rest of the world by the Atlantic and the Pacific Oceans, they developed unique cultural

1

traditions. The physical environment of the Americas is immensely varied. Climatic conditions range from polar to tropical, and the terrain includes high mountain ranges and open plains, deserts and swamps. As in Africa (see chapter 12), geophysical diversity fostered the growth of many different cultures. Eskimo peoples of the Arctic north still hunt walrus and seal, as they have done for centuries, and carve intricate and elaborate details on ivory and bone. Indians of the North American plains depended for their livelihood on herds of buffalo, which provided not only food, but also leather for clothes and tents.

Comprising hundreds of independent tribes and cultures, Native Americans developed distinctive mythologies to explain natural phenomena. These were given visual expression in the decoration of ceremonial clothes, statuettes, carved wooden totem poles, and a host of other objects.

Early Farmers

Sometime around 7000 B.C.E., nomadic hunters in Central America began to settle in agricultural communities based on the cultivation of maize. This fast-growing crop required relatively little effort to produce

high yields and was capable of supporting large populations, especially in Mexico and Peru, where it was most intensively grown. The expansion of agriculture in turn gave rise to larger towns and cities. It is not surprising that the major civilizations of pre-Columbian America emerged from such sites. In Mesoamerica (present-day Mexico, Guatemala, El Salvador, Belize, and western Honduras), a series of cultures flourished from as early as 1200 B.C.E. until the Spanish conquest: the Olmec, the Zapotec, the Maya, the cities of Teotihuacán and El Tajin, the Toltec, the Mixtec, and the Aztec. Farther south (in Colombia, Ecuador, and Peru),

1. Quetzalcoatl (detail). *Museo Missionario Etnologico, Vatican. Stone. Ca. 1400 C.E. The feathered serpent Quetzalcoatl was one of the most powerful deities in Mesoamerican mythology.*

2. Seated boy. *Wadsworth Athenaeum, Hartford, Connecticut. Stone. Olmec sculptors displayed a high degree of technical skill in their small figures carved from semiprecious stones with metal tools.*

3. Colossal head. *La Venta, Mexico. Basalt. Before 400 B.C.E. Archaeologists have found more than ten of these giant heads, all slightly different; they are among the most impressive remains of the ancient Olmec civilization.*

2

3

the Quimbaya, Tolima, Moche, and Inca peoples developed their own distinctive cultures. The peoples in both regions were dominated by rigidly organized theocratic states, and their art developed above all in a religious context. The enormous scale of their architectural monuments reflected the relative leisure of a peasant class, which not only provided a large and inexpensive workforce but also diminished the need to develop the kind of tools used for construction in Europe and Asia. Instead of iron or metal, pre-Columbian Americans used flint and hard stone, such as obsidian, for the cutting of building blocks, for killing, and even for shaving. The wheel, which played such an important role in the West, was used for toys but not exploited for its practical potential.

The Olmec

The oldest known pre-Columbian civilization is that of the Olmec, who inhabited the tropical forests of Mexico around the Gulf of Mexico and dominated the area between about 1200 and 500 B.C.E. The Olmec are believed to have established the key characteristics of later Mesoamerican societies: extensive trade, the division of society into commoners and elites, the worship of fertility gods, and monumental architecture. Many of the elements commonly associated with major Mesoamerican civilizations were present in Olmec culture, including hieroglyphic writing, ritual calendars, ceremonial ball games, human sacrifice, and the building of pyramids. Mountains of human construction, which also appear in the architecture of ancient Mesopotamia (see chapter 2) and Egypt (see chapter 3), reflected the importance of height and scale as a visual expression of the relationship between humans and gods. The two major

4

4. Ball game player. *Museo Nacional de Antropologia, Mexico City. Found in the west of Mexico, this figure probably represents a player in the ritual ball game, an essential element in the majority of Mesoamerican cultures. Played with a rubber ball, the game seems to have involved ritual sacrifice.*

5. Funerary mask. *Museo Nacional de Antropologia, Mexico City. Wood and mosaic. Ca. 300–650 C.E. The elaborate pattern and brightly colored pieces of stone on this funeral mask from Teotihuacán reflected the status of its owner.*

5

6. Funerary mask. *Museo Etnografico di Castello d'Albertis, Genoa. Serpentine. Ca. 250–750 C.E. Stylized masks of the human face were designed to be placed over the head of a corpse in burials at Teotihuacán.*

6

THE LEGEND OF THE FEATHERED SERPENT

The image of the feathered serpent, a mythical creature embodying the attributes of a bird and a snake, occurs throughout the art and architecture of Mesoamerica.

It is generally considered a representation of the god Quetzalcoatl, known in Maya mythology as Kukulkan. A deity associated with the creative forces of nature, Quetzalcoatl was particularly important for agriculture and variously worshiped as the god of vegetation, rain, or wind. In some mythologies, it was wor-

shiped as the power behind human creation itself. An important deity for the Toltec, Quetzalcoatl was represented in its emblematic butterfly form on the giant caryatids that supported the main temple in Tula.

The circular temples at Tula, Tenochtitlán, and possibly Teotihuacán, otherwise rare in Mesoamerican civilizations, were invariably associated with the

cult of Quetzalcoatl. In Aztec mythology, the royal founder of the Toltec city of Tula adopted the name of Quetzalcoatl in honor of the god.

Driven out of his city and traveling to the eastern coast, he set sail on a raft of serpents and was reborn as the planet Venus, the morning star. To reinforce their divine status, Aztec monarchs claimed descent from Quetzalcoatl, the

departed ruler. According to legend, however, Quetzalcoatl promised to return to claim his inheritance. In fact, he prophesied the return of powerful white men that would be able to reconquer the throne and usher in a new golden age.

When the Spanish conquistador Hernán Cortés and his soldiers landed in Mexico (1519), they were well received by the Aztec emperor, Montezuma, who believed that Cortés was the reincarnation of Quetzalcoatl.

7. Quetzalcoatl. *Museo Missionario Etnologico, Vatican. Stone. Ca. 1400 C.E. Curvilinear and stylized detailing was a characteristic feature of Mesoamerican art.*

8. Temple of Quetzalcoatl. *Xochilalco, Mexico. The use of incised decoration was a common element in Mesoamerican architecture.*

8

9. Quetzalcoatl. *Musée de l'Homme, Paris. Images of Quetzalcoatl are varied, reflecting its different divine manifestations, but the deity is recognizable by the combination of a forked serpent's tongue and bird's feathers.*

7

9

sites of Olmec culture, La Venta and San Lorenzo, have revealed evidence of a highly organized society dominated by priests, and of a well-developed artistic tradition. The earliest known stone sculptures date from around 1250 B.C.E. Highly skilled Olmec craftsmen used stone implements to carve jade, serpentine, and other semiprecious stones into delicate figurines, many of which have the distinctive feline features of the jaguar, a central image of physical power in Mesoamerican culture. At La Venta, mosaic pavements were carefully buried as offerings to the earth-god. The most dramatic Olmec remains are a series of colossal stone heads measuring nearly 10 feet (3 meters) high. Current knowledge of Olmec culture is severely restricted by the inability to decipher its writing system, and the precise function of many of the objects found is difficult to ascertain. It remains clear, however, that the Olmec had a major influence on later developments in Mesoamerica.

Architecture and Ceremony

The classic period of Mesoamerican civilization—from about the second to the tenth century B.C.E.—saw the rise of a series of powerful states in the region. While the Maya (see below) were emerging as the dominant power in Guatemala and Belize to the east, the theocratic city-states of Teotihuacán and El Tajin were flourishing in the west. With a population estimated at more than 200,000, Teotihuacán (ca. 100–750 C.E.) was a major economic and religious center located northeast of present-day Mexico City. It was laid out in a formal grid plan that focused on three massive temples, raised on pyramids and oriented toward the four points of the compass. The so-called Temple of the Sun stood on a platform more than

10. Caryatid columns. *Tula. Tenth–thirteenth century. These anthropomorphic columns, about 15 feet (5 m) high, depict Toltec warriors and were originally designed to support a temple roof.*

10

11. and 12. Cups. *Terracotta. These cups from Coclé in Panama, featuring stylized animal designs in two colors on a pale background, reflect the influence of Andean art.*

11

12

200 feet (60 m) high. Like the Hellenistic and Roman emperors, the rulers of Teotihuacán combined grandiose ceremonial approaches with imposing architectural monuments to reinforce the power of the state. Built of stone, brick, and rubble, the city's temples, palaces, and other buildings were elaborately carved and decorated with both hieroglyphic script and formalized curvilinear animals and birds that recall the Olmec style. The ruins of the city-state of El Tajin include eleven courts for the playing of a ceremonial ball game, an important element in Mesoamerican religious worship. Much of what we know

about the game, which seems to have involved ritual sacrifice, comes from the elaborate decoration at the courts of El Tajin.

In southern Mexico, the influence of the Olmec was similarly reflected in the Zapotec and later the Mixtec civilizations. The Zapotec city of Monte Alban, contemporary with Teotihuacán, was also designed to relate directly to the four points of the compass and centered on a large open space surrounded by temples, a ball court, and other buildings. Excavations have revealed a wide variety of sculptured reliefs and elaborate terracotta urns, as well as wall paintings in underground tombs.

The Maya

Farther south, the Maya emerged as rulers of a large empire that, at its height (ca. 250–900 C.E.), controlled most of the Yucatán Peninsula of Mexico as well as Guatemala, Belize, and western Honduras. Highly developed astrological and mathematical skills reflected the Maya fascination with life, death, and the continuity of existence. They devised a basic solar calendar of 365 days, superimposing a ritual calendar of 260 days, and counted years beginning from 3113 B.C.E. (much as Christians begin counting from the year of

13. Huitzilopochtli.
The warrior god of the Aztecs, Huitzilopochtli was worshiped with offerings that included human hearts and blood.

14. Funeral mask. *Museo di Antropologia, Florence. Before 550* C.E.

15. Funeral mask. *Museo Nacional de Antropologia, Mexico City. Masks carved in semiprecious stones, like this Mayan mask of turquoise, have long been prized by Europeans. The high demand has resulted in many forgeries.*

Christ's birth). Stone stelae were erected to mark the passing of each fifty-two-year cycle, when the two calendars coincided, as well as other important events. These stelae, the earliest of which were painted, featured reliefs depicting the current ruler and his ancestors. Dates and inscriptions were carved in a distinctive hieroglyphic script, which can now be read, for the most part. Maya religious practices appear to have centered on the calendar and different religious practices and rituals corresponded to the cycles of the year and sacrifices to the gods. Human sacrifice, which played a vital role in later Mesoamerican civilizations, was practiced along with animal sacrifice and other rituals. Reflecting the rigid and hierarchical nature of Maya society, ceremonial centers such as Palenque and Uxmál were laid out in formal grid plans. Their vast scale reinforced Maya power and prestige. Uxmál, for example, covered 250 acres. Not cities in the conventional sense, they were inhabited by priests and other members of the ruling classes, while common people lived in surrounding areas.

As in the case of other Mesoamerican civilizations, religious ceremonies played a central role in Maya culture, and the architecture was designed deliberately to impress. Facing vast plazas, from which the people watched, massive temples were erected atop wide-based stone pyramids with long staircase approaches. Temples and palaces were decorated with sculptured reliefs and wall paintings that depicted stylized figural and animal motifs as well as elaborate geometrical patterns. The use of jade among the Maya was associated with rulers and other elite personages, who were buried with jade masks, headdresses, and jewelry. The Maya civilization collapsed during the ninth century for reasons that are still unclear,

15

16

16. Standing figure. *Museo Luigi Pigorini, Rome. Originally painted in blue, red, and brown, the elaborate headdress and jewelry were intended to convey the status of the figure.*

although the appearance at Chichén Itza of sculptural and architectural details bearing close resemblance to Toltec remains at Tula (see below) suggests the possibility of an invasion from the north.

The Toltec

Teotihuacán was destroyed in 750 C.E. and, soon thereafter, invaders from the north created a new empire in west-central Mexico. An ancient Mesoamerican people, the Toltec dominated the region from the tenth to the mid-twelfth century. They established their capital at Tula (ca. 980), the center of a thriving trade network that reached as far south as Colombia. Dominated by military leaders rather than priests, the Toltec stressed the importance of human sacrifice in religious worship. Although they adopted the classic Mesoamerican model of vast ceremonial plazas with massive monumental buildings, Toltec architecture also gave visual expression to the unique character of the regime. Massive statues of Toltec warriors supported the roof of one temple, and Toltec sculptural reliefs show a marked preference for more aggressive and angular forms than the rounded figure styles of Teotihuacán.

The Aztecs

A new wave of invasions from the north resulted in the destruction of Tula (1168 C.E.) and the dismemberment of the Toltec Empire into a series of small warring states. It was from these that the Aztecs emerged as the dominant force in the region during the fourteenth century, and indeed the warrior culture of the Toltecs acted as a powerful precedent for the new regime. The Aztecs established their capital at Tenochtitlán (1345) in central Mexico. Laid out in a grid plan, the city was connected to the mainland by causeways,

17

17. Palace. *Palenque, Mexico. One of the major centers of Maya civilization, the ruins of Palenque include this monumental palace as well as temples. The scale of the architecture gave visual expression to the power of its rulers.*

18

18. Architectural detail. *Uxmál, Yucatan. Elaborate geometrical designs, carved on the façades of both temples and palaces, were typical of Maya architecture.*

19. Seated figure. *Museo Luigi Pigorini, Rome. Stone. The Quimbaya tribes of Colombia are known for their small figures in terracotta and metal.*

20. Platform of the Eagles, detail with snake head. *Chichén Itza. Ca. 1200. An important center of Maya culture, Chichén Itza also contains later ruins that strongly resemble the Toltec city of Tula.*

19

with fresh water provided by aqueducts. Destroyed by the Spanish in 1521, Tenochtitlán became the site of modern Mexico City. The Spanish were duly impressed by what they found. Their eyewitness accounts describe a large metropolis with paved streets and thriving marketplaces; grand palaces surrounded a central walled precinct containing the city's great pyramid temples and courts for the ritual ball game. The Spanish were also impressed by the statues and ornaments of gold, silver, precious, and semiprecious stones that were used to decorate important buildings. But the Spanish were less complimentary about the religious practices of the Aztecs. Ruled by a priest-king, the Aztec Empire was held together by military force and a religion whose central rite was human sacrifice. According to some accounts, the dedication of the temple of the war god Huitzilopochtli (1487) occasioned the sacrifice of more than 20,000 prisoners of war. Spring was celebrated with the flaying of a young man and the use of his skin to dress another, symbolizing the natural cycle of growth and renewal. The importance of these rituals was given visual expression in meticulously detailed statuettes, reliefs, and paintings of the events that decorated the temples and palaces of the city.

Peru and the Inca

In South America, archaeological research has revealed evidence of a number of different cultures that flourished in Colombia, Ecuador, and Peru beginning about 3,000 years ago. Named after the village where the ruins of an important temple were discovered, the Chavin culture dates to ca. 1250 B.C.E. Later descendants of the Chavin were the Moche (or Mochica) tribes (fl. ca. 100 B.C.E.–700 C.E.), whose

20

21. Hunchbacked figure. *Museo Nacional de Antropologia, Mexico City. Terracotta.*

22. Portrait vase. *Museo Luigi Pigorini, Rome. Terracotta. Ca. 100 B.C.E.–700 C.E. These stirrup-spouted portrait vases were common in the Moche pottery of South America.*

23. Castillo. *Chichén Itza. Before 1050 C.E. Like the majority of the temples of Mesoamerica, this pyramid structure was deliberately oriented so that its four façades faced directly north, south, east, and west.*

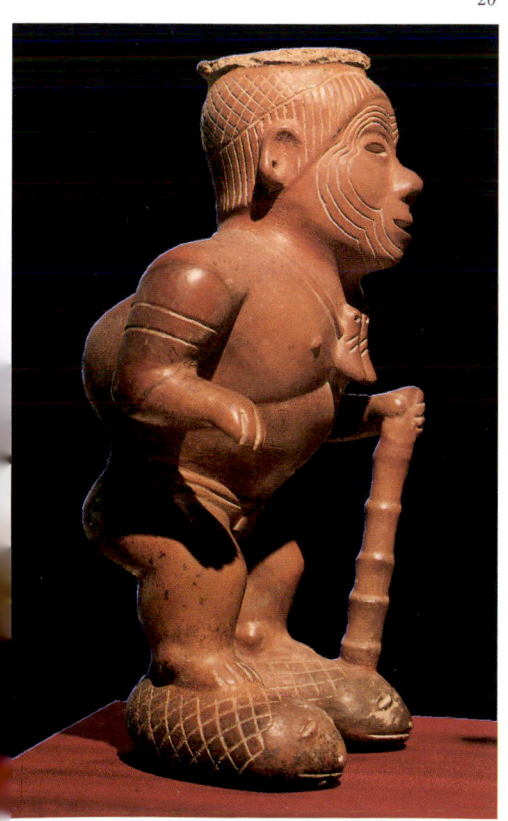

21

22

23

pottery styles and decorative motifs were clearly derived from Chavin prototypes. Moche art includes a range of stirrup-spout pottery, in the form of human heads and animals, as well as masks and headdresses made of metal.

The major pre-Columbian civilization of South America was undoubtedly the Inca Empire. Originally a tribe from the Peruvian highlands, the Inca established their capital at Cuzco in the fifth century. The major territorial expansion occurred in the fifteenth century under Pachacuti (r. 1438–1471) and his successors. At its peak, the empire stretched along the Andes Mountains and to the east, from Ecuador to southern Chile and including parts of Bolivia and Argentina. Controlling an estimated 12 million people, the empire was linked by 3,750 miles (6,030 km) of roads, along which llama trains carried the nation's goods and runners carried official messages. The rugged natural terrain made the Inca excellent engineers. From complex systems of terraces and irrigation channels for the cultivation of maize to the ingenious fitting of stone blocks in architectural monuments, the Inca gave visual expression to their mastery over nature. Denied personal property, the Inca people were obliged to provide labor for their divine rulers, whose power and prestige were reflected in the monumental scale of Inca architecture. The legendary wealth of the Inca was based on the ready availability of gold and silver, which lined the interiors of important buildings, including the Temples of the Sun and Moon at Cuzco. Highly efficient and rigidly organized, the Inca Empire lacked the military skills and technology necessary to withstand the Spanish invasion, and in 1533 it was incorporated into the Catholic dominions of Spain.

24. Anthropomorphic pendant. *Gold. The prevalence of gold in the art of Mesoamerica and the Andes gave rise to the legend of El Dorado, the city of gold, which inspired European fortune hunters to plunder the newly discovered continent.*

25. Poporo. *Gold. The smooth rounded surfaces of this urn were typical of Quimbaya metalwork.*

26. and 27. Machu Picchu. *Peru. High in the inhospitable Andes, this Inca city was protected by its precipitous site. Never found by the Spanish, Machu Picchu was discovered in 1911.*

26

24

25

27

CHURCH AND STATE WERE CLOSELY LINKED in the Spanish Empire. The Spanish state had been born of the Christian defeat of the Moors, or Reconquest, completed in the late fifteenth century. Philip II (r. 1556–1598) was a powerful champion of the Counter-Reformation, enforcing Catholicism in the Spanish Netherlands and focusing on Protestantism as the source of political rebellion against Spanish rule. In the American colonies, Spanish authority was reinforced by the imposition of Christianity on indigenous cultures. Rich and powerful, Spain dominated the political affairs of Europe

CHAPTER 36

SPAIN AND THE CATHOLIC EMPIRE

Art in the Spanish Dominions

in the sixteenth century. But the cost of maintaining its hegemony proved high. The wars to retain control of the Netherlands were enormously expensive, and ultimately resulted in failure. Equally unsuccessful and a further drain on resources were attempts to stem the rising power of France in the late seventeenth century. The financial problems were exacerbated by an extravagant aristocracy, which made little effort to invest in the infrastructure of the Spanish economy. The decline was hastened by Philip III (r. 1598–1621), who inherited Philip II's empire but not his capacity for personal government. Delegating political power

1

to leading aristocrats, he set a pattern for his successors, Philip IV (r. 1621–1665) and Charles II (r. 1665–1700), who were increasingly divorced from the affairs of state. Charles II died without an heir, and the demise of Hapsburg Spain was completed when Louis XIV of France installed his nephew as the nation's first Bourbon king, Philip V, in 1700.

Philip IV

Philip III had left his father's monastic palace, the Escorial, for Madrid, and the city came to be dominated by a wealthy aristocratic elite. The *plaza mayor* was designed as a setting for court ceremonies, including bullfights and the inquisitorial trials by fire. Philip IV's chief minister, the Count–Duke Olivares, sought to limit expenditures, but a politics of austerity was hardly compatible with the propagation of an image of power, and his efforts met with little success. The Spanish monarchs avoided political and economic matters and devoted themselves to leisure. Philip IV's architectural projects included a summer palace, the Buen Retiro (begun 1629), and a hunting lodge, the Torre de la Parada (begun 1636). Philip IV's choice of Olivares as chief minister also had important repercussions in cultural matters. A leading patron in his hometown of Seville, Olivares encouraged Sevillian dramatists, poets, historians, and artists at court. Among them was Diego Velázquez, appointed court painter to Philip IV (1623).

Velázquez at the Spanish Court

Velázquez (1599–1660) made two extended trips to Italy on behalf of Philip IV (1629–1631, 1649–1651); those tours and the opportunity to study Titian's paintings in the royal collection had a decisive influence on his style. While in Italy, Velázquez bought

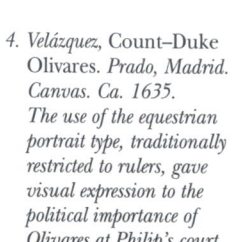

2. *Velázquez,* Philip IV. *Prado, Madrid. Canvas. Ca. 1635. Velázquez's skill as a portrait artist developed in an enormous variety of images he painted of the king.*

3. *Velázquez,* Prince Baltasar Carlos on Horseback. *Prado, Madrid. Canvas. Ca. 1635.*

4. *Velázquez,* Count–Duke Olivares. *Prado, Madrid. Canvas. Ca. 1635. The use of the equestrian portrait type, traditionally restricted to rulers, gave visual expression to the political importance of Olivares at Philip's court.*

1. *Peter Paul Rubens and Jan Brueghel,* Infanta Isabella. *Prado, Madrid. Canvas. Ca. 1610. Fashionably dressed and bejeweled, the daughter of the king of Spain and wife of the governor of the Spanish Netherlands was portrayed with her rural retreat, the Château Mariemont, in the background.*

works on behalf of Philip IV by Titian, Veronese, and Tintoretto. In the tradition of Philip II, the king collected Venetian paintings to promote an image of culture at the Spanish court. This was in marked contrast to attitudes at the French court of Louis XIV, where Venetian artists were considered too emotional in their use of form and color.

Velázquez's main task at the court of Philip IV was painting portraits of the king, his family, and his courtiers, including dwarfs and jesters. Influenced by Titian's early portraits, Velázquez adopted the standard types associated with royalty—equestrian portraits, full-length portraits, and hunting portraits. To reflect the diminished status of the Spanish monarchy, however, he experimented with new interpretations of these forms. His equestrian portrait of Philip IV, for example, deliberately avoided the expression of imperial power for which the type had been designed. In the case of Olivares, his equestrian portrait instead reinforced the minister's all-important role in affairs of state. If indeed these paintings were as true to their subjects as they appear to be, they also satisfied another basic requirement of good portraiture as defined by Velázquez's master, Francisco Pacheco, in his treatise *The Art of Painting*. Pacheco's insistence that a portrait should also be a good painting in terms of execution, color, and form reflected a growing belief that the artist's contribution was more important than the subject matter.

Images of Spanish Power

Many of the royal portraits were commissioned for the Torre de la Parada and Buen Retiro. Following another precedent established by Philip II, these palaces were also decorated with scenes from Ovid's *Metamorphoses* and other classical

5. *Velázquez*, Don Sebastian de Morra. *Prado, Madrid. Canvas. Ca. 1644. Trained in Seville, Velázquez (1599–1660) was appointed court painter in Madrid (1623). His many court portraits included a series of Philip IV's dwarfs.*

5

6. *Velázquez, The Surrender of Breda. Prado, Madrid. Canvas. Before 1635. Contrasts between the victorious Spaniards on the right and the conquered Bredans on the left focus the viewer's attention on the ceremony—the handing over of the keys to the city—at the center.*

6

7. *Juan Bautista Maino, The Recovery of Bahia. Prado, Madrid. Canvas. Ca. 1630. Maino's record of this Spanish victory in America was one of the few court paintings that could faithfully portray Spanish royal power during the decline of the Hapsburgs.*

7

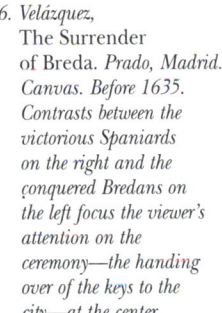

myths, commissioned from Peter Paul Rubens, the court painter of Philip's brother Fernando, governor of the Spanish Netherlands. Images of national power, so popular with monarchs in ascendancy, seemed inappropriate in this period of dynastic decline. Nevertheless, one room in the Buen Retiro was decorated with scenes of Spanish victory. Velázquez's dignified and stately *Surrender of Breda* commemorated one of the rare successes of Spanish forces in the Netherlands, even though the Dutch had recaptured the city almost immediately. More powerful was Maino's *Recovery of Bahia*, which commemorated a Spanish victory

in America and showed Philip IV crowned by victory and Olivares trampling Heresy, Anger, and War. The deaths of his wife (1644) and his heir, Prince Baltazar Carlos (1646), led Philip to choose a new wife, with whom he had more children. Velázquez's masterpiece *Las Meninas* (1656) portrayed his daughter, the Infanta Margherita, together with her maids (*meninas*), servants, a dog, and a dwarf. Velázquez himself appears at the left of the canvas in his role as court artist, and the faces of the king and queen are reflected in the mirror on the back wall. Intended as a court portrait for the royal apartments, the image was remarkable

for its informality and avoidance of all references to imperial power. The image of Velázquez with his instruments of craft— brush, palette, and easel—underscored the rising status of the artist and growing respect for creative talent.

Religious Art in Spain

Religious art in seventeenth-century Spain was produced in a variety of forms and under very different circumstances. Dramatic altarpieces provided images that celebrated the triumph of the Catholic Church. Francisco de Zurbarán was a close

8. *Velázquez, Las Meninas. Prado, Madrid. Canvas. 1656. In this celebrated work, Velázquez recorded an informal and relaxed moment in everyday court life: posing before an artist.*

8

contemporary of Velázquez, but his patrons were mainly provincial monasteries. The contrast between the styles of the two artists reflected the increasing seclusion of the court at Madrid. The success of the Counter-Reformation and revived power of Catholicism inspired new subjects and new interpretations, which found a ready market in Spain. The *Immaculate Conception* by Bartolome Murillo was one of many images of this controversial doctrine produced in seventeenth-century Spain. With regard to this subject, Pacheco's treatise on art laid down guidelines that called for a combination of reality and symbolism.

Recognizing that the crescent moon, commonly associated with the Immaculate Conception, is in fact a segment of a sphere, he encouraged painters to depict the two horns pointing down. Murillo, however, was clearly less interested in physical reality, and his image expressed spiritual rather than scientific truth.

The Spanish Netherlands

The rise of Protestantism in northern Europe was fiercely opposed by the Spanish rulers of the Netherlands, who saw it not only as heresy but also as a threat to their authority.

Protestantism thus became the focus of political rebellion, and localized riots soon developed into open war (1568–1648). With the Peace of Westphalia (1648), the northern provinces achieved independence and established the Republic of the Netherlands (see chapter 37). The southern provinces, however, had been reconquered by Spain. Philip II had installed his daughter, Isabella, and her husband, Archduke Albert of Austria, as rulers of the Spanish Netherlands (1598). A truce (called in 1609) provided the monarchs with an opportunity to give visual expression to the restoration of Spanish authority. Architects, sculptors, and

9. *Bartolomé Murillo,* The Immaculate Conception. *Prado, Madrid. Canvas. Ca. 1678. Giving visual expression to the reaffirmation of this controversial doctrine, Murillo (1618–1682) followed contemporary recommendations for the representation of the Immaculate Virgin, including an association with the crescent moon.*

10. *Francisco de Zurbarán,* Lying in State of St. Bonaventure. *Louvre, Paris. Canvas. Ca. 1629. Drawing inspiration from Rome, Zurbarán (1598–1664) created an image that expressed the religious fervor of the age in this work for the Franciscan church of St. Bonaventure in Seville.*

11. *Rubens,* The Raising of the Cross. *Cathedral, Antwerp. Panel. Ca. 1609–1610. Violence and drama gave visual expression to the power of Roman Catholicism in its defense against Protestant heresy in the Netherlands.*

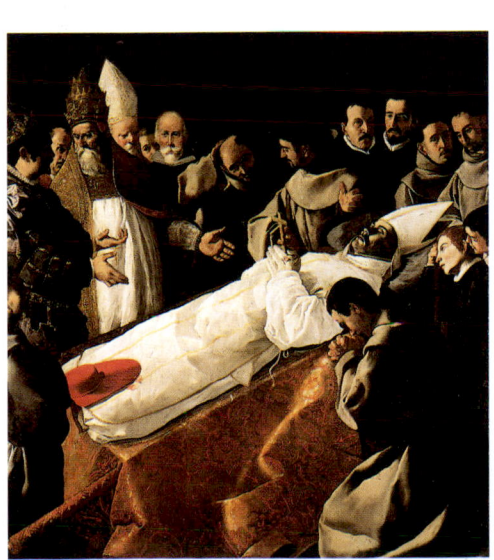

9

10

11

A painter, designer, scholar, and diplomat knighted by Charles I of England, Sir Peter Paul Rubens (1577–1640) was immensely successful. He was trained as a painter in Antwerp before traveling to Italy (1600–1608) and service with the Gonzaga dukes of Mantua.

While in Italy, Rubens studied both classical art and contemporary painters, especially Michelangelo and Caravaggio, and learned much about the use of rich colors from Venetian artists such as Titian and Veronese.

While on a diplomatic mission to Madrid, he copied the works created by Titian in the Spanish royal collection. Deeply influenced by his Italian experience, Rubens was appointed official painter at the Hapsburg court in Antwerp, developing a dramatic and sensuous style that established him as the leading and most sought-after artist in northern Europe.

His skill at organizing complex poses into powerful, dynamic, but harmonious compositions was put to good use in religious and secular commissions, which were indeed quite numerous.

Known for his fondness for the female figure, Rubens frequently exploited his ability to capture the texture of flesh. In his later years, however, his style became calmer. His marriage (1630) to Hélène

Fourment, many years younger than Rubens, inspired an informal portrait of the couple with his son (see figure 12). This painting is set in an austere landscape that contains classically inspired elements.

With his purchase of a country estate, the Château de Steen, Rubens cultivated an interest in landscape, and his free, calm, and atmospheric style stood in marked contrast to the formal classical landscapes of Lorrain and Poussin (see chapter 38).

12. *Rubens*, Rubens and Hélène Fourment with Rubens's Son. *Alte Pinakothek, Munich. Panel. Ca. 1635–1638.*

14. *Rubens,* The Consequences of War. *Palazzo Pitti, Florence. Canvas. 1638. Drama and disorder gave visual expression to the state of seventeenth-century Europe.*

15. *Rubens*, Justus Lipsius and His Three Disciples. *Palazzo Pitti, Florence. Canvas. Ca. 1612. Rubens was closely associated with the intellectual circle of the reconverted Catholic humanist Justus Lipsius, seated under the bust of the Stoic philosopher Seneca. Rubens portrayed himself at the left.*

12

13. *Rubens*, The Judgment of Paris. *Prado, Madrid. Panel. 1638–1639. Rubens's ideals of feminine beauty were reflected in this depiction of the three goddesses, Juno, Minerva, and Venus. Paris was to choose Venus as the loveliest, thereby provoking the Trojan War.*

13

painters were encouraged to return to the Netherlands to contribute to the new image of the Spanish Hapsburg court. Foremost among these was Rubens, whose family was from Antwerp. Before his appointment by Albert (1609), Rubens had been employed as court painter by the Gonzaga family in Mantua (1603–1608). Significantly, he had also received religious commissions in Rome through Albert's influence. Unlike Velázquez in Madrid, Rubens painted very few court portraits. The Spanish reconquest of the Netherlands could be expressed more effectively through the reinforcement of Catholic faith.

The Defeat of Protestantism

The wars had caused havoc. In Antwerp, iconoclast rioters had stripped churches of their statues and altarpieces (1566–1567). Spanish soldiers had sacked the city and burned the town hall (1576), and the Protestant government had whitewashed church walls (1581). The city was finally retaken after a long siege (1585). Protestants were banished, and Catholicism triumphed. With the support of the Jesuits, Albert and Isabella's regime ensured that the southern provinces remained firmly Catholic as a bastion against the Protestant Dutch

Republic. In Antwerp, ecclesiastical and municipal authorities commissioned altarpieces from Rubens for the new churches, including thirty-nine canvases for the ceiling of the Jesuit church (1620). In these works, his dramatic and powerful style captured the exuberance, grandeur, and dynamism of Italian Baroque in images that gave visual expression to the renewed power of Catholicism.

Ruben's fame as a court painter earned him commissions throughout Europe. As a diplomat, as well as an artist, in the service of Isabella, he participated in peace negotiations in Spain and England,

14

16

16. Rubens, Triumphal Entry of Cardinal Infante Ferdinando of Austria into Antwerp. *Uffizi, Florence. Panel. Ca. 1635. Originally destined for a career in the Church, Philip IV's brother was then appointed to lead the Spanish armies in their fight against the Dutch Republic. Rubens's painting of the Infante's entry into Antwerp used a dramatic pictorial space to reinforce the triumphal theme.*

15

and obtained commissions at both courts. In France, Marie de' Medici commissioned him to paint a cycle of pictures that would glorify herself and her husband, Henri IV (see chapter 34). Rubens's output was tremendous. His works for private patrons ranged from portraits and classical themes to allegories of the wars that had ravaged Europe. His *Consequences of War* depicted Europe dressed in black and stripped of jewels and ornaments, holding an orb that symbolized Christianity. Much of his work was executed by assistants in his Antwerp studio, however, as the master limited himself to providing designs and supervision.

Rubens was immensely successful and could afford to acquire his own collection of paintings—including thirty-six by Titian, Veronese, and Tintoretto—as well as statues, ivories and medals.

The Spanish in America

Convinced of their cultural superiority, the Spanish conquerors in America imposed their own political, economic, and religious organization on the indigenous tribes. Christianity was an essential element in the exercise of Spanish authority in America, as it had been in the Netherlands. Conquest was given visual expression in the destruction of pagan temples and the construction of new Christian churches. Often built on the same sites as the old temples, the latter were invariably located in a prominent position. The churches also introduced a new architectural style to America. Unknown before the Spanish conquest, the arch and classical orders replaced the post-and-lintel construction of indigenous buildings. Superior both technically and intellectually in the eyes of the Spanish, these new buildings reinforced the inferiority of the old culture and the dominant power of the new regime.

17. Rubens, The Rape of the Daughters of Leucippus. *Alte Pinakothek, Munich. Canvas. Ca. 1616–1619. Classical themes were not subject to the Church's ban on nudity in religious art. Rubens's exploitation of the sensuousness of flesh was a hallmark of his style.*

17

PROTESTANT PREACHERS STRESSED THE virtues of thrift, hard work, sobriety, and morality as the true way to salvation. Their message had a particular appeal in the urban centers of the Netherlands, where these same virtues were encouraged to promote mercantile wealth and civic prosperity. But Protestantism was heretical in the eyes of the Catholic Spanish rulers of the Netherlands. Ruthlessly suppressed by Philip II (1555–1598), it became the focus of a bitter struggle for political freedom (1568–1648). Spain kept control of the south (see chapter 36)

CHAPTER 37

THE DUTCH REPUBLIC

The Golden Age of Dutch Art

but the northern provinces, led by Prince William of Orange (1579), split away to form a Protestant Dutch Republic. Independence, effectively recognized in a truce (1609), was finally accepted by Spain (1648).

United under the leadership of the House of Orange, political power was concentrated in the hands of the Protestant mercantile elite in quasi-autonomous centers like Amsterdam, Haarlem, Leiden, and Delft, each sending representatives to the States-General in The Hague. Catholic worship was forbidden in public, but it

1

was accepted in private, and this atmosphere of religious toleration encouraged mass immigration of persecuted minorities from other parts of Europe, notably the Jews.

Prosperity and Independence

The new Republic prospered. Ships of the Dutch East India Company (founded in 1602) exploited the new sea routes to the East, and the Amsterdam Stock Exchange (founded in 1609) provided a forum for merchants, artisans, tradesmen, and farmers to invest their newfound wealth. By the end of the seventeenth century, the Dutch had the highest per capita income in Europe.

Commercial wealth dominated the Republic and a new class of patrons emerged, conscious of their political and financial achievements. Above all, the Dutch promoted their own national identity, their language, and their history to emphasize their independence. The contrast with the absolutist courts elsewhere in Europe was marked, and this was given visual expression in their art and architecture.

Images of Power

The Dutch cities celebrated their independence and prosperity with massive programs of artistic patronage, designed as propaganda to promote the power of the new Republic. Grandiose market halls, weigh houses, and other commercial buildings provided expressions of mercantile wealth. As the prime image of civic power, the town halls provided an arena for competition among centers as each asserted its own identity within the Republic. Decisions relating

1. Rembrandt,
The Company
of Captain Cocq
(The Night Watch).
*Rijksmuseum, Amsterdam.
Canvas. 1642. One of six
portraits commissioned
by the militia in
Amsterdam to decorate
the banqueting room
of the Musketeer's Hall,
Rembrandt's image was
notable for its innovations
in composition.*

2. Hendrick de Keyser, Tomb
of Prince William I.
*Nieuwe Kerk, Delft.
Marble. Commissioned
1614. Although a
Catholic, Prince William
of Orange objected to
Philip II's dictating the
private beliefs of his
subjects, and, under his
leadership, the northern
provinces formed the
Union of Utrecht (1579),
which formed the basis
of the independent
Dutch Republic.*

3. Houckgeest, Interior
of the Nieuwe Kerk,
Delft. *Mauritshuis,
The Hague. Canvas.
1651. Stripped of their
Catholic decoration,
the plain interiors of
Dutch churches reinforced
the importance of
Protestant belief in
the new Dutch Republic.*

to their design, construction and decoration were taken by the city councils. To commemorate the 1609 truce, the States-General in The Hague commissioned a series of paintings illustrating the Batavian victory over Roman imperial armies. A north German tribe, the Batavians had successfully rebelled against Roman domination, and they provided an ideal image for the Dutch victory over Spanish rule. Batavia (now Jakarta) was the name given to the main Dutch East India Company trading station in Java (1619).

Amsterdam Town Hall

Amsterdam was now a center of world trade. Her economic power and wealth were reflected in a formal town plan of canals and streets, designed to accommodate the city's growing population. It was no coincidence that Amsterdam's Town Hall was begun in the same year as Spain formally recognized the Republic, marking the end of the long struggle for freedom (1568–1648).

The simple classical architecture with its carefully chosen program of sculptural and painted decoration expressed the peace, prosperity, and independence of the new régime. The imagery was distinctively Dutch, and scenes of the Batavian victory proclaimed the nation's independence. Other historical subjects included Old Testament or classical leaders who had excelled in the civic virtues of loyalty, honesty, and bravery. Flinck's *Marcus Curtius Dentatus Who Scorned His Enemy's Gold and Chose a Meal of Turnips* was a typical example of the Dutch use of obscure Republican Roman themes to give visual expression to their victory over tyranny. These decorative programs

4. Van der Heyden, View of the Town Hall, *Amsterdam. Louvre, Paris. Canvas. 1668. This view of Amsterdam by Jan van der Heyden (1637–1712) depicts the city's new town hall, begun in 1648. This prestigious building gave visual expression to the aspirations of the new Republic in a program of classical architecture and allegorical sculptural decoration.*

5. Flinck, Marcus Curtius Dentatus Who Scorned His Enemy's Gold and Chose a Meal of Turnips. *Royal Palace (formerly Town Hall), Amsterdam. Canvas. 1656. This painting by Govert Flinck (1615–1660) was intended to convey an explicitly Republican and moral message. The theme was unusual in the context of European seventeenth-century art, and its choice deliberate. Anti-foreign domination and anti-royalist, it provided ideal propaganda for the new régime.*

Arguably the greatest artist of the Dutch School, Rembrandt Harmenszoon van Rijn (1606–1669) was born in Leiden but spent most of his working life in Amsterdam, where he established himself as a successful portrait painter to the wealthy merchants of the new Dutch Republic.

His numerous self-portraits provided him with the opportunity to experiment with contrasts of light and shade, facial expressions, poses, and costumes. Applying his new ideas to portraits of civic officials and individuals as well as to his religious and mythological works, Rembrandt's compositions were markedly less formal than was usual, and he placed considerable emphasis on individual character.

In his later years the style of his paintings, etchings, and drawings changed. The drama of his *Deposition* (1633) gave way to the more contemplative mood of his painting of two biblical figures embracing, often described as *David and Absalom* (1642) and his *Bathsheba* (1654). Explanations for this change have been sought in the death of three of his four children together with his wife, Saskia (1642), and increasing financial problems, which resulted in his bankruptcy (1656). Rembrandt's religious works reflected his devout Protestantism. In contrast to Rubens, his Catholic contemporary, he avoided displays of religious fervor and concentrated on portraying the depths of human emotions and the inner, private feelings of his biblical characters. It must, however, be kept in mind that the quite rich collection of works attributed to Rembrandt has been, for some time now, carefully re-examined and reconsidered What has resulted is that many of the works once thought to be of Rembrandt have been attributed to other artists.

6

6. Rembrandt, Self-Portrait. Louvre, Paris. Canvas. 1660.

8

8. Rembrandt, Bathsheba. Louvre, Paris. Canvas. 1654. Rembrandt's emphasis on the deeper feelings of biblical characters in his religious scenes was illustrated by the pensive Bathsheba as she contemplated the contents of a letter from King David.

7

7. Rembrandt, Biblical Figures Embracing. Hermitage, St. Petersburg. Canvas. 1642.

were exceptionally unusual in the context of seventeenth-century European art. Consciously different from royalist or papal propaganda, they were the result of painstaking research of the Ancient Roman texts of Livy, Tacitus, and Plutarch to find images that not only asserted the new Republican régime but also its determination to resist foreign domination.

Religious Art

The Catholics proclaimed their faith in huge altarpieces and decorative programs. But the Protestants generally upheld the Biblical ban on the worship of images. They had little use for religious art in their churches, and it was restricted to a civic or private context. Rembrandt's scenes of the Passion were commissioned by Prince Frederick Henrick for his palace at The Hague. The preference for Old Testament themes in the Dutch Republic was another aspect of the distinction between Catholic and Protestant beliefs. Old Testament scenes were generally used by the Catholic Church as prefigurations for events in the lives of Christ or the Virgin.

To the Protestant Rembrandt and other Dutch painters, the Old Testament was as much the Word of God as the New Testament. Moreover the Old Testament characters, like the Dutch Protestants, were also awaiting salvation, and, as members of God's chosen race, the Jews provided a parallel for the Dutch achievement. Expressing the internal feelings of his characters, Rembrandt's interpretation of religious themes had little in common with the religious fervor of Roman Baroque art. Indeed, few Dutch artists showed any interest in Italian styles of the age.

9. Rembrandt, Deposition. Alte Pinakothek, Munich. Canvas. 1633. An early work by Rembrandt, this was no Baroque expression of religious glory. Contrasts of light and shade emphasized the reality of the scene.

9

Portraiture

Portraiture was in high demand by the citizens of the new Republic. A portrait not only conveys a form of immortality upon the sitter, but it also communicates much about the society in which it was commissioned. The two images most closely associated with absolute power in seventeenth-century Europe, the full-length individual and equestrian portraits, were comparatively rare in Dutch art. But portraits that expressed family unity and marital harmony were common. Also popular were the official portraits commemorating civic duties in the military, scientific, and charitable institutions of the Protestant state. The Dutch cities had their own militias for security and defense. It was common practice for these companies to commission paintings to commemorate their term of office, each member paying to have his own portrait included. Rembrandt's *Night Watch* was paid for by the company of Captain Frans Banning Cocq and portrayed him with his lieutenant and men. But Rembrandt's interpretation of the theme was new. Giving precedence to the pictorial composition, he was criticized for not paying enough attention to the portraits. The questioning of traditions in religion and art was part of a more general desire to broaden the frontiers of knowledge. Scientific research that was banned by the Catholic Church was not restricted in the Dutch Republic. Annual lectures on anatomy were given by the praelectors of the Surgeon's Guilds in Amsterdam, Leiden, and Delft, and their position was commemorated in official portraits of these lectures. Again, Rembrandt's composition and interpretation of the theme were new. Noticeably less formal, Rembrandt grouped the members of the Guild around a cadaver placed at an angle to the picture plane and emphasized their scientific absorption in the subject.

10. Frans Hals, Officials of the Company of St. Hadrian. *Frans Hals Museum, Haarlem. Canvas. 1633. One of the leading painters in the Dutch Republic, Frans Hals (ca. 1580–1666) settled in Haarlem and concentrated on portraiture.*

10

11. Pieter Jacobs Codde, Portrait of a Couple. *Mauritshuis, The Hague. Panel. 1634. Usually commissioned to celebrate a marriage, this portrait type was popular in the Dutch Republic.*

11

12. Adriaen van Ostade, Family Portrait. *Louvre, Paris. Panel. 1654. Severe and simple, this portrait by the Haarlem painter Adriaen van Ostade (1610–1685) reinforced the virtues of Puritan family life. The roses in the foreground symbolize the pleasures and the pain of love.*

12

One of the most important duties of the Dutch burgher was the fulfilling of his charitable obligations to society. It was the moral duty of wealthy merchants and their wives to help those less fortunate than themselves, and they were expected to serve as Regents and Regentesses in the management of old people's homes, orphanages, poorhouses, lunatic asylums, leper hospitals, and houses of correction. Group portraits of these officials provided visual proof of their charitable actions, as well as gave painters, like Frans Hals, the opportunity to experiment with composition and technique.

Frans Hals and Vermeer: Light and Color

In addition to Rembrandt, the golden age of Dutch painting can boast of two other important protagonists: Frans Hals and Jan Vermeer, who both experimented with a quite original and innovatory pictorial language.

In particular, Hals specialized in portraits and moved in the direction of extraordinary representational freedom. At first, in around 1620, he dedicated his efforts to depicting popular themes, thus allowing himself to emphasize the more realistic aspects. Over time, Hals increasingly developed his light-filled brushstrokes that emphasized, above all, the psychological traits of those portrayed. Then with the group portrait, which was used to commemorate official reunions or representatives of social institutions, Hals gave his figures incredible intensity in their facial and corporeal gestures.

Jan Vermeer, who was about forty years younger than Hals, was able to revolutionize the use of light: in his works light amazingly takes on concreteness. Faithful to reality, the images of Vermeer are permeated, thanks to the brilliant use of light that is oftentimes characterized

13

15

13. Frans Hals, Regents of the Hospital of St. Elizabeth, *Haarlem. Frans Hals Museum, Haarlem. Canvas. 1641.*

14. Rembrandt, Anatomy Lesson of Dr. Tulp. *Mauritshuis, The Hague. Canvas. 1632. This traditional portrait type recorded an annual lecture on anatomy. The lecture in this case was given by Dr. Nicolaes Tulp in January 1632, and he was distinguished from his audience by his tool of office-surgical scissors.*

15. Frans Hals, Regentesses of the Old Men's Home, *Haarlem. Frans Hals Museum, Haarlem. Canvas. Ca. 1664. Hals's skill as a portraitist was reflected in the careful observation of the individual characteristics of these group portraits that recorded the sitters' involvement in charitable work.*

14

by very pure intensity and transparency, with the elegance of poetry. At times he used windows to allow light to enter into his settings, which were enriched by objects or persons from everyday life.

Townscapes, Seascapes, and Landscapes

The bulk of the pictures produced in the Dutch Republic were painted for the open market. Foreign visitors commented on the extent of art ownership. Townscapes, seascapes, and landscapes recorded the context of Dutch life and reflected the urban, maritime, and agricultural sources of her wealth. Less prestigious than historical subjects or portraiture, they were carefully composed and did not faithfully reproduce reality. They also had deeper levels of meaning. Storms and shipwrecks were a reminder of the vagaries of fortune. Calm and rough seas were also metaphors for success and failure in love.

Inspired by ideas found in Ancient Roman literature, urban and rural life were often contrasted in terms of the obligation to fulfill one's civic responsibilities and freedom from these duties.

Morality and Dutch Genre

Our perception of these images is hampered by a need to understand their allegoric or symbolic content, which would have been easily read at the time of their creation. This is particularly true of the scenes of everyday life (genre), also produced for the open market. Personifications of the seasons, elements, or virtues were well established in seventeenth-century Europe and usually portrayed in terms of idealized beauty. But the mercantile culture in the Netherlands had transposed these figures into ordinary people.

16. *Vermeer,* View of Delft from the Rotterdam Canal. *Mauritshuis, The Hague. Canvas. 1658. Careful attention to detail reinforced the reality of this townscape by the Delft painter Jan Vermeer (1632–1675).*

16

18. *Jacob van Ruisdael,* View of a River. *Mauritshuis, The Hague. Canvas. 1665. The naturalistic landscapes of Dutch artists like Jacob van Ruisdael (ca. 1628–1682) were an important influence on the development of landscape artists in France and England.*

17. *Jan van Goyen,* The Mouth of a River. *Mauritshuis, The Hague. Panel. 1655. Jan van Goyen (1596–1656) specialized in the landscapes and seascapes that were so popular in the Dutch Republic.*

17

18

Many of the pictures of Dutch interiors included symbols designed to convey a moral message, its power reinforced by the recognizable visual detail and setting. Vermeer's *The Letter* relates much about the interior of a middle-class Dutch house, but it was intended to convey something more specific. Music and love were associated in contemporary literature, and the seascape on the wall behind reflected its content. Steen's *The Merry Company* depicted men, women, and children of all ages enjoying themselves. But the paper held by the old woman contained the words of a popular song on how children imitate the habits of the elders. These elders were not setting a very good example. De Hooch's painting of a woman drinking with soldiers contained another moral sermon on the effects of alcohol. The woman's posture and her glass, held at a slight angle, suggested that she had drunk too much. The implications of this were reinforced by the painting above the fireplace, which portrays Christ and the adultress. Other images were more explicitly sexual. Metsu's hunter carries a dead partridge and a gun, but it would be a mistake to think that all he has to offer is food. The Dutch word for bird was also a slang term for sexual intercourse and the gun, a common symbol for the penis.

Images of *Vanitas*

The Dutch made important contributions to the developing science of botany, and the rare species found in the East were avidly collected. The popularity of flower paintings in the Republic testified to this interest. Although each plant was faithfully represented, the composition was imaginary and often included flowers that bloomed at different seasons. But these pictures were not painted solely as aesthetic compositions.

19

19. *Vermeer*, Woman Reading a Letter. *Rijksmuseum, Amsterdam. Canvas. Ca. 1670.*

20

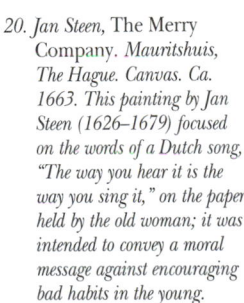

21

20. *Jan Steen*, The Merry Company. *Mauritshuis, The Hague. Canvas. Ca. 1663. This painting by Jan Steen (1626–1679) focused on the words of a Dutch song, "The way you hear it is the way you sing it," on the paper held by the old woman; it was intended to convey a moral message against encouraging bad habits in the young.*

21. *Pieter de Hooch*, Woman Drinking with Soldiers. *Louvre, Paris. Canvas. 1658. Careful attention to the details of a typical Dutch interior reinforced the moral message contained in this scene by Pieter de Hooch (1629–after 1684).*

They also had a didactic purpose. The symbolic language of flowers has a long history. Lilies, roses, and carnations had been traditionally used as Christian symbols for purity, love, and resurrection. But flowers decay, and this message was reinforced by Van Beyeren, who added an open pocket watch to his composition to express the transience of their beauty. Other symbols regularly used by Dutch painters to give visual expression to the vanity of human life included skulls and soap bubbles. The tulip was fashionable and expensive until its market crashed (1637), and it too became a symbol of vanitas.

22

22. Gabriel Metsu, The Hunter's Gift. *Uffizi, Florence. Panel. Ca. 1660. The partridge was a common symbol of lust in seventeenth-century Dutch art and literature. Metsu (1629–1667) reinforced the message with other similar images in this scene.*

23. Van Beyeren, Vase of Flowers. *Mauritshuis, The Hague. Canvas. Ca. 1660. The tulip was both fashionable and expensive until its market collapsed (1637), and it became a symbol of vanitas. Like other Dutch flower painters, Van Beyeren (ca. 1620–1690) studied his flowers from life, but their combinations were not necessarily realistic, and it was common to find the blooms of different seasons together.*

23

ALTHOUGH THE ART MARKET IN seventeenth-century Europe was dominated by patrons and artists at the courts of absolutist monarchs and the papacy in Rome, it was not exclusively so. Increasing wealth, leisure, literacy, and intellectual freedom among the middle classes encouraged the patronage of the arts. Mercantile patrons in the Dutch Republic had stimulated the development of new ideas in the arts that gave visual expression to their own distinctive society (see chapter 37). Elsewhere, middle-class patrons found images that were more appropriate for their particular culture than the overwhelming

CHAPTER 38

STYLES, SUBJECTS, AND PATRONS

New Ideas in Seventeenth-Century Art

displays of extravagance and opulence created to reinforce the supremacy of spiritual and temporal power. The religious and social upheavals of the previous century had made a profound impact on the development of philosophical and scientific thought. Rational explanations were now sought for issues previously answered by reference to the Bible, and the value of the pagan cultures of antiquity were re-examined in the light of this new approach. While not immediately threatening established authority, these new ideas were expressed in the development of a number

1

of different artistic styles and themes that had important implications for the development of art.

Caravaggio and the Caravaggesques

The desire to express the fervor of religious belief that had resulted in the exuberant, grandiose, and illusionistic works of Baroque Rome (see chapter 33) also inspired Caravaggio. Michelangelo Merisi da Caravaggio (1571–1610) was born near Milan and trained with a local painter before going to Rome (ca. 1590). After painting a series of genre scenes, portraits, and mythologies, he obtained his first major commission, the decoration of the Contarelli Chapel in San Luigi dei Francesi in Rome (1597) with three scenes from the life of St. Matthew: *St. Matthew and the Angel,* the *Calling of St. Matthew,* and the *Martyrdom of St. Matthew.* Caravaggio's interpretation of these scenes was innovatory. In his *Calling of St. Matthew,* Christ's face is almost entirely in the dark, a shaft of light illuminating the edge of his halo and, above all, the hand that points across the scene at Matthew. This departure from tradition was not generally approved of in Rome, where the need to proclaim the supernatural power of the Catholic Church was seen as paramount. Caravaggio earned more disapproval by deliberately emphasizing the ordinariness of the figures he depicted. His unsophisticated settings, his preference for portraying simple, often ugly people rather than the idealized and beautiful personifications of religious faith, set him apart from his contemporaries. His use of a woman drowned in the Tiber as a model for his *Death of the Virgin* was particularly criticized and, like many of his works, it was rejected by Church

1. Caravaggio, Bowl of Fruit. *Pinacoteca Ambrosiana, Milan. Canvas. 1596. This still life was commissioned by Cardinal Federico Borromeo, a major figure in the Counter-Reformation (see chapter 30).*

2. Caravaggio, The Calling of St. Matthew. *San Luigi dei Francesi, Rome. Canvas. 1599–1602. One of a cycle of three paintings on the life of St. Matthew, commissioned by Matteo Contarelli for his chapel in the French church in Rome, this painting illustrates Caravaggio's skill at using chiaroscuro to enhance the drama of the subject. Lighting up Christ's hand rather than his face, Caravaggio recorded the moment when Jesus called St. Matthew from his occupation as a tax collector for the Romans to become one of the apostles.*

2

authorities. In 1606, as a result of a violent quarrel, Caravaggio was forced to leave Rome and move to Naples. His late paintings show a greater intensity of feeling, heightened by the use of *chiaroscuro*. It was works like his *Adoration of the Shepherds,* with its emphasis on the simplicity of the scene, which were of such influence in northern Europe. But his paintings were utterly different from those of his contemporaries in Rome. Exploiting contrasts between light and shade to give drama to his works, Caravaggio stressed the physical reality of his characters by depicting them as simple, ordinary people. His style was unpopular in Rome, but it inspired artists in northern Europe. Catholic patrons in France and the Netherlands responded to this desire to emphasize the human drama of religious events. Foremost among his followers, known as the Caravaggesques, was La Tour, whose patrons were mainly middle-class, local government officials in Lorraine. Lacking all pretensions of grandeur, La Tour's *Christ and St. Joseph in the Carpenter's Shop* depicted a very ordinary artisan and a youth, using a simple candle to light up Christ's face and so focus on him rather than the larger figure of Joseph.

The Le Nain Brothers

Middle-class patronage in France also influenced the development of new types of secular imagery. The three Le Nain brothers, whose separate identities have not yet been fully established, specialized in portraiture. Their patrons included civic government officials in Paris and also members of their own class, the new bourgeois landowners. Capitalizing on the financial problems of the French peasantry, the urban middle classes bought up land. This new form of investment had the added advantage of classical parallels. Cicero, Virgil, and Pliny had all

3. *Caravaggio,* Boy with a Bowl of Fruit. *Galleria Borghese, Rome. Canvas. 1593.*

4. *Caravaggio,* Adoration of the Shepherds. *Museo Nazionale, Messina. Canvas. 1609. Caravaggio (1571–1610) exploited the dramatic potential of chiaroscuro, the contrast between light and shade, and his style formed the fundamental influence on the development of the so-called Caravaggesques in northern Europe.*

5. *Georges de la Tour,* Christ and St. Joseph in the Carpenter's Shop. *Louvre, Paris. Canvas. Ca. 1645. The French painter Georges de la Tour (1593–1652) developed a simple, naturalistic style, carefully observing the effects of light to emphasize the important elements in his scenes.*

6. *Louis (?) Le Nain,* La Charrette. *Louvre, Paris. Canvas. Ca. 1640. A scene of the rural bourgeoisie by one of the Le Nain brothers reflected the new middle-class investment in land in seventeenth-century France.*

POUSSIN AND CLASSICISM

Nicolas Poussin (1594-1665) trained as a painter in Paris before going to Rome (1624), where he worked with major Baroque artists and obtained a commission to paint an altarpiece for St. Peter's (the *Martyrdom of St. Erasmus*, now in the Vatican).

First he visited Venice. Returning to Paris only on a few rare occasions, Poussin moved to Rome, where he died. Around 1630 his style changed dramatically, and the severe, classical manner he adopted was a marked contrast to his contemporaries. The same was also true of the classical themes of his paintings. Instead of the mythological *poésie* popularized by imitators of Titian or the classically inspired allegories of state power, Poussin's patrons preferred scenes from the history of Republican Rome.

His painting of *The Continence of Scipio* (formerly in the collection of Earl of Derby, now in the Pushkin Museum in Moscow) related the story of Scipio's treatment of a beautiful girl, whom he received as a prize after his capture of Carthage. Restoring her unviolated to her fiancé, his act reinforced the moral, austere, and virtuous image of Republican Rome.

Poussin's brilliant treatment of the theme deserves special mention for its narrative clarity. Seated on a throne, Scipio was presented in the act of returning the captured bride to her groom, and the clear composition of the figures emphasized logic, rationality, and proportion.

This intellectual approach was very different from the emotional fervor and intensity of Baroque Rome, and Poussin's work was a rather fundamental and essential influence on the development of the neoclassical movement with painters like Jacques-Louis David in the eighteenth century (see chapter 43).

7

9

8

10

owned farms, and the Ancient Roman virtues of frugality and morality were cultivated by their French followers. Often described as a scene of peasant life, *La Charrette* was not intended to portray the rural poor. On the contrary, their clothes betray their middle-class status, wealthy enough to afford shoes, even for the baby.

Poussin

Other artists responded to an increasingly archeological interest in antiquity. Poussin's early career brought him from France to Rome (1624), where he obtained a prestigious commission for an altarpiece in St. Peter's. But he opted out of the main arena. Contact with Cassiano del Pozzo, secretary to Cardinal Francesco Barberini (see chapter 33), led to a dramatic change in both the style and the content of his paintings.

Cassiano's passion for antiquity had resulted in a huge collection of drawings of the remains of Ancient Rome, and his archeological approach to the ruins was a foretaste of the neoclassical movement that developed in the eighteenth century (see chapter 41). Poussin's works reflected these new ideas. Austere and intellectual, his paintings were clearly inspired by the sculptural remains of antiquity. Commissions from Richelieu and Louis XIII established his reputation in France, and his style was much admired by the French Academy. But his major French patrons came from the intellectual middle-class circles in Paris who had revived the classical philosophy of Stoicism. Giving visual expression to the austere and moral ideals associated with Stoicism both in his style and choice of subject-matter, Poussin's paintings were a distinct contrast to the extravagant and luxurious images associated with the court.

7. *Nicolas Poussin,* The Ashes of Phocion. *Collection of Earl of Derby, Knowsley, Lancashire. Canvas. 1648. The layout of this scene of Phocion's wife gathering his ashes reflected Poussin's application of simple logic to pictorial composition.*

8. *Nicolas Poussin,* The Continence of Scipio. *Moscow, Pushkin Museum. Canvas. Ca. 1650.*

11

11. *Stefano da Verona,* Madonna of the Rose Garden. *Museo di Castelvecchio, Verona. Panel. Early fifteenth century. Nature was the source of a wealth of symbolic imagery for the medieval world and its artists.*

9. *Nicolas Poussin,* The Israelites Gathering Manna. *Louvre, Paris. Canvas. 1638. Poussin applied his classically inspired style to religious works that were a marked contrast to the exuberant Baroque of his contemporaries like Rubens or Bernini.*

10. *Nicolas Poussin,* Narcissus and Echo. *Louvre, Paris. Canvas. Between 1629 and 1633. Probably painted shortly after Poussin came into contact with the Roman antiquarian Cassiano del Pozzo, this picture illustrated his development of a more* all'antica *style.*

12

12. *Pieter Brueghel,* The Fall of Icarus. *Musée des Beaux-Arts, Brussels. Canvas. 1558. Ships, the plow, and other carefully observed details created a naturalistic setting for this mythological scene by Pieter Brueghel the Elder (ca. 1528–1569).*

The Development of the Classical Landscape

Poussin was also a key figure in the emergence of landscape as an independent art form in seventeenth-century Europe, an event of great significance in the history of art. Landscapes were not new. They had long provided the background for religious and classical scenes, as well as portraits. Images like Stefano da Verona's *Virgin of the Rose Garden* or Brueghel's *Fall of Icarus* called specifically for an outdoor setting. Much of the natural detail in Stefano da Verona's painting had a symbolic meaning that reinforced its message: the enclosed garden itself was a symbol of Mary's virginity, the roses reflected her sinlessness, and the peacocks symbolized immortality. The recognizable details in Brueghel's landscape enhanced the reality of the scene taking place. But neither of these images was a landscape per se. The idea of painting a landscape for itself had its roots in antiquity and in the descriptions of classical art in Ancient Roman literature. The seventeenth-century Dutch school of landscape painters (see chapter 37) and others like Rubens were at least partly influenced by this tradition. Rubens's interest in the vitality of nature and the effects of the weather and light were recorded in idealized settings.

There is scant evidence of artists reproducing what they actually saw in seventeenth-century landscapes. The growing archeological interest in antiquity also inspired another school of landscape painters, who developed a set of rules for composition and structure in order to create an image that evoked the spirit, if not the reality, of the classical world. Imposing reason and order on the creation of idealized beauty was a deliberate attempt to give the landscape an intellectual content. Known as the classical landscape, this type was developed by artists in Rome,

13. *Albrecht Dürer,* View of Arco. *Louvre, Paris. Paper. 1495. Dürer's watercolor sketches of his travels were an important step in the development of landscape as an independent genre.*

14. *Annibale Carracci,* Landscape with the Flight into Egypt. *Galleria Doria-Pamphili, Rome. Canvas. Ca. 1604. Carracci's evocative use of landscape provided a setting for this biblical story.*

15. *Rubens,* Return of the Peasants from the Fields. *Palazzo Pitti, Florence. Canvas. 1635–1638. Rubens's interest in landscape painting developed toward the end of his life, and he imbued his scenes with vitality and movement.*

14

13

15

above all Poussin and another French painter, Lorrain. Pictorial space was divided into three distances, graded by changes in color and linked by features frequently classical in inspiration, such as temples or ruins. Order was enhanced by carefully balancing areas of light and shade. Both Lorrain and Poussin followed these rules but their results were different. Poussin's intellectual, cold and austere approach reflected his interest in the heroic image of antiquity. Lorrain's atmospheric, lyrical, and calm paintings evoked the more pastoral themes of Roman poetry.

16

17

16. Claude Lorrain, Landscape with a Mill. *Galleria Doria-Pamphili, Rome. Canvas. 1648. Lorrain (1600–1682) used carefully contrived repoussoir elements, including both man-made and natural features, to lead the viewer into his picture.*

17. Claude Lorrain, Port with the Villa Medici. *Uffizi, Florence. Canvas. 1637. Subtle and lyrical, Lorrain's approach to landscape was very different from the classical heroism of Poussin.*

18

18. Nicolas Poussin, Summer (Ruth and Boaz). *Louvre, Paris. Canvas. 1660–1664. This biblical story enabled Poussin to exploit his idea of formal landscape composition, arranging his buildings and trees with subtle color gradations to create a sense of depth.*

THE EIGHTEENTH CENTURY

Looking at all aspects of Western Civilization, the eighteenth century was the golden age of reason and hence of the great achievements in politics and knowledge. There were many and different artistic trends in this century that was characterized by great vitality; artists and architects traveled frequently from one country to another—and ventured even as far as imperial Russia. The frivolous, ornate Rococo tastes (popular and widespread mainly in France and Spain) that took over from the Baroque of the previous century were offset by a renewed interest in classical antiquity. The Neoclassical style, as expressed so fully in Winckelmann's theories and Canova's art, was augmented by the archaeological discoveries in Italy and Greece. Artists and intellectuals spent long periods in Italy during their "grand tours" (the "compulsory" cultural journey for young people of the upper classes and for intellectuals in general). The century of the Enlightenment and of revolutions saw the birth of new museums throughout Europe, and the existing ones were systemically reorganized. Great encyclopedias and treatises on antiquity were also published. In addition, a new artistic genre developed, mainly in Italy and England: caricature and political satire. In the Far East great masters were perfecting architecture and the decorative arts with increasingly sophisticated techniques such as prints and porcelain that aroused the great interest and enthusiasm of the West.

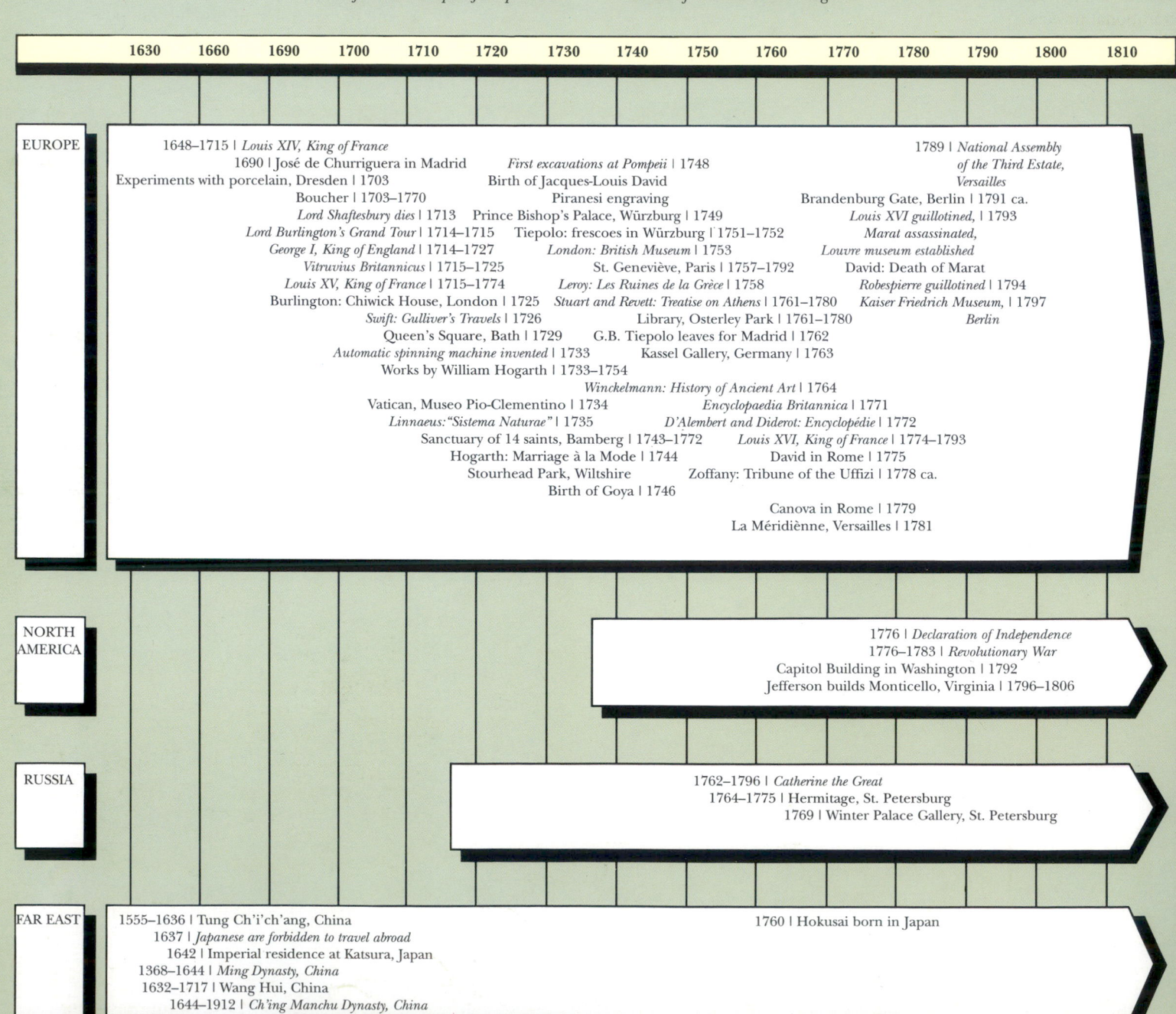

| | 1630 | 1660 | 1690 | 1700 | 1710 | 1720 | 1730 | 1740 | 1750 | 1760 | 1770 | 1780 | 1790 | 1800 | 1810 |

EUROPE

1648–1715 | *Louis XIV, King of France*
1690 | José de Churriguera in Madrid
Experiments with porcelain, Dresden | 1703
Boucher | 1703–1770
Lord Shaftesbury dies | 1713
Lord Burlington's Grand Tour | 1714–1715
George I, King of England | 1714–1727
Vitruvius Britannicus | 1715–1725
Louis XV, King of France | 1715–1774
Burlington: Chiwick House, London | 1725
Swift: Gulliver's Travels | 1726
Queen's Square, Bath | 1729
Automatic spinning machine invented | 1733
Works by William Hogarth | 1733–1754
Vatican, Museo Pio-Clementino | 1734
Linnaeus: "Sistema Naturae" | 1735
Sanctuary of 14 saints, Bamberg | 1743–1772
Hogarth: Marriage à la Mode | 1744
Stourhead Park, Wiltshire
Birth of Goya | 1746

First excavations at Pompeii | 1748
Birth of Jacques-Louis David
Piranesi engraving
Prince Bishop's Palace, Würzburg | 1749
Tiepolo: frescoes in Würzburg | 1751–1752
London: British Museum | 1753
St. Geneviève, Paris | 1757–1792
Leroy: Les Ruines de la Grèce | 1758
Stuart and Revett: Treatise on Athens | 1761–1780
Library, Osterley Park | 1761–1780
G.B. Tiepolo leaves for Madrid | 1762
Kassel Gallery, Germany | 1763
Winckelmann: History of Ancient Art | 1764
Encyclopaedia Britannica | 1771
D'Alembert and Diderot: Encyclopédie | 1772
Louis XVI, King of France | 1774–1793
David in Rome | 1775
Zoffany: Tribune of the Uffizi | 1778 ca.
Canova in Rome | 1779
La Méridiènne, Versailles | 1781

1789 | *National Assembly of the Third Estate, Versailles*
Brandenburg Gate, Berlin | 1791 ca.
Louis XVI guillotined, | 1793
Marat assassinated, Louvre museum established
David: Death of Marat
Robespierre guillotined | 1794
Kaiser Friedrich Museum, | 1797 *Berlin*

NORTH AMERICA

1776 | *Declaration of Independence*
1776–1783 | *Revolutionary War*
Capitol Building in Washington | 1792
Jefferson builds Monticello, Virginia | 1796–1806

RUSSIA

1762–1796 | *Catherine the Great*
1764–1775 | Hermitage, St. Petersburg
1769 | Winter Palace Gallery, St. Petersburg

FAR EAST

1555–1636 | Tung Ch'i'ch'ang, China
1637 | *Japanese are forbidden to travel abroad*
1642 | Imperial residence at Katsura, Japan
1368–1644 | *Ming Dynasty, China*
1632–1717 | *Wang Hui, China*
1644–1912 | *Ch'ing Manchu Dynasty, China*

1760 | Hokusai born in Japan

THE WORD "ROCOCO" WAS FIRST USED at the end of the eighteenth century as a term of abuse to describe the frivolous and decorative style associated with the aristocratic elite of pre-Revolutionary France. But it was not uniquely French. In Austria, Germany, Italy, and Spain the grandeur of seventeenth-century Baroque was replaced by a new approach that exploited its decorative potential. Adopted by the Church as well as by absolute monarchs and aristocrats as an expression of wealth and status, this artificial style epitomized the self-complacency of traditional powers in early eighteenth-

CHAPTER 39

EXTRAVAGANCE AND FRIVOLITY

The Development of Rococo Art

century Europe, ignoring or unaware of the increasingly vociferous opposition around them. Rococo art and architecture was imaginative and original. Dispensing with the formal rules of classical ornament, it promoted an image that was markedly less popular in intellectual circles or in Protestant England and the Dutch Republic.

Rococo Art in France

In his old age Louis XIV (1643–1715) rejected the grandeur of the Baroque established by Colbert and Lebrun as an expression of his absolute power

1

(see chapter 34) in favor of a more relaxed and pleasure-seeking image. The formal classical rules of the Academy were rejected. The earlier emphasis on drawing and the intellect, typified in the work of Poussin, was replaced by a desire for color and sensual effect as used by Rubens and the Venetian artists, notably Titian. The Poussinistes and the Rubénistes debated the superiority of their own approach. But fashionable court society opted for pleasure, and Louis XIV's successor, Louis XV (1715–1774), developed the themes of leisure and luxury as an image for his court. Above all, it was a decorative style and found

its best expression in the large quantities of furniture, porcelain, and silver produced for its ornamentation. Intimacy and informality were reflected in smaller rooms, decorated with intricate detail. Light, elegant pastel colors replaced the rich, heavy, and dark interiors of the seventeenth century. Straight lines were broken with curves and arabesques. Elaborate naturalistic ornament further distracted the eye from architectural boundaries. The prevalence of shell motifs, or *rocaille*, gave the style its name, Rococo. Increasing trade with the East stimulated a fashion for Chinese lacquer, porcelain, and silk.

This reflected the growing interest in asymmetrical elegance and oriental ornament became an important feature of Rococo design.

Watteau and Boucher

A new generation of painters responded to these ideas. Rejecting the historical and religious subjects preferred by the classical academicians, they also avoided the dramatic style of Baroque art. Watteau's series of paintings exploring the theme of Cythera, the island of Love, was typical. Influenced by the mythological

1. François Boucher, Diana at Her Bath. *Louvre, Paris. Canvas. 1757. Boucher's elegant and intimate painting of Diana had little in common with the proud image of the Virgin Huntress promoted by Louis XIV.*

2. Jean Antoine Watteau, L'Enseigne de Gersaint. *Schloss Charlottenburg, Berlin. Canvas. 1720. Elegant, informal, and relaxed, Watteau's style was typically Rococo.*

3. Boffrand, Salon de la Princesse. *Hôtel de Soubise, Paris. 1736–1739. The grandiose interiors of the Baroque gave way to the lighter elegance of Rococo.*

4. Jean Antoine Watteau, Embarkation for Cythera. *Schloss Charlottenburg, Berlin. Canvas. 1717. Jean Antoine Watteau (1684–1721) owed much to Venetian artists in his use of color.*

Intimate, pretty, affectionate, and, to our eyes, often frivolous, Rococo portraits have a distinctive charm. Their informality provides a marked contrast to the dignified, pompous, and glorified images of Baroque power.

Two of the leading portrait painters at the court of Louis XV, both Jean Marc Nattier (1685–1766) and François Boucher (1703–1770) had been trained in the Baroque style. Nattier, in particular, had worked on engravings of Rubens's *Marie de' Medici.* But the death of Louis XIV (1715) and the accession of Louis XV inevitably imposed a different character on the French court, which was reflected in new approaches to portraiture and, above all, to stylistic change.

Nattier's painting of Marie Leczinska, wife of Louis XV, made no effort to present her as the Queen of France, resplendent in the jewels and clothes of state. On the contrary, this quiet, smiling portrait is remarkable for its informality of pose and gesture, for the delicate treatment of the texture of her skin, and for the exquisite detailing of lace.

Boucher's portrait of Madame de Pompadour, the official mistress of Louis XV, was equally informal. Daughter of a wealthy financier, she was arguably the leading patron of the Rococo fashion at the French court. Boucher's skill at capturing her elegant idleness was reflected in her elaborate dress and tiny feet and the rustic setting of the scene. His nude portrait of an unofficial mistress of the French court made no attempt to mask pleasure behind an allegorical façade.

Deliberately provocative, this portrait gave visual expression to the atmosphere of amorous amusement and playfulness that characterized the leisured noble court of Louis XV.

EXTRAVAGANCE AND FRIVOLITY

5

6

5. *François Boucher,*
Louise O'Murphy.
Alte Pinakothek, Munich.
Canvas. 1752.

6. *François Boucher,*
Madame de Pompadour.
Victoria & Albert Museum,
London. Canvas. 1758.
The patronage of the
mistress of Louis XV firmly
established the reputation
of Boucher (1703–1770)
at the French court.

7. *Jean-Marc Nattier,* Marie
Leczinska. *Louvre, Paris.*
Canvas. 1748. Nattier
(1685–1766) worked
at the French court from
1740, where his skill as
a portrait painter earned
him many commissions.

7

poésie of Titian and Veronese, he depicted a peaceful, dreamy, and idyllic world peopled by carefree insubstantial individuals whose sole aim appeared to be pleasure. The Academy named them *fêtes galantes*, a new term to reflect their innovatory style and subject. His *L'Enseigne de Gersaint* showed a more realistic event, the appreciation and purchase of works of art, but treated it with the same lack of formality and grandeur. Other artists emphasized the intimate content of mythological scenes in contrast to the heroic image promoted earlier. Boucher's employment by Madame de Pompadour, the officially recognized

mistress of Louis XV, established his reputation at the court at Versailles, and his work included designs for Sèvres porcelain and tapestries. His *Diana at Her Bath* was hardly the image of a powerful goddess. Intimate and sensual, it was more like a scene in a boudoir than Mount Olympus. The boudoir theme was developed further in his portrait of one of Louis's less official mistresses. This playful nude, with her delicate coloring and hedonistic pose, captured the spirit of Rococo art and gave visual expression to the frivolity and luxury of Louis's court.

Tiepolo at the Courts in Würzburg and Madrid

Similar developments took place throughout Europe. At some courts, French Rococo had a direct influence. The Elector of Bavaria, who had been in exile in France, returned to Munich (1714) and adopted French Rococo as the image for his renewed power. His court architect Cuvilliés was sent to France for training in the new style. His decorative schemes for the Elector's palace interiors were even more fanciful and frivolous than those in France. In other places, the growing passion for decoration

8. *Giambattista Tiepolo,* Sacrifice of Iphigenia. *Villa Valmarana ai Nani, Vicenza. Fresco. 1757. Putti balanced on moving clouds and incidental details like the man's hand on a column deliberately distracted from the intense drama of the scene.*

8

9. *Johann Balthasar Neumann,* Prince-Bishop's Palace, Kaisersaal. Würzburg. *1749–1754; frescoes by Tiepolo, 1751–1752. Extravagant and luxurious, the design of this interior gave visual expression to the power and prestige of its patron.*

9

was reflected in styles that evolved more directly from seventeenth-century Baroque. The immense palace of the Prince-Bishop of Würzburg was typical in its extravagant use of ornament as an expression of wealth and power. The grandeur and scale of the Kaisersaal had little in common with the intimacy of French Rococo interiors, but it reflected the same desire to disguise the straight lines of classical architecture with frivolous gilded ornament. The Prince-Bishop commissioned a Venetian artist, Tiepolo, to paint more explicit statements of his power. Like the architecture, the subjects of the frescoes recall the heroic imagery of the Baroque. Above the main staircase, Tiepolo painted the *Four Continents* paying homage to this petty ruler, whose territory in no way justified the theme. But the style was distinctly different. Tiepolo's skill at combining the illusionism and theatricality of Baroque art with a lighter range of colors and frivolous detail to create ephemeral images of the past and present was much in demand with aristocratic patrons in Venice. He was also commissioned to decorate the throne room in the new royal palace in Madrid with an apotheosis of the Spanish monarchy.

Rococo and Religion

The decorative potential of Baroque was also exploited in a religious context. In Germany a series of new pilgrimage churches proclaimed the power of the Catholic faith. The plan of the church of Vierzehnheiligen was basically a Latin cross, but its simplicity was disguised with curves and elaborated by the use of ovals. The ambiguities of the plan contributed to the fantasy world created inside. White and gold, asymmetrical and curvaceous, this stuccoed and gilded interior provided a setting for worship that consciously aimed

EXTRAVAGANCE AND FRIVOLITY

10

11

12

10. *Giambattista Tiepolo,* Asia. *Prince-Bishop's Palace, Würzburg. Fresco. 1751–1752. The Venetian artist Tiepolo (1696–1770) was commissioned to fresco much of the interior of the palace, including the ceiling of the grand ceremonial staircase, which was decorated with personifications of the four continents.*

11. *Giambattista Tiepolo,* The Glorification of Spain. *Palacio Reale, Madrid. Fresco. 1762–1770. Tiepolo's use of light colors, his emphasis on elegant details, and his complex poses were typical of his style.*

12. *Goya,* The Sunshade. *Prado, Madrid. Canvas. 1777. Designed for a tapestry intended for the dining room in the royal palace, this cartoon by Goya (1746–1828) displayed an elegance and frivolity that was markedly different from his later works (see chapter 45).*

to transport believers into a celestial paradise. In Spain and her territories in America, new heights of ornamentation produced a similar effect. Frenzied and excessive, the altarpieces, façades, and decorative schemes of José de Churriguera and his followers, whose style is known as Churrigueresque, abandoned all pretence of conformity to classical rules. Lavish detail covered every possible surface as elaboration took precedence in the creation of images to overwhelm the worshiper with the power of his religion.

13

14

14. *Johann Balthasar Neumann,* Altar. *Vierzehnheiligen Pilgrimage Church. 1743–1772. It is hard to find a straight line in this extravagant fantasy.*

13. *Johann Balthasar Neumann,* Vierzehnheiligen Pilgrimage Church, interior. *1743–1772. Extravagance and complexity combined with light colors and gilded detail, this church was contemporary with the music of Mozart.*

15

15. *José de Churriguera,* Altar. St. Stephen's, Salamanca. Gilded wood. 1693–1696. *Increasing elaboration gave visual expression to the power of the Catholic Church in Spain.*

THE MING EMPERORS (1368–1644) re-established Chinese rule after a century of foreign domination by the Yan Dynasty, reinforcing it by a deliberate revival of Chinese tradition. Confucianism had emphasized adherence to the standards of the past and respect for authority. But under the Ming Dynasty this was interpreted as extreme conservatism together with conformity to a set of petty rules within a complex hierarchical system. The Great Wall, built by the first Emperor, Shih-huang-ti (221–207 B.C.E.), was refaced and strengthened. Emperor Yung-lo (1403–1425) moved his court to Peking,

CHAPTER 40

NEW EMPIRES IN THE FAR EAST

China and Japan

the old Mongol capital, and laid out a new palace, the Forbidden City, that enclosed the earlier imperial buildings. In both style and technique, Chinese architecture had changed little since the T'ang Dynasty (618–906), and this consistency gave visual expression to the importance of continuity in Chinese culture despite dynastic change. The Ming buildings were no exception.

The Ming Dynasty

Ming imperial art is often derided for its lack of originality. But this was precisely what the

Emperors expected of their court artists, who modeled their work on older styles. Moreover, their emphasis on extravagance in material, color, and technical skill reinforced imperial prestige.

The same attitudes were displayed in the decorative arts, like lacquer work and cloisonné enamel, that reached unprecedented heights of luxury under the Ming Emperors. Outside the immediate court circle, artists were freer to develop their own styles. This was one of the reasons that Tai Chin left the court, and his style was influenced by the Che school of professional landscape artists. Amateur scholar-painters of the Wu school continued the traditions established under the Sung and Yan Dynasties (see chapter 14). Artists like Shen Chou typically added a poem to their paintings, reinforcing its intellectual context. Tung Ch'i-ch'ang developed a critical theory of painting that established the superiority of the scholarly tradition (southern school) over the professional painters (northern school), in particular those associated with imperial patronage. The corruption of the Ming court made it unable to withstand the invasion of the Manchus, who had established their kingdom on the northeastern borders of China.

The Ch'ing Dynasty

The Manchu Ch'ing Emperors were the last of the imperial dynasties in China (1644–1912). Although they forbade intermarriage with the Chinese, they encouraged Chinese officials to remain in control of the civil service and used both languages on official documents, coins, and seals. But they did insist that the Chinese mandarins adopt their custom of the pigtail. As foreigners themselves, they were more open to ideas from abroad. Through the advice of a Jesuit missionary, the decoration of the Ch'ing summer palace owed much

1. Screen. Victoria & Albert Museum, London. Lacquer. Early eighteenth century. Decorated with animals and plants that had symbolic meaning in the Chinese religion, the stylized detail and richness of color reflected the increasingly elaborate tastes of the Ch'ing Dynasty.

2. Imperial crown. Ming Dynasty, sixteenth century. Intricate, elaborate, and, above all, expensive, the jeweled imperial phoenix crown gave visual expression to Ming prestige.

3. Temple of Heaven. Peking. Early fifteenth century. Walled off inside Peking, the Imperial City contained the imperial palace and the major religious buildings, the Altar of Heaven, and the Hall of Annual Prayers (the Temple of Heaven).

2

4

4. Great Wall. China. Begun third century B.C.E. Begun by the First Emperor, Ch'in Shih-Huang-ti (see chapter 4), the Great Wall was faced with stone during the Ming Dynasty.

3

to Versailles. Court artists were influenced by Western painting. But the scholar-painters rejected foreign ideas. Wang Hui was one of a number of painters who concentrated on reinterpreting the styles of the old masters. Others, such as the Individualists, developed their original ideas in the Chinese idiom. The luxury of the Ch'ing court continued the pattern established under the Ming Emperors. Prestige and wealth were expressed in expensive materials and exceptional standards of craftsmanship. The scale of demand for the decorative arts encouraged the imperial court to set up workshops inside the palace for the manufacture of elaborate lacquer work, enameled glass, and jade as well as for the production of court robes.

The Chinese Ceramic Industry

Chinese culture under the Ming and Ch'ing Emperors is best expressed in the development of ceramics. Porcelain had first been made in China during the T'ang period (618–906). Court patronage under the Sung Emperors (960–1279) had established its popularity, and their intellectual culture was reflected in simple monochrome wares. The porcelain industry expanded under the Ming Dynasty. The imperial factory at Ching-Té-Chén, supervised by a palace official, responded to the demand for luxury at court, supplying as many as 70,000 pieces a year. The demand for copies of Sung ware reflected the status of tradition in Ming society, but the bulk of porcelain production expressed the more opulent tastes of the imperial court, with elaborate shapes and multicolored decoration in turquoise, dark blue, and purple. Under the Ch'ing Emperors the decorative options were widened as new glazes and colors were developed, such as ox-blood red or imperial yellow. The dominant

5. Box. *Victoria & Albert Museum, London. Painted lacquer. 1600. Decorated inside and out, the intricate detail of the ornament was typical of the elaborate tastes of the Ming Dynasty.*

6. *Tai Chin*, Life on the River. *Smithsonian Institution, Freer Gallery of Art, Washington, D.C. Ink on paper. Fifteenth century. Developing his style from the old Sung tradition of landscape painting, Tai Chin (ca. 1390–1460) created evocative scenes of rivers, trees, and boats.*

6

7. *Wang Hui*, Pavilions Under the Pines. *Victoria & Albert Museum, London. Ink and color on paper. Ca. 1700. This landscape by Wang Hui (1632–1717) included Chinese scholars at work on their pursuit of culture.*

5

7

use of bright green led to its European name, *famille verte.*

Chinese ceramics inspired pottery production throughout Europe and Asia. During the sixteenth century Portuguese and Dutch traders had returned from China with blue and white porcelain. Its high value in Europe ensured its continued production in China. Export wares were produced to satisfy European tastes. Special commissions even included the coats of arms of European nobility. Factories in England, France, and especially at Delft in Holland produced imitations, but it was not until the discovery of the secret of porcelain manufacture in

Dresden (1703) that Europeans could produce anything that paralleled the excellence of the Chinese wares. The popularity of these wares declined in the nineteenth century as European factories began making their own porcelain.

Japan

China played a formative role in the development of Japanese culture. Buddhism reached Japan in the sixth century, where it coexisted with the local Shinto religion and introduced a new artistic tradition. Chinese culture was perceived as superior and was

adopted by the Japanese emperors to reinforce their power. Chinese script was adapted to their language, and Japanese intellectuals imitated Chinese poetry and painting styles. By 900 the emperor was little more than a religious figurehead, and real power was vested in an aristocratic family, the Fujiwara, who acted as regents. The wealth and prestige of the Fujiwara were reflected in their private chapel, with its wall paintings and gilded image of the Buddha. The Fujiwara regency was too weak to resist the increasing power of the warrior-families (samurai). It was overthrown by Yoritomo (1085), who established control at Kamakura. His military dictatorship was

9

8. Imperial Robe. *Victoria & Albert Museum, London. Silk. Early nineteenth century. Chinese symbols of ranks were just as distinctive as the stripes and other details of Western military uniforms: bird motifs for civilian officials, animals for military officials, and five-clawed dragons for the imperial family.*

9. Blue and white vase. *Victoria & Albert Museum, London. Porcelain. Mid-fourteenth century. Blue and white Chinese porcelain was exported through Asia to the West. Its material, style, and decoration had a fundamental influence on the development of ceramics in countries ranging from Persia to Britain.*

8

given imperial recognition with the title Shogun. This so-called Kamakura period saw the consolidation of warrior society in Japan and the rise of the Zen sect of Buddhism.

Zen Buddhism

Zen Buddhism (Chinese, ch'an) was also imported from China. Its appeal to the culture of the professional warriors, the samurai, lay in its emphasis on rigorous self-discipline and rigid behavioral codes in the search for the ultimate truth. One of the peculiarities of this intuitive religion is that words provide only an inadequate explanation.

Zen Buddhism became an essential element in Japanese culture.

The Kamakura shogunate (1333) was replaced by another military dictatorship, the Ashikaga shogunate (1336–1573), who ruled from the Muromachi district of Kyoto, the imperial capital. Under the pervasive influence of Zen, ostentation was rejected in favor of simplicity as an expression of prestige. This was not only a reflection of austerity but also an aesthetic principle in its own right. Japanese Zen painters looked to the Ch'an artists in China for inspiration, creating subtle landscapes with basic materials: brush, ink, and absorbent

paper. But landscape was not only painted; it was also built. In Japan landscape gardening and the art of flower arranging developed as a consciously contrived aid to the Zen belief in contemplation as part of the quest for truth in nature. These gardens often incorporated natural features, others were entirely man-made, and some consisted solely of pebbles, moss, and trees arranged deliberately to convey an inner meaning. Cultural life in the Muromachi period was typified by the Shogun Yoshimasa (1449–1474), who abdicated to lead a life of elegance in his Silver Pavilion, where he wrote poetry,

10. Vase. *Victoria & Albert Museum, London. Porcelain. Ca. 1500. Thin strips of clay were used to separate the glazes and allow elaborate floral and animal motifs to be used successfully.*

11. Phoenix Pavilion. *Byodoin, Kyoto. Completed 1053. Part of a complex of buildings commissioned by the Regent Fujiwara Yorimichi (994–1074), this elaborate wooden pavilion housed a large gilded image of Buddha.*

12. Golden Pavilion (Kinkaku-ji). *Kyoto. 1398, rebuilt in 1964 after a fire. Commissioned by Shogun Ashikaga Yoshimitsu, this pavilion was designed to hold his art collection and to provide a shelter for the spiritual contemplation of the landscape garden through its seasonal and daily changes.*

11

10

12

appreciated the meaning of Chinese Sung paintings and porcelain, discussed calligraphy, and contemplated his landscape garden. His cultural advisor, the Zen monk Noami, a connoisseur, landscape gardener, and painter, introduced him to a new art form, the Tea Ceremony. The aesthetic appreciation of this ritual involved not only the tea and the texture of the ceramic tea-bowl but also its carefully contrived setting. In deliberately simple, rustic houses divided by painted screens, devotees left their worldly cares behind and contemplated the spiritual beauty of their architectural surroundings, a painting, or a flower arrangement.

The Edo Period

The rise to power of Ieyasu, the first of the Tokugawa Shoguns (1576–1867), marked the end of Ashikaga control. Ieyasu moved his headquarters out of the imperial capital, Kyoto, to Edo (modern Tokyo). External and internal threats to the new power were forcibly dealt with. European influence, which had begun with the arrival of the Jesuits (1543) and merchants, was halted by the expulsion of all Christians (1624) and a ban on Japanese going abroad (1637). Vassal lords were obliged to spend several months each year at Edo and to leave members of their families behind as permanent hostages when they returned to their estates. Designed to ensure the survival of the shogunate, this practice also encouraged the development of Edo as the cultural center of Japan. Its luxury stimulated the rise of mercantile wealth, which reached unprecedented standards.

The ritual of the Tea Ceremony continued and the simplicity of the teahouses deliberately contrasted with the ostentation of the imperial palaces and shogun castles. Instead of the subtle, Zen-inspired landscapes, these public buildings

13. Dry landscape garden. *Ryoanji, Kyoto. Constructed in the 1480s. Giving visual expression to the Zen quest for truth in nature, these landscape gardens are difficult for a Westerner to appreciate.*

14. Oribe ware. *National Museum, Tokyo. Terracotta. Seventeenth century. Deliberately rough and heavy, these ceramics were designed to stimulate sensual perception.*

13

14

were decorated with screens covered in gold-leafed paper and painted with scenes that concentrated on the more dramatic qualities of nature. This colorful and extravagant style, known as the Kano school, reflected the growth of mercantile wealth. The rise of a secular urban culture in the seventeenth and eighteenth centuries found expression in the development of wood block prints, depicting scenes from contemporary town life, including actors, beauties, and courtesans.

In 1853 Japan was finally forcibly reopened to the outside world by American warships. As the Emperors looked to the West for models of imperial power, so Japanese artists studied and developed Western styles of painting. But Japan had much to offer to the West. Japanese prints had a considerable impact in nineteenth-century Europe, and the spiritual simplicity of the teahouses has provided inspiration for modern architecture.

15

16. Imperial villa. *Katsura. 1642. Deliberately simple and undecorated, this villa was designed as a spiritual retreat from the formality of court life.*

15. *Hasegawa Tohaku,* Pines. *National Museum, Tokyo. Ink on paper. Late sixteenth century. The composition, contrasting details, and forms of this screen reflected an intellectual contemplation of nature, not a realistic depiction of an actual scene.*

16

Printing developed in China during the eighth century, and the earliest surviving printed book, a copy of the *Diamond Sutra*, is dated 868 and embellished with sophisticated woodcut illustrations. By the fourteenth century, long before this technique had been developed in the West, Chinese printers had begun to produce woodblock illustrations in color, using as many as five different tones. Like other aspects of Chinese culture, the technique of woodblock color printing spread to Japan.

The Japanese *Ukiyo-e* prints, "pictures of the floating world," depicted scenes of everyday life, and their popularity reflected the growth of middle-class wealth and leisure in seventeenth-century Edo (Tokyo). Initially simple black outlines, these woodblock prints were occasionally hand-colored and were effectively color printed only in the early eighteenth century. By 1850 the use of gold and silver illustrated a desire for increasing opulence. Concentrating on the beautiful courtesans of the day, Japanese artists used stylized curves and flat blocks of color to convey extravagance and often eroticism and sensuality, creating highly elaborate and detailed images of leisure. The growing popularity of the Kabuki theater and its actors provided another important source of material for these prints, as did landscape, which was depicted with detail and elegance and which clearly reflected the love and admiration of the Japanese for nature. These colorful and highly decorative prints became enormously influential and greatly sought after in the West when trading links with Japan were forcibly re-established by the United States Navy (1853). As a result, Japanese goods, including prints, flooded European and American markets (see chapter 47).

17

17. Sotatsu, Matsushima (Pine Islands). *Smithsonian Institution, Freer Gallery of Art, Washington, D.C. Ink on paper. Early seventeenth century. Wealth and power, expressed in gilded paper and the forces of nature, were typical of the developing taste for luxury at court.*

18. Courtesan with Attendants. *Victoria & Albert Museum, London. Paper. Ca. 1750.*

18

THE SCALE AND GRANDEUR OF ANCIENT Rome has exercised a profound influence on the evolution of European civilization. In the fourth century B.C.E., Christianity was openly practiced under the Emperor Constantine and became the official state religion under Theodosius I. The art, literature, and philosophy of the late Roman Empire thus became an integral part of the Christian heritage. It was this aspect of Roman culture that inspired Charlemagne, the founder of the Holy Roman Empire, and the medieval papacy. The patrons of the Italian Renaissance and the artists who worked for them, seeking new

images of wealth and prestige, directed their attention to the classical past, adapting the styles, themes, and architectural language of pagan antiquity to the exigencies of their times. Direct contact with Italian art and architecture influenced the rulers of Spain, France, and England, who adopted the style to promote their own politics of power. By 1600, archaeological interest in the ruins of Rome led to the systematic excavation of statuary and other objects. Newly excavated statues enriched the collections of popes and the papal court in Rome, while patrons elsewhere had to be content with casts. The copies commissioned by Francis I

(r. 1515–1547) and Louis XIV of France (r. 1643–1715) were impressive in quality and variety but no substitute for the originals. The Baroque sculptor Giovanni Bernini encouraged other artists to study classical figure styles, and the foundation of the French Academy in Rome (1666) enabled French artists to study classical works firsthand. The increasingly scholarly attitude toward antiquity in seventeenth-century Rome was reflected in the collection of precise and detailed drawings of ancient ruins made by the antiquarian Cassiano del Pozzo. This more specifically archaeological approach gathered momentum during the eighteenth century and formed the basis of the movement known as neoclassicism.

The Grand Tour

By the mid-1700s, a trip to Italy had become an indispensable element in the education of artists as well as patrons. Rome was the cultural mecca of Europe and an indispensable stop on the Grand Tour for visitors from north of the Alps. The trip from England by Lord Richard Boyle Burlington in 1714–1715 was typical; he left London for Rome accompanied by a tutor and a painter to record the sights of the tour, returning home via Venice and Paris with 878 crates of souvenirs that ranged from a Roman porphyry vase to Parisian gloves. Wealthy English visitors stimulated the tourist trade in Rome, as they avidly acquired copies, prints, and paintings of the remains of antiquity. Specialists in such works, like the Italian etcher and architect Giovanni Piranesi and his partner, the Scottish painter and antiquarian Gavin Hamilton, set up lucrative businesses to capitalize on the demand; especially popular were Piranesi's series of topographical engravings of Ancient Rome, published in *Vedute di Roma* (Views of Rome, 1748–1755).

1. Johann Zoffany, Tribune of the Uffizi. *Royal Collection, Windsor. Canvas. 1772–1778. Connoisseurs now worshiped at the altar of art. Zoffany's detailed painting of English tourists admiring the Medici collection included such recognizable works as Titian's* Venus of Urbino *and the antique* Medici Venus.

2. Giovanni Antonio Dosio, View of Ancient Roman Remains. *Uffizi, Gabinetto dei Disegni e delle Stampe, Florence. Ca. 1562. The architect and sculptor Giovanni Antonio Dosio (1533–1609) passionately studied the ruins of Ancient Rome and published a volume of drawings titled* Urbis Romae aedificiorum illustrium quae supersunt reliquiae *(1569).*

2

3

3. Giovanni Battista Piranesi, View of the Roman Forum. *Uffizi, Gabinetto dei Disegni e delle Stampe, Florence. Ca. 1762. A grazing area for cattle during the Middle Ages, the Roman Forum began undergoing systematic excavations in the eighteenth century. It was not brought fully to light until the nineteenth.*

4. Piranesi, The Campo Marzio. *Uffizi, Gabinetto dei Disegni e delle Stampe, Florence. 1762. Dramatic and awe-inspiring, the views of Ancient Rome published by Piranesi (1720–1778) were emotive rather than factual recreations.*

4

Excavations in Italy, Greece, and Asia Minor

Classical sites in and around Rome were systematically investigated by those aware of the ready market for their finds. Hadrian's Villa at Tivoli was a particularly fruitful site. The excavations at Pompeii (begun 1748) and Herculaneum (begun 1738) also provided neoclassical artists and architects with new sources of inspiration. Farther south, the French architect Jacques-Germain Soufflot (1713–1780, see chapter 43) surveyed the Greek temples at Paestum (1750). The new interest in Ancient Greek culture was one of the key elements of eighteenth-century neoclassicism that distinguished it from earlier revivals. The first book specifically devoted to Greek architecture was Leroy's *Les Ruines des Plus Beaux Monuments de la Grèce* (1758), which was soon followed by James Stuart's and Nicholas Revett's *Antiquities of Athens* (1762). The latter two had made a trip to Greece (1748–1753) financed by the Society of Dilettanti in London, one of many clubs founded in the eighteenth century to promote classical culture. Stuart and Revett took a strong position against artists like Piranesi, whose drawings of ancient monuments were intended to impress rather than to inform. Their own rationalistic approach, which emphasized the accuracy and informational content of visual documents, characterized the new attitude of eighteenth-century culture toward antiquity. Other enthusiastic travelers recorded the Roman imperial architecture at Baalbek and other sites in the Middle East. Although the books they published constituted important sources of inspiration for neoclassical architects, travel to Greece and Asia Minor proved too hazardous to threaten the preeminent position of Rome as the center for classical studies.

5

6

5. *Bernini*, Apollo and Daphne. *Galleria Borghese, Rome. Marble. 1622–1625. Himself inspired by classical sculpture, Bernini (1598–1680) urged other artists to draw from antique statues.*

6. *Joseph Severn*, Shelley at the Baths of Caracalla. *Keats-Shelley Memorial House, Rome. Canvas. 1845. The remains of Ancient Rome were a major inspiration to academic archaeologists as well as to poets, painters, and architects.*

On August 24, 79 C.E., the spectacular eruption of Mount Vesuvius on the eastern shore of the Bay of Naples buried the towns of Pompeii, Herculaneum, and Stabiae under 20–23 feet (6–7 meters) of volcanic ash and debris. The event was vividly described by Pliny the Younger, who witnessed the catastrophe, in a letter to the Roman historian Tacitus. Although the existence of Pompeii was long known, the site was never systematically explored until the mid-eighteenth century. The first major excavation, financed by the king of Naples, Charles Bourbon, was undertaken in 1748. The discoveries stimulated enormous excitement among the growing circles of neoclassical theorists, architects, designers, painters, and sculptors throughout Europe. The lightness of the volcanic ash, which had suffocated many residents, nevertheless preserved their bodies and protected buildings from damage. The removal of ash thus revealed whole human remains, the body of a watchdog, and such paraphernalia of everyday life as children's toys, election posters, and tables set for breakfast. The excavations also brought to light an unprecedented range of architecture, complete with painted decoration. Stimulating the greatest interest were the private houses and villas, whose rooms and interior halls provided a whole new repertoire of ornamental motifs, painting styles, and other decorative details that fueled the growth of a major fashion for the antique. Other decorative items of interest to both archaeologists and designers ranged from combs and jewelry to sculpted portraits, coins, and bronze lamps. However, we must also keep in mind the importance of the excavation at Herculaneum and the exploration of the grandiose temples at Paestum.

7

7. Casa dei Vettii, mural decoration. *Pompeii. IV style, ca. 70 C.E.*

8

8. "Furietti" Centaur. *Museo Capitolino, Rome. Marble. Roman copy of Greek original. One of two centaur statues found (1736) by Monsignor Alessandro Furietti in his excavation of Hadrian's Villa, this was sold by his heirs to Pope Clement XIII for the Museo Capitolino.*

Collections and Museums

Like the medieval acquisition of relics, eighteenth-century collections of antiquities played an important role in enhancing the status of their owners. In Rome, the major source of classical remains, antiquity was big business. Cardinal Albani, who promoted classical studies for both intellectual and financial gain, sold his collection of sculpture to Pope Clement XII for the new papal museum at the Capitol (1734). Clement XIV also purchased what he could to augment the extraordinary papal collection, which he moved to a new museum in the Vatican palace (ca. 1770). Stringent efforts were made to forbid the export of original works, but the laws were only partially effective. Prices soared as demand increased, and independent excavators, like Hamilton, had a powerful incentive to sell their finds to English, French, German, and Russian aristocrats eager to amass their own private collections. One of the few important collections of classical sculpture outside Rome had been assembled by the Medici popes and cardinals in the sixteenth century. Removed from their Roman villa to Florence (ca. 1780), these works formed the nucleus of the great collection at the Uffizi.

Outside Rome, excavations at the cities of Pompeii and Herculaneum were financed by the king of Naples, who at once acquired his own collection of antique art and conferred an image of classical prestige on the institution of the monarchy.

Greece Versus Rome

At the intellectual level, scholars debated the relative merits of Ancient Greece and Ancient Rome. The Italians had a vested interest in defending Rome's claim to superiority. Piranesi stressed its Etruscan origins, but others regarded Roman culture

9. Anton Sminck van Pitloo, The Temples of Paestum. Museo di Capodimonte, Naples. Canvas. 1830. The new interest in Greek rather than Roman culture was an important feature of eighteenth-century neoclassicism and distinguished it from earlier classical revivals.

10. Simonetti, Museo Pio-Clementino, Octagon. Vatican. Begun 1773. Designed to house the major statues of the Vatican collection, this museum included special niches for the Laocoön, the Apollo Belvedere, the Hermes, and three sculptures by Canova.

10

9

11

11. Hubert Robert, Pont du Gard. Louvre, Paris. Canvas. Exhibited at Salon of 1787. Minuscule human figures and low-lying clouds enhance the grandeur of Ancient Roman engineering.

Antonio Canova (1757–1822) and Bertel Thorvaldsen (ca. 1770–1844) were arguably the two greatest exponents of neoclassical sculpture. Raised by his grandfather, a stonecutter and mason, Canova moved from his home near Venice to Rome (1780), where he soon came under the influence of the new archaeological interest in antiquity. Thorvaldsen, a Dane by birth, won a scholarship to study in Rome, arriving there in 1797. Promoting the revival of the classical ideals of beauty, both Canova and Thorvaldsen rejected the idiosyncrasies of Roman, Renaissance, and Baroque interpretations of Ancient Greek sculpture. Under the influence of Winckelmann, who recommended that artists should imitate the spirit of antiquity, they emphasized adherence to rules of proportion in representing the human figure. Both were partial to subjects from Homer and other Greek authors. Their choice of balanced poses, often with the weight resting on one leg, was directly inspired by their study of classical Greek sculpture. Their cold, pure style was deliberately depersonalized and lacking in emotion. In contrast to classical Greek sculptors, however, they typically left the eyeballs of their figures uncarved and unpainted. Much in demand as artists of the new style, both Canova and Thorvaldsen obtained commissions for major monuments. The former carved portraits of Napoleon and tombs for Popes Clement XIV (1783) and Clement XIII (1787). Thorvaldsen, whose commissions included monuments to Pope Pius VIII (1823) and Lord Byron (1830), left his works and collections to the city of Copenhagen. Over time, Thorvaldsen's style moved away from Canova's, and was aimed at an ideal of timeless beauty.

12. Antonio Canova, Cupid and Psyche. *Louvre, Paris. Marble. 1787–1793. Pure and idealized, the sculptural style of Antonio Canova (1757–1822) developed under the influence of the German scholar Johann Joachim Winckelmann, who called on artists to imitate the spirit of classical art rather than slavishly copying it.*

12

as a derivative of Greek civilization. With respect to architecture, the debate focused particularly on the difference between Roman structures based on the arch and vault, which were more technically advanced, and the simpler Greek post-and lintel constructions, admired for their purity of form. Those who argued for Hellenistic supremacy disapproved of the decorative use of the classical orders in Rome. Foremost among the Grecophiles was Johann Joachim Winckelmann, a German scholar whose passion for antiquity had brought him to Rome (1755), where he became a librarian in the service of Cardinal Albani.

The cardinal's outstanding collection of antiquities gave Winckelmann the opportunity to study classical art firsthand and inspired him to write *Thoughts on the Imitation of Greek Works of Art in Painting and Sculpture* (1755) and *History of Ancient Art* (1764). Landmarks in the history of art, Winckelmann's texts analyzed the subject for the first time in terms of stylistic development. Like Plato, he believed that there is a close correspondence between the artistic style of a work and the moral values of the society that produced it.

Winckelmann's circle included the painters Hamilton and Anton Raphael Mengs and the sculptor Antonio Canova, whom he encouraged to imitate the spirit of antiquity rather than merely copy its remains. Mengs's *Parnassus* (1761), commissioned for Cardinal Albani's villa, is widely regarded as the first neoclassical painting; the work is conspicuous in its lack of the illusionistic devices that characterized Baroque ceiling decoration. The preference for Greek culture was also reflected in the choice of Greek subject matter. Many of Hamilton's and Canova's works were inspired by Homer's epics, the *Iliad* and the *Odyssey*. Canova had come to Rome (1779) to study the Baroque sculpture of Bernini but, under

13

14

13. Bertel Thorvaldsen, The Entry of Alexander into Babylon (detail). *Palazzo del Quirinale, Rome. Marble. Early nineteenth century.*

14. *Canova, Venus Italica. Palazzo Pitti, Florence. Marble. Finished 1812. This copy of the Medici Venus was made to replace the original, which had been removed to Paris by Napoleon.*

15. *Canova,* Tomb of Clement XIII. *St. Peter's, Vatican. Marble. 1783–1792. Neoclassical artists such as Canova emphasized intellectual and moral ideals rather than the emotional fervor of the Baroque.*

15

the influence of Hamilton, developed a passion for antiquity. Cold, austere, and elegant, his style constituted an unavoidable point of reference for an entire generation of artists.

Taste and Connoisseurship

The importance attributed by patrons and artists to knowledge of the classical world led to the birth of a critical approach based on aesthetic criteria. Many antique statues that had been valued purely as illustrations of historical or mythological themes now were appreciated for their beauty.

Works of art came to be judged on the basis of aesthetic merit. *Tribune of the Uffizi*, by Johann Zoffany, celebrated this new concept of connoisseurship with a group of English tourists admiring the major works in the Medici collection. The heroes of the scene are the connoisseurs themselves, whose gestures and poses reflect their knowledge, appreciation, and taste. Good taste became the essential distinguishing characteristic of a true gentleman. As judge and critic, his ability to recognize quality in art set him apart from the masses. In this way he could continue to reinforce his superior position in a society in which increasing wealth had

blurred the traditional boundaries between classes. Subtle and intangible, good taste was a sign of status and an effective instrument of social advancement.

16

16. *Hubert Robert,* Imaginary View of the Grande Galerie in the Louvre in Ruins. *Louvre, Paris. Canvas. 1796. One of the first curators of the Louvre, the French landscape architect and painter Hubert Robert (1733–1808) envisioned a glorious future for contemporary architecture, itself invested with the grandeur of classical ruins.*

17

17. *Angelica Kauffmann,* Francesco and Alessandro Papafava. *Private collection, Frassanelle. Canvas. Ca. 1800. A skilled portraitist and friend of Winckelmann, Angelica Kauffmann (1741–1807) was a founding member of the British Royal Academy of Art. Her portrait of the Papafava Brothers deliberately enhanced their status as arbiters of taste.*

CHAPTER 42

THE RULE OF TASTE

British Art in the Eighteenth Century

THE DEATH OF QUEEN ANNE (1714) marked the end of the Stuart Dynasty and the start of a new era of prosperity for Great Britain. The accession of her distant cousin, the elector of Hanover, as George I (r. 1714–1727) settled the issue of Protestant succession, and the religious disputes that had played such a major role in sixteenth- and seventeenth-century British politics finally faded into the background. The power of Parliament had established the role of the constitutional monarch (1689), and the new dynasty made little effort to impose its authority on the citizenry. Cultural tastes were dictated by a powerful Whig aristocracy whose investments in trade, agriculture, and banking stimulated a period of major economic expansion. Trade ties with America, the West Indies, Africa, and India were soon to make Britain the wealthiest nation in Europe. The enclosure of farmlands and new techniques in cultivation vastly increased the potential for wheat production. With the introduction of crop rotation, the winter-feeding of animals, and scientific methods of sheep breeding, English agriculture underwent a veritable revolution. At the same time, the desire to increase industrial productivity led to the invention of the first spinning machines

1

(patented 1738) and new techniques for the smelting of iron ore, which provided the basis for the Industrial Revolution of the nineteenth century.

In the artistic realm, these developments contributed to the emergence of a distinctive British style. The contemporary European preferences for Baroque and Rococo, with their overtones of Roman Catholicism and absolutist monarchies, held little appeal for the British aristocracy. But the idea that good taste was synonymous with classical culture had been established by Charles I and his architect, Inigo Jones (see chapter 34), who had created an English style based on the works of the sixteenth-century Italian architect Andrea Palladio. The new aristocratic patrons of eighteenth-century England returned to this theme to give visual expression to their power and prestige.

The Appeal of Palladio

Even disregarding the precedent set by Charles I, Palladio's architecture carried a particular appeal for the aristocracy of eighteenth-century Britain. Many of Palladio's patrons had been Venetian patricians, forced by economic circumstances to develop the agricultural potential of the mainland as a new source of wealth (see chapter 29). The British upper classes also relied on their land, and their agricultural innovations contributed to the growing prosperity of the nation as well as to their personal fortunes. Palladio's villas, with their regular symmetrical plans, simple proportions, and temple façades, provided an unobtrusive interpretation of classical style that was a distinct contrast to the opulence of Baroque or Rococo and that had obvious appeal to the British aristocracy. The impetus for the development of the new Palladian style in Britain came largely from one man, Lord Richard Boyle Burlington.

1. Joshua Reynolds, Daughters of Sir William Montgomery Adorning a Term of Hymen. *Tate Gallery, London. Canvas. 1774. Reynolds was deeply influenced by the renewed interest in classical antiquity and traveled to Rome to study it.*

2. Andrea Palladio's Four Books of Architecture. *Frontispiece to the 1738 English edition. Isaac Ware, the publisher of this translation of I* Quattro libri dell'architettura, *sought to improve on two earlier editions of the work, which, he claimed, had not done justice to the original. Copying his frontispiece directly from the first edition of Palladio's text (1570), Ware dedicated his edition to Lord Burlington (1694–1753), the leading figure behind the Palladian revival in eighteenth-century England.*

3. Colin Campbell, Stourhead. *Wiltshire. 1721. A central block fronted by a temple façade and flanked by side wings was a distinctive feature of Palladio's villas adapted by Palladian architects in eighteenth-century Britain, such as Colin Campbell (ca. 1676–1729).*

4. Richard Boyle Burlington, Chiswick Villa. *London. 1725. Lord Burlington adapted Palladio's style to suit the unique demands of the British climate and culture, adding chimneys, raising the dome, and installing a complicated staircase.*

An immensely wealthy Whig aristocrat, Burlington had visited Italy on his Grand Tour of 1714–1715 (see chapter 41), but it was his second trip (1719), specifically for the purpose of studying Palladio's architecture, that proved decisive in the present regard. During his tour, Burlington annotated his copy of Palladio's treatise, *I Quattro libri dell'architettura* (The Four Books of Architecture), and commissioned precise drawings of the most notable buildings.

Returning to England with the material for a radical change in style, Burlington commissioned a new façade for his London residence from the Scottish architect Colin Campbell. The latter had made his mark with *Vitruvius Britannicus* (1715–1725), a collection of architectural engravings that included numerous buildings designed by Inigo Jones and earned him a considerable reputation for his own designs for country houses. Burlington designed Chiswick Villa, a pleasure retreat located just outside London, in a style that amounted to a British interpretation of Palladio's Villa Capra (see chapter 29). Burlington substituted Corinthian capitals for Ionic capitals, copying those of the Temple of Castor and Pollux in Rome, a building singled out for special praise by Palladio. The new style imposed rules of classical symmetry, regularity, and proportion on what was seen as the irrationality of Baroque design. Restrained, sober, and dignified, it gave visual expression to the role of the upper classes in the creation of a new world power.

Landscape

The English Palladian style was not restricted to architecture. Landscape designers abandoned the formality of Baroque gardens, with their ornate and stylized hedges, in favor of a deliberately constructed informality. Open vistas of parkland dotted

5

6. *James Paine,* Kedleston Hall, north front. *Derbyshire. Begun 1759. The combination of temple front and dome in this design by James Paine (ca. 1716–1789) was a hallmark of Palladian architecture.*

5. *Henry Flitcroft and Sir Henry Hoare,* Gardens at Stourhead. *Wiltshire. Begun ca. 1744. A study in contrived informality, the gardens designed by Henry Flitcroft (1697–1769) for Stourhead, the residence of Sir Henry Hoare, centered on an artificial lake. A number of buildings were located on the grounds, including this tiny Pantheon, designed to evoke the spirit of antiquity.*

6

with seemingly natural clusters of trees became an essential feature of the aristocratic landscape. A cunningly contrived ditch, the *ha-ha*, prevented livestock from coming too close to the house while still allowing an uninterrupted view. Some gardens were inspired by classical literature. The Virgilian landscape at Stourhead, for example, was deliberately designed to evoke the spirit of antiquity with inscriptions, grottoes, and temples carefully positioned to create a series of contrasting views; it was, in effect, a three-dimensional version of a classical landscape by Claude Lorrain (see chapter 38).

Landscape painting also flourished in eighteenth-century Britain, following distinctive new directions. The rural scenes of Thomas Gainsborough (1727–1788), while in some ways similar to those of the French Rococo artist Jean Antoine Watteau (see chapter 39), were not composed according to the classical rules established in France or Italy; nor did they depict the idle pleasures of the rich. Like the British poetry of the period, Gainsborough's landscapes reflected nostalgia for a lost paradise. Other artists, both in Britain and elsewhere, painted landscapes that emphasized the sublime

beauty and awesome power inherent in the forces of nature.

British Portraiture

The importance of land as the foundation of British wealth was also reflected in portraiture. The enclosed fields, grazing sheep, and sheaves of corn that formed the setting of Gainsborough's *Mr. and Mrs. Andrews* were a deliberate reference to the revolution taking place in English agriculture. They also reflected the sitters' wealth and social status. Other patrons requested simpler images: paintings that

7

8

7. *Thomas Gainsborough,* Sunset: Carthorses Drinking by a Stream. *Tate Gallery, London. Canvas. Ca. 1759–1762. Although commissioned mainly as a portraitist, Thomas Gainsborough (1727–1788) painted many nostalgic and evocative landscapes. His works have superficial similarities to those of the French Rococo artist Watteau, but Gainsborough's rural and rustic themes are very different from Watteau's depictions of leisured wealth.*

8. *Gainsborough,* Mr. and Mrs. Andrews. *National Gallery, London. Canvas. Ca. 1750. In this early portrait by Gainsborough, the positioning of the sitters and the setting itself reflect the wealth born of Britain's agricultural revolution in the eighteenth century.*

9

9. *George Stubbs,* A Lady and Gentleman in Their Carriage. *National Gallery, London. Canvas. 1787. In addition to the couple seated in a late-model carriage, this portrait features a careful rendering of the horses. George Stubbs (1724–1806) was popular as a horse painter and wrote a treatise titled* Anatomy of a Horse *(1766).*

depicted their houses and estates or the leisure pursuits associated with the landed aristocracy, such as hunting and horse racing. Moving to Bath (1759), Gainsborough soon became the preferred painter in fashionable town society. The simple naturalism of his earlier portraits was replaced by a grander manner, inspired by the seventeenth-century court portraits of Van Dyck; the style reinforced the prestige of his patrons with direct reference to tradition.

A successful artist in those days also had to be a good businessman. In addition to employing a team of assistants and students, he was responsible for promoting his work in a highly competitive market. At Bath, Gainsborough charged sixty guineas for a full-length portrait, while in London the prices were much higher. Sir Joshua Reynolds (1723–1792), arguably the leading portrait painter of the period, could charge more than double that amount. In his *Discourses on Art*, a series of lectures presented to the students of the Royal Academy (1769–1790), Reynolds expressed his belief that history and religious paintings were superior to portraiture. But portraiture was what fashionable British society demanded, and the art market was dominated by that genre. More than half the paintings exhibited at the annual exhibitions of the Royal Academy during the late eighteenth century were portraits; about one quarter were landscapes.

Reynolds and the Royal Academy

Founded in 1768, the Royal Academy initially consisted of forty members—leading practitioners of painting, sculpture, and architecture—known as the Academicians. Among the founding members were Gainsborough, Reynolds, William Chambers, Johann Zoffany, and Angelica Kauffmann (see chapter 41). Reynolds was elected the first president, and Chambers was appointed

10. Reynolds, Master Hare. *Louvre, Paris. Canvas. Ca. 1788. Commissioned by Master Hare's aunt, Reynolds conveyed all the charm and innocence of childhood in this portrait of a two-year-old boy.*

11

12

10

11. Gainsborough, Mrs. Graham. *National Gallery, Edinburgh. Canvas. 1775–1776. Gainsborough's later portraits reflected the status of his new patrons in the fashionable society of Bath and London.*

12. Reynolds, Commodore Augustus Keppel. *National Maritime Museum, London. Canvas. 1752–1753. In this portrait, Sir Joshua Reynolds (1723–1792) depicted his subject in the dignified pose of the Apollo Belvedere.*

Famous for the curative properties of its natural spring waters, Bath has been popular as a spa and resort since Roman times. During the Middle Ages, the town expanded as a center of the region's wool industry. In the eighteenth century, Bath suddenly developed into a fashionable retreat from the rigors of modern life for London high society. Capitalizing on this change in circumstance, the architect John Wood the Elder (1704–1754) and his son, John Wood the Younger (1728–1782), transformed the medieval city into a modern urban center, designed in a style that reflected the prevailing taste for classical architecture. The focuses of the plan were the Baths and the Assembly Rooms, where card parties and festival balls were held to entertain visitors. The center was linked to residential districts by wide new streets, lined with elegant houses decorated with columns, pediments, and other richly carved classical details. Residential squares followed a wide variety of designs. The rectangular plan of Queen's Square (1729), for example, contrasted with the oval shape of the Circus (begun 1754), which was clearly reminiscent of the Colosseum in Rome. However, these classically inspired features were adapted and reduced in scale in order to create a suitable proportion for the town. Beyond the Circus was the Royal Crescent (1767), an imposing curved row of terraced houses articulated with Ionic columns to make it look like a single grand palace. The projects conceived by the two Woods for Bath were an important realization of contemporary ideas on urban planning and had a decisive influence on the design of squares and streets in eighteenth-century London.

13

13. John Wood the Younger,
Royal Crescent. *Bath.*
1767–1775.

14

14. *William Chambers,*
Somerset House.
London. Begun 1776.
On his return from a
trip to Italy, Sir William
Chambers (1723–1796)
was appointed
architectural tutor to
the prince of Wales
and soon established
himself as the leading
neoclassical architect
in the intellectual circles
of London.

treasurer. Established to promote quality in the British arts, the Academy hosted an annual exhibition that was open to nonmembers and set up a school in which students were taught by the Academicians themselves.

Reynolds, too, responded to the fascination with classical culture that swept Europe during the eighteenth century. After training in London with the portrait artist Thomas Hudson, he traveled to Rome (1750) to study antique sculpture and the masterpieces of the High Renaissance. In doing so, Reynolds developed a new language for portraiture that reflected the growing importance of taste as the distinguishing mark of a gentleman. By adopting the poses of ancient statues or by the use of mythological allusion, he conferred a new type of dignity on his patrons and effectively raised the status of portraiture to a classical art form. His *Discourses on Art* established a distinctive British school of art and theory. Thanks to his immense success as an artist, Reynolds, the son of a country schoolmaster, was accepted into the fashionable elite of London society. His rise in social status reflected the importance of the artist as an arbiter of taste.

The Influence of Neoclassicism

The growing interest in the remains of antiquity (see chapter 41) and its influence on European culture followed in the wake of the Palladian revival. But whereas Palladian architects viewed Ancient Rome in the context of Palladio's texts and works, neoclassical designers took their ideas directly from a variety of classical sources. Arguably the most successful promoter of the new fashion was the Scottish architect Robert Adam. With his brother, James, Adam ran a profitable business importing antique copies from Rome

15

15. Johann Zoffany, The Academicians of the Royal Academy. *Royal Collection, London. Canvas. 1772. The German artist Johann Zoffany (1733–1810) earned success as a royal artist. His painting of the life class at the Royal Academy reinforced the status enjoyed by artists as arbiters of that indefinable quality–taste. The picture includes portraits of many of the leading artists of the day: Zoffany himself sits on the left with his palette; Reynolds, with his ear trumpet, stands in the center; and Chambers, the treasurer of the Academy, is behind him.*

for his clients in England. Developing a repertoire of neoclassical motifs derived from the ruins at Pompeii, Diocletian's palace at Split, and other ancient sites, Adam established himself as the leading designer and architect for the wealthy upper classes, eager to redecorate their houses in the new style. His projects included not only architecture and interior decoration but also designs for furniture and carpets to match the scheme for each room. Other architects took a more scholarly approach to antiquity. One of the first neoclassical architects to visit Greece, James Stuart published drawings of the monuments there (1762, see chapter 41) and designed copies of Athenian monuments for the garden at Shugborough. Chambers, the first treasurer of the Royal Academy, designed a series of classically inspired buildings for the royal palace at Kew, including a replica of the Roman Temple of the Sun at Baalbek.

The Rule of Taste

The key role of Lord Burlington in establishing a distinctive aristocratic culture in Britain was recognized by his contemporaries. The idea that taste was the distinguishing feature of a gentleman was condemned by the satirist William Hogarth (see chapter 44) but exalted by the influential Lord Shaftesbury (1671–1713). According to the latter, taste is the touchstone of truth, arrived at through long and rigorous study; affectation is reprehensible. Wealth had blurred the boundaries between the classes, and taste was now the sole means of distinguishing the code of behavior, conduct, manners, and preferences of a true gentleman. Typically, perhaps, Shaftesbury offered no precise definition of taste. After all, a true gentleman would have known what he meant!

16. *Robert Adam,* Osterley Park, library. *Middlesex. 1766–1773. Adam (1728– 1792) used his first-hand experience of the remains of antiquity to develop a distinctive and highly decorative style that he applied to stuccoed ceilings and walls, furniture, mantelpieces, and bookcases.*

16

17

17. *James Stuart,* Design for a Painted Room in Spencer House. *British Museum, Department of Prints and Drawings, London. Paper. 1759. James Stuart (1713–1788) was a key figure in the new interest in Ancient Greece. He visited Athens with Nicholas Revett (ca. 1721–1804), and the two architects published an influential series of drawings and descriptions of Greek monuments.*

CHAPTER 43

PHILOSOPHERS, HISTORIANS, WRITERS, and scientists in the Age of Enlightenment applied reason to their thirst for knowledge of a wide range of human experiences. Daily newspapers, which had first appeared in the late seventeenth century, now became widely available in Europe and America. The Swedish naturalist Carolus Linnaeus published his systematic classification of the plant world (1751). Diderot's French *Encyclopédie* (1751–1752) was followed by the *Encyclopedia Britannica* (1771). The British Museum was founded in London (1753) to house the collection of books, manuscripts, and objects of natural

FROM FASHION TO REVOLUTION

Neoclassicism, 1750–1800

history bequeathed to the government by the physician and naturalist Sir Hans Sloane. Ranging from fossils to coins and antiquities, his collection was augmented by the royal manuscript library (1756) and sculptures from the Parthenon in Athens known as the Elgin Marbles (1816). Renewed interest in the cultures of antiquity inspired such seminal works of history as Johann Winckelmann's *History of Ancient Art* (1764) and Edward Gibbon's *Decline and Fall of the Roman Empire* (1776–1788). It also stimulated a new awareness of the political systems of democratic Greece and Republican Rome. The excavation of Pompeii (begun 1748) and

1

other ancient sites broadened the repertoire of classical ornamental motifs, stimulating the growth of a fashion that had a major effect on architecture, sculpture, painting, and the decorative arts. The new passion for antiquity was the focus of a growing reaction to Rococo (see chapter 39). Undulating curves and decorative excesses were replaced by straight lines and harmonious symmetry in the language of classical architecture.

The French Court

Extravagant and frivolous, Rococo had provided an ideal image for the court of Louis XV (r. 1715–1774), but this overt expression of wealth and leisure was inevitably criticized as decadent. Responding to the rising tide of neoclassicism, Louis XV and his courtiers replaced one fashion with another. After all, classical culture was well established as an appropriate style for monarchic or imperial power, and its revival also expressed nostalgia for the age of Louis XIV and past French glory (see chapter 34). The church of St. Genevieve in Paris, commissioned by Louis XV from the architect Jacques-Germain Soufflot, proclaimed its classical inspiration with a free-standing temple front. Madame de Pompadour, Louis XV's mistress and former patron of Rococo, commissioned the Petit Trianon, a retreat in the royal gardens at Versailles. Small and intimate, its scale recalled Rococo design, but its decorative motifs were inspired by antiquity. Moving in the same direction, Louis XVI (r. 1774–1793) commissioned the redecoration of a series of apartments at Versailles for his wife, Marie Antoinette, after the birth of the dauphin (1781). This display of extravagance and opulence, however, concealed the disastrous financial situation of the French state, one of the critical factors in the eventual demise of the monarchy. The financiers who remained

1. Sèvres plate for Catherine the Great of Russia. *Musée des Ceramiques, Sèvres. Late eighteenth century. The neoclassical emphasis on luxury and extravagance was not unlike that of Rococo design, but the motifs changed. Classical cameos and acanthus leaf scrolls replaced seashells and naturalistic ornament.*

2. *Jacques-Germain Soufflot, St. Genevieve (now Panthéon). Paris. 1757–1792. Fluted Corinthian columns supporting a pediment emphasized the classical inspiration of this church, renamed the Panthéon after the French Revolution (1789). The architect, Jacques-Germain Soufflot (1713-1780), had accompanied Madame de Pompadour's brother on his Grand Tour to Italy.*

3. Carl Gotthard Langhans, Brandenburg Gate. *Berlin. 1788–1791. Formal and regular, the language of classical architecture provided images of imperial and military power throughout late eighteenth-century Europe.*

committed to preserving the ailing regime gave visual expression to their own wealth and status, as well as their loyalty to the king, in luxurious palaces decorated in the style adopted by the court.

Morality in Painting

The attack on the decadence of Rococo was also directed at painting, which was criticized as decadent for its appeal to the senses and emotions. Neoclassical art, by contrast, appealed to the intellect; it was not only an aesthetic style, but also a statement of ethical and civic principle. The frivolous subject matter and elegant style of Rococo art were rejected, as the Academy urged a return to the classical ideals of history painting. It encouraged the choice of themes that promoted public duty, civic virtue, and loyalty to the state and its institutions—themes that amounted to propaganda for a regime in which corruption was rampant and implementation of badly needed fiscal reforms was resisted.

The major exponent of the new style in late eighteenth-century France was Jacques-Louis David (1748–1825), who was trained in Rome and developed a severe figure style based on close study of classical sculpture. In *Oath of the Horatii*, commissioned by Louis XVI, David's austere and heroic interpretation of a theme from Roman history reinforced a moral message. The scene depicted the three Horatii Brothers taking an oath, on swords held by their father, to defend Rome in a fight to the death against the Curatii; the latter were the chosen representatives of the Albans, who were then at war with Rome. The Horatii and Curatii families were related by marriage; thus, the painting reinforced the importance of loyalty to the state over family ties. A similar theme lay behind David's *Brutus Receiving the Bodies of His Sons*; Brutus had ordered the death of his own sons after discovering their

4. Richard Mique, The Queen's Cottage. *Versailles. Begun 1783. Marie Antoinette commissioned Richard Mique (1728–1794) to build a rural hamlet as a retreat for her court in the park at Versailles. It included a mill and a dairy as well as this "cottage."*

5. Mique, Temple d'Amour. *Parc du Trianon, Versailles. 1778. Elegant and decorative, this circular temple was typical of the new classical image promoted at the court.*

6. La Méridienne. *Versailles. 1781. The ornamental detail of this room, decorated by Louis XVI for his wife to celebrate the birth of the dauphin, was inspired by antiquity.*

Jacques-Louis David (1748–1825) trained as a painter in Paris before winning the prestigious Prix de Rome in 1775 and traveling to Italy from 1775 to 1780. Under the influence of the austere and intellectual neoclassical ideals promoted by Johann Joachim Winckelmann (see chapter 41), Canova, and Mengs, David studied and drew from antique sculptures. Profoundly impressed by these pieces, he created a new and distinctive figural

DAVID AND NEOCLASSICISM

style by imitating their poses, forms, and even costumes. After his return to France, David soon imposed himself as the leading neoclassical artist of the period. Responding to the demand for morality in art, David's paintings were simply constructed and notable for their narrative clarity. Exaggerated heroic gestures, clas-

sically inspired poses, cool balanced colors, and austere architectural backgrounds reinforced the morality of the historical subject matter. Directly involved with the politics of the French Revolution, David was imprisoned after the execution of Robespierre (1794) but returned to favor with the rise of Napoleon, who made him one of the official painters of his new regime (see chapter 45).

plot against the state. In the context of absolutist, monarchic France, loyalty to the state ultimately meant fidelity to the king. After the Revolution, however, the significance of these paintings took on an entirely different meaning.

The French Revolution

Classical art and architecture were entirely consonant with political structures that were neither imperial nor monarchic. Vehemently opposed to either system, the literatures of democratic Greece and Republican Rome encouraged demands

7

8

7. *Jacques-Louis David,* Oath of the Horatii. *Louvre, Paris. Canvas. 1785. David's austere and heroic style of painting reflected the new preference for morality in art.*

8. *David,* Brutus Receiving the Bodies of His Sons. *Louvre, Paris. Canvas. 1789. David's deliberate use of simple, strong Doric columns reinforced the moral theme of his painting. The scene depicts the return of the bodies of Brutus's sons after their execution for conspiracy. Brutus's role in their deaths symbolized the importance of loyalty to the state over family ties.*

9

9. *David,* Oath of the Tennis Court. *Versailles. Ink and brown wash. Commissioned 1790. In this sketch for a large painting commemorating a decisive moment in the French Revolution, the compositional scheme is based on logical criteria, with no display of emotional fervor.*

for greater representation in government and inspired the concept of political egalitarianism. The revival of classicism in eighteenth-century France revived these principles as well, just as it had in the Italian city-states of the fourteenth century and the new Dutch Republic in the seventeenth century. If the French Revolution was waged on behalf of these ideals, neoclassicism would give them visual expression.

By 1788, incompetence, corruption, and fear of change had made the French monarchy effectively powerless, at once alienated from conservative opinion for instituting reforms and criticized by the more progressive factions for failing to get them passed. The situation was exacerbated by a financial crisis precipitated by the cost of supporting the American colonies in their war of independence against the British and by a series of disastrous harvests at home. At Versailles in June 1789, the Third Estate (Commons) reconstituted itself as the National Assembly, an act that inspired a popular uprising in the streets of Paris. Joined by reformist elements among the nobility and clergy but denied access to its customary hall, the new Assembly met in the royal tennis court and swore an oath to establish a constitution. This historic moment was recorded in a celebrated canvas by David, whose heroic style was soon identified with the call for *liberté, egalité, fraternité*.

The birth of the republic was attended by extraordinary violence. A shaky constitutional monarchy ultimately foundered, with such issues as representation of the poor and the abolishment of feudalism highlighting a deep split in French society. Louis XVI, tried and convicted of treason, was executed by the guillotine (1793), as were many members of the aristocracy and the upper bourgeoisie. Even the leaders

10. David, Death of Marat. Musées Royaux des Beaux-Arts, Brussels. Canvas. 1793. David's painting of the assassinated hero of the French Revolution and martyr to the cause deliberately recalled images of the dead Christ. The date on the painting, L'an deux, alluded to the year of the new regime.

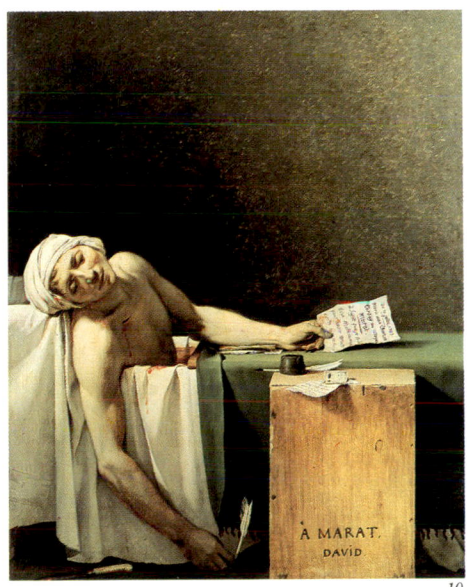

10

11. Etienne-Louis Boullée, Design for a Temple to Reason. Uffizi, Gabinetto dei Disegni e delle Stampe, Florence. 1793–1794. Rational and logical, the use of the pure sphere by Etienne-Louis Boullée (1728–1799) gave visual expression to the worship of reason.

11

of the Revolution did not escape the Reign of Terror; Marat was assassinated (1793) and Robespierre executed (1794). To consolidate its power, the new Republic nationalized ecclesiastical property and abolished the privileges of anyone who had enjoyed the benefits of the Catholic Church. Even the Gregorian calendar was abolished; traditional months were replaced by twelve months with thirty days each and no Sundays, designated by classically inspired names pertaining to the seasons, such as *Fructidor* (August-September) and *Germinal* (March-April). Faith in the Divinity was replaced by the worship of Reason. The church of Notre-Dame in Paris was renamed the Temple of Reason (1793); Louis XV's church of St. Genevieve was designated as the Panthéon, its bell-towers and sacristies dismantled.

David set up the Commune of the Arts (1793) in place of the old Academy, and neoclassicism now took on clear republican overtones. But the financial crisis inherited from the *ancien régime* and the effective siege of France by the united European monarchies left republican institutions in a precarious position and opened the way for the rise to power of Napoleon Bonaparte (see chapter 45).

Russia

Dominated by the Orthodox Church, tsarist Russia had inherited its religious, political, and cultural traditions from the Byzantine Empire and had long remained deeply suspicious of the West. But the expansionist policies of Peter the Great (r. 1682–1725) established Russia as a major power in Europe, a position reinforced by his efforts to westernize Russian culture. His campaign found visual expression in the new capital of St. Petersburg, whose imperial palaces, the Peterhof and the Winter Palace, were designed by French and Italian architects

12

14. *Jean-Baptiste Vallin de la Mothe*, Pavilion, central hall. *Hermitage, St. Petersburg. 1764– 1775. Commissioned by Catherine the Great from the French architect Jean-Baptiste Vallin de la Mothe (1729– 1800), the Hermitage Pavilion struck a balance between Baroque and neoclassical styles.*

14

12. *Luigi Premazzi*, View of the southeast corner of the Hermitage. *1861. After the great fire of 1837, the Hermitage was reconstructed (1839–1852) under the supervision of Vassili Stasov, in imitation of the original.*

13

13. The Winter Canal. *Hermitage, St. Petersburg. Mid-eighteenth century.*

in the contemporary Baroque style. Elizabeth (r. 1741–1762), Peter's daughter, employed the Italian Bartolomeo Rastrelli to redesign the Peterhof, Winter Palace, and old imperial palace at Tsarkoe Selo on the massive Baroque scale of Versailles (see chapter 34).

Catherine the Great (r. 1762–1796) continued the policy of expanding political and cultural ties with Western Europe, and the rising tide of neoclassicism was inevitably reflected at her court. She commissioned an English architect to design a new royal pavilion at Tsarkoe Selo, with a park landscaped in imitation of a British noble estate and filled with copies of classical statues. She expanded her already vast collection of antique casts with copies of all the major classical sculptures in Rome and Florence. The Italian architect Giacomo Quarenghi designed an imitation of Raphael's Vatican Loggias for the Hermitage, complete with *all'antica* decoration. Quarenghi further established the neoclassical style in St. Petersburg with a series of buildings that included the State Bank and the Hermitage Theater. Catherine's successors continued her efforts to create a Western European image, but the increasing isolation of court culture from its Russian roots would become a factor in the success of the Bolshevik Revolution (1917).

Neoclassicism and American Independence

On the other side of the Atlantic, meanwhile, thirteen British colonies were rebelling against the economic and political domination of the monarchy. In the *Declaration of Independence* (1776), Thomas Jefferson—inspired by classical concepts of liberty—affirmed for the first time that every person has certain inalienable rights, including freedom from oppression. The war for independence (1776–1783) was inevitable.

15

15. Bartolomeo Francesco Rastrelli, Winter Palace, principal staircase. St. Petersburg. 1753–1762. This grand ceremonial staircase was part of the extravagant Baroque remodeling of the Winter Palace undertaken by the Italian architect Bartolomeo Francesco Rastrelli (ca. 1700–1771).

16

16. Giacomo Quarenghi, Raphael's Loggia. Hermitage, St. Petersburg. 1783–1792. Quarenghi (1744–1817) had studied under the neoclassical painter Anton Mengs in Rome before being invited to Russia to work for Catherine the Great.

The American victory was commemorated in the decoration of city halls throughout the newly independent states. Especially common were portraits of the military hero General George Washington, like the one commissioned from John Trumbull by the city council of Charleston, South Carolina. Given broad discretion in his choice of theme, Trumbull opted to paint Washington at the crucial moment of devising his plan for the Battle of Trenton, the first important American success of the war and a major boost to morale. Washington's solemn and heroic pose was likely inspired by figures on the frieze of the Parthenon; at the same time,

the artist took particular care with the authenticity and details of the general's clothes. The intellectual content of the picture was completely lost on the council, which rejected the portrait and requested Trumbull to paint a less extravagant, more down-to-earth image.

Like the Romans before them, the new Americans preferred a less idealized, more direct image to commemorate the reality of their achievement. Equally Roman in inspiration was the design of the prime image of the new America, the federal capital. Named as well for the nation's revolutionary hero, the city was designated as an

independent district—the District of Columbia—to avoid interference by individual states. Conceived by the French architect Pierre-Charles L'Enfant, the urban plan was based on a rigid grid system with grand triumphal vistas centering on the Capitol, the seat of constitutional government. Both in name and style, the Capitol consciously recalled that ancient symbol of freedom, the Capitol in Rome. Formal, ordered, and above all rational, L'Enfant's plan for Washington, D.C., gave visual expression to the rule of reason, the guiding principle of the Enlightenment.

17. *Thornton, Hallet, Latrobe, Walters, and others,* Capitol. *Washington D.C. Central block 1792–1827, dome and wings 1851–1865. The preeminent architectural symbol of American democracy, the Capitol gives visual expression to national aspirations in both scale and design.*

17

19

18. *Thomas Jefferson,* Monticello. *Charlottesville, Virginia. 1796–1806. The author of the Declaration of Independence (1776) and third president of the United States, Thomas Jefferson (1743–1826) was also a leading architect of his time. His designs were deeply influenced by neoclassicism and Roman architecture.*

18

19. *George Trumbull,* General George Washington at the Battle of Trenton. *Yale University Art Gallery, New Haven, Connecticut. Canvas. 1792. Trained in England, Trumbull engaged his talents in the service of his new country with a series of portraits of George Washington.*

THE INEXORABLE INCREASE IN ECONOMIC power among the bourgeoisie of eighteenth-century Europe encouraged the development of middle-class political and cultural aspirations. Questioning the long-established authority of Church and State, the libertarian ideals of Jean-Jacques Rousseau and others Enlightenment philosophers led ultimately to the French Revolution (1789). Rococo, the fashion that flourished in royal circles at the beginning of the century as a visual expression of aristocratic leisure and privilege, was eagerly adopted by bourgeois patrons who wished to associate themselves with the upper levels of

CHAPTER 44

ART, POLITICS, AND SOCIETY

Middle-Class Art, 1700–1800

society. Others rejected it outright.

In reality, neither the frivolous extravagance of Rococo nor the heroic nobility of neoclassicism was entirely appropriate to the expression of middle-class values. In the sociocultural context of the bourgeoisie, the same reaction to the luxury at court and the same growing desire for morality that stimulated the development of the austere styles and themes of neoclassical art (see chapter 43) found expression in distinctive middle-class preferences. The reaction took many forms, ranging from naturalistic depictions of everyday life to more direct satirical attacks.

1

The Growth of Genre

"Genre" art is the term commonly used to designate the depiction—often in smaller works—of scenes from everyday life in ordinary surroundings. In eighteenth-century Italy, Giuseppe Maria Crespi and other artists recorded the idiosyncrasies of contemporary bourgeois and peasant life; one of Crespi's best-known genre paintings shows a young woman searching her clothes for a flea, a pest which at the time afflicted individuals regardless of social conditions. Pietro Longhi painted scenes of street markets, domestic interiors, and exhibits of exotic animals, in which the Venetian bourgeoisie and aristocracy are represented without the least idealization. This preference for informality over ceremony, for the ordinary rather than the grand, was an important feature of middle-class culture and found expression in other areas, especially theater. It is noteworthy as well, however, that the *Porter* and other works by Giacomo Ceruti documented working-class conditions in Brescia and Milan without explicit comment on the social problem of poverty.

Whereas French Rococo artists recorded the boudoirs and pleasure gardens at court, now painters like Claude Gillot, Jean-Baptiste-Siméon Chardin, and Jean-Baptiste Greuze focused their attention on the events of everyday life in a very different setting. In addition to a representation of the inconveniences of urban travel, Gillot's *Quarrel of the Cab Men* can be understood as an ironic comment on the extravagant fashions and excessive formalism in court society. Chardin, himself of bourgeois origin, painted intimate scenes of domestic interiors that emphasized the moral virtues of thrift and hard work. The works of Greuze, praised by Diderot as "morality in paint," reinforced the natural virtue and honesty of the poor. His *Village Betrothal* stressed the importance of

1. Bartolomeo Bimbi, Espalier of Citrus Fruits. *Palazzo Pitti, Florence. Canvas. Early eighteenth century. The growing interest in scientific research during the Age of Enlightenment was reflected in a more analytical approach to the painting of flowers and plants.*

2. Giuseppe Maria Crespi, The Flea. *Louvre, Paris. Canvas. Ca. 1725. Giuseppe Maria Crespi (1665–1747) came from a family of painters. His intimate paintings of domestic life were notable for their attention to quaint details, like the dog on the pillow.*

3. Giacomo Ceruti, The Porter. *Brera, Milan. Canvas. Ca. 1760. Minutely observed details in this portrait of a farm boy indicate the painter's interest in the ordinary affairs of everyday life.*

4. Pietro Longhi, The Rhinoceros. *Ca' Rezzonico, Venice. Canvas. 1751. Recording the fascination of Venetians for a rhinoceros brought to the city in 1751, Pietro Longhi (1702–1785) was less concerned with the depiction of wealth.*

family ties in an accurate depiction of rural life. The somber and muted colors of the family's clothes stood in marked contrast to the elegant, pastel shades that characterized Rococo scenes of aristocratic life. The trend toward naturalistic depiction became evident in sculpture as well. The works of Jean-Antoine Houdon, whose statue of Voltaire evidenced none of the heroic idealization of neoclassical portraiture, were prominent in that regard.

Hogarth

To ridicule the eccentricities and foibles of contemporary English society, many turned to satire. This form quickly became a powerful weapon in the hands of such artists as the poet John Gay, whose *Beggar's Opera* (1728) attacked political corruption; the novelist Jonathan Swift, whose *Gulliver's Travels* (1726) warned of pride, avarice, and other human failings; and by the paintings and etchings of William Hogarth (1697–1764). Working explicitly in the comic tradition, Hogarth developed several series of narrative paintings conceived as single dramatic presentations with moral overtones. The series *The Harlot's Progress* (1732), *The Rake's Progress* (1734–1735), and *Marriage à la Mode* (1743–1745) charted the progressive decline of their subjects through greed, immorality, and the squandering of natural talent. His *Election* series was a stinging indictment of corruption in public life. Consistent with his views on the political and social problems of his day, Hogarth did not create these works under the commission of a specific patron but published them as collections of engravings. Little appreciated by the social elite and outside the mainstream of of artistic development in England, his skill as a portrait painter brought commissions mainly from his own circle of middle-class philanthropists. His treatise, *Analysis of Beauty* (1753), emphasized

5

6

5. Jean-Baptiste Chardin, The Diligent Mother. *Louvre, Paris. Canvas. 1740. This hardworking mother embodied the virtues of middle-class family life. The distinction between her milieu and the life at court is reinforced by the use of somber, muted colors.*

6. Jean-Baptiste Greuze, The Village Betrothal. *Louvre, Paris. Canvas. Ca. 1760. Hailed by Diderot as "morality in paint," the works of Jean-Baptiste Greuze (1725–1805) displayed careful attention to the details of bourgeois manners, clothes, and interiors.*

7. Claude Gillot, The Quarrel of the Cab Men. *Louvre, Paris. Canvas. Ca. 1710. Claude Gillot (1673–1722) captured the banality of this everyday incident in the diverse reactions of the cab drivers, passengers, and passersby.*

8. Jean-Antoine Houdon, Voltaire. *Hermitage, St. Petersburg. Marble. Copy of original (1778) made for Catherine II of Russia in 1781. Jean-Antoine Houdon (1741–1828) studied in Rome, but his naturalistic sculpture portraits show a far greater concern with personality than the idealized and heroic images of neoclassicism.*

7

8

In a series of six paintings titled *Marriage à la Mode* (1745), William Hogarth narrates the progress of young Lord Squanderfield and his wife from the drawing up of their marriage contract and their pursuit of separate pleasures, to his death in a duel with his wife's lover and her death by suicide. The essential elements of the story are all present starting from *The Marriage Contract* (below). Hogarth's choice of name for each character contributes to the understanding of his narrative. In need of money to complete the unfinished Palladian mansion visible through the rear window, the gouty old Lord Squanderfield has decided to marry his idle son (far left) to the daughter of a wealthy alderman. The two fathers are seated at the table, discussing the terms of the contract; the lord holds his family tree, the alderman, his empty moneybags with his daughter's dowry. The future Lord Squanderfield deliberately ignores his young bride, who is engaged in intimate conversation with the lawyer Silvertongue, soon to become Lady Squanderfield's lover. Hogarth's scene portrays the greed, ostentation, and preoccupation with money on which the alliance between the two families was based and that ultimately led to its tragic end. His message is reinforced by the poses, gestures, and clothing of the individuals, as well as in the settings of his scenes. A satirical attack on the unnecessary and exaggerated extravagance of the aristocracy and on the snobbish aspirations of the wealthy bourgeoisie, the series was intended as an indictment of the manners and affectations of his time. However in these paintings, Hogarth elaborated a more sophisticated style in respect to his other more popular and caricatural works.

9

10

9. William Hogarth,
Marriage à la Mode I,
The Marriage Contract.
*National Gallery, London.
Canvas. 1744.*

10. Hogarth, The Conduit
Children's Recital.
*Galway Collection, Dorset.
Canvas. 1731–1732.
One of the leading artists in
eighteenth-century England,
William Hogarth (1697-
1764) applied his talents
to satirical critiques of
contemporary society
as well as more
conventional images
such as this elegant
"conversation piece."*

the role of the artist above that of the patron or the connoisseur and attacked the elitist idealism of the Palladians and the Rule of Taste (see chapter 42). In his painting *O The Roast Beef of Old England* (1748–1749), Hogarth conveyed his profound antipathy for France, its absolutist monarchy, the affected manners of its inhabitants, and its Church institutions.

Caricature and Politics

Caricatura developed in seventeenth-century Italy as an art form that aimed to divert and amuse its audience by exaggerating the facial characteristics of political, religious, and literary personalities and the wealthy English aristocrats who visited Italy on the Grand Tour. In early eighteenth-century England, however, the genre of caricature became an instrument of virulent political satire that reflected a freedom of expression unknown in the rest of Europe. British caricature formed an important outlet for dissent against cultural, social, and political elitism. From the intellectual posturing of members of the Royal Academy of Arts to city merchants who aped the manners of the aristocracy, from the corrupt behavior of political leaders to the morals of society ladies, the British establishment was subject to brutally satiric portrayal. Thomas Rowlandson and James Gillray, the acknowledged masters of print caricature and fathers of modern political cartooning, attacked every element of entrenched power and took every opportunity to hold it up to ridicule. The royal family came in for especially harsh treatment. While the leading portraitists of the period sought to convey the dignity and position of their royal sitters, cartoonists produced images that were far more widely seen and consistently emphasized the gluttony, extravagance, and moral failings of their subjects. George III

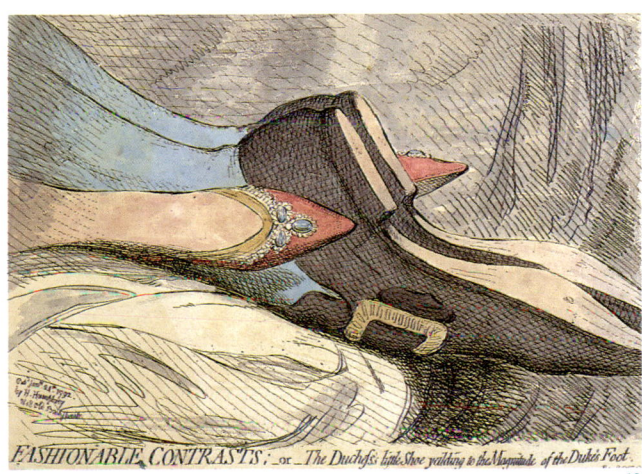

FASHIONABLE CONTRASTS;—or—The Duchess's little Shoe yielding to the Magnitude of the Duke's Foot.

12

11

11. Hogarth, O The Roast Beef of Old England (Calais Gate). *Tate Gallery, London. Canvas. 1748. Inspired by a trip to France and his arrest outside the Calais Gate on charges of spying, Hogarth included a self-referential figure on the left in the process of sketching.*

12. James Gillray, Fashionable Contrasts, or The Duchess's Little Shoe Yielding to the Magnitude of the Duke's Foot. *British Museum, London. Hand-colored etching. 1792. One of the leading political cartoonists in England, James Gillray (1757–1815) aimed this satirical and somewhat malicious attack at the recent marriage of the philandering son of George III, the duke of York, to the dainty Princess of Prussia.*

13. Pier Leone Ghezzi, Giovanni Mario Crescimbeni. *Biblioteca, Vatican, MS Ottob.lat. 3112, f.1br. The art of caricature developed in seventeenth-century Italy for the purpose of amusement, as exemplified by this cartoon of the poet Crescimbeni by Pier Leone Ghezzi (1674–1755).*

13

sadly commented to his son that other European monarchs were treated with respect by their subjects, while the English royal family could expect to be attacked on the most tenuous grounds.

Venice and the *Vedutiste*

Topographical scene paintings, a genre know as *veduta* ("view"), had already undergone various experiments by the end of the seventeenth century, especially in the representation of antique ruins, often in an unreal and idealized atmosphere. But it was in eighteenth-century Venice that the *veduta*, as a faithful representation of reality, became a prominent form of expression for dedicated practitioners. Unlike the townscapes produced by seventeenth-century Dutch painters (see chapter 37), Venetian view paintings generated a large foreign market, stimulated by the city's growing importance as a stop on the Grand Tour. The *vedute* were intended as visual records of Venice's historic monuments, landmark churches, and picturesque alleyways and canals. More imaginative interpretations than factual records, these views were engraved in vast quantities to satisfy the flourishing tourist market.

Only the wealthiest visitors could afford to commission paintings of the city. Foremost among the foreign patrons was the British consul, Joseph Smith. His patronage of Antonio Canaletto (1697–1768) established that painter as one of the leading *vedutiste* and earned him an invitation to work in England. During that time (1746–1756), Canaleto produced views of London, Windsor, and other locations for the British aristocracy. The *vedute* also proved popular among German visitors to Venice, who were as eager as the British to import the genre. Canaletto's nephew and pupil, Bernardo Bellotto, was appointed court painter (1747)

14. *Francesco Guardi,* City View. *Hermitage, St. Petersburg. Panel. Mid-eighteenth century. Francesco Guardi (1712–1793) specialized in topographical views, or* vedute, *an art form much in vogue with English and other foreign visitors to Venice.*

15. *Bernardo Bellotto,* Pirna from the Right Bank of the Elbe. *Hermitage, St. Petersburg. Canvas. 1747. Bernardo Bellotto (1720–1780) painted views of Pirna and other sites near Dresden for Count Heinrich Brühl, minister to Augustus III, the elector of Saxony.*

14

15

to the elector of Saxony, Augustus III; his views of Dresden and surrounding areas continued the Venetian tradition in high form.

As evidenced in a wide variety of forms and styles, images of contemporary life became a prominent theme of European art during the course of the eighteenth century. Their importance as a source of artistic inspiration became paramount with the emergence of the nineteenth-century Realist movement (see chapter 47).

16. Antonio Canaletto, View of St. Mark's and the Doge's Palace, Venice. *Uffizi, Florence. Canvas. Ca. 1730. Arguably the best-known Venetian* vedustista, *Antonio Canaletto (1697–1768) worked extensively for the English market.*

17

16

17. Guardi, View of the Island of San Giorgio Maggiore, Venice. *Hermitage, St. Petersburg. Canvas. Mid-eighteenth century.*

THE NINETEENTH CENTURY

The nineteenth century in Europe began with the rise of Napoleon. When his reign ended in 1815 Europe was in great upheaval. The ideals of the Enlightenment, and the previous century's confidence in reason, were replaced by uncertainty, doubt, and psychological introspection. After the triumphalistic art of the Napoleonic era, new tendencies inspired by emotions and sentiment began to make inroads throughout Europe. In Spain, Goya expressed the sense of contradiction and anguish, the fear of war and its disasters in paintings that were at times solar and serene, and at others, tormented and dark. One of his most famous series of engravings bears one of the most significant titles of the entire century: The Sleep of Reason Produces Monsters. In literature and philosophy, as in art, Romanticism led to a break with the cultural world linked to the study of classicism. Now color, shape, and composition were being studied for the new dramatic possibilities they offered. The painted landscape was radically changed. Man faced nature with doubt, aware only of its immense power (a clear example can be seen in the works of Caspar David Friedrich of Germany). In Europe, as in America, this era was marked by revolutionary changes in the industrial, social, and economic spheres that, in turn, were reflected in architecture and the visual arts in general. Great artistic freedom, impassioned experiments in the field of color and shape led to the birth of a very important movement: Impressionism.

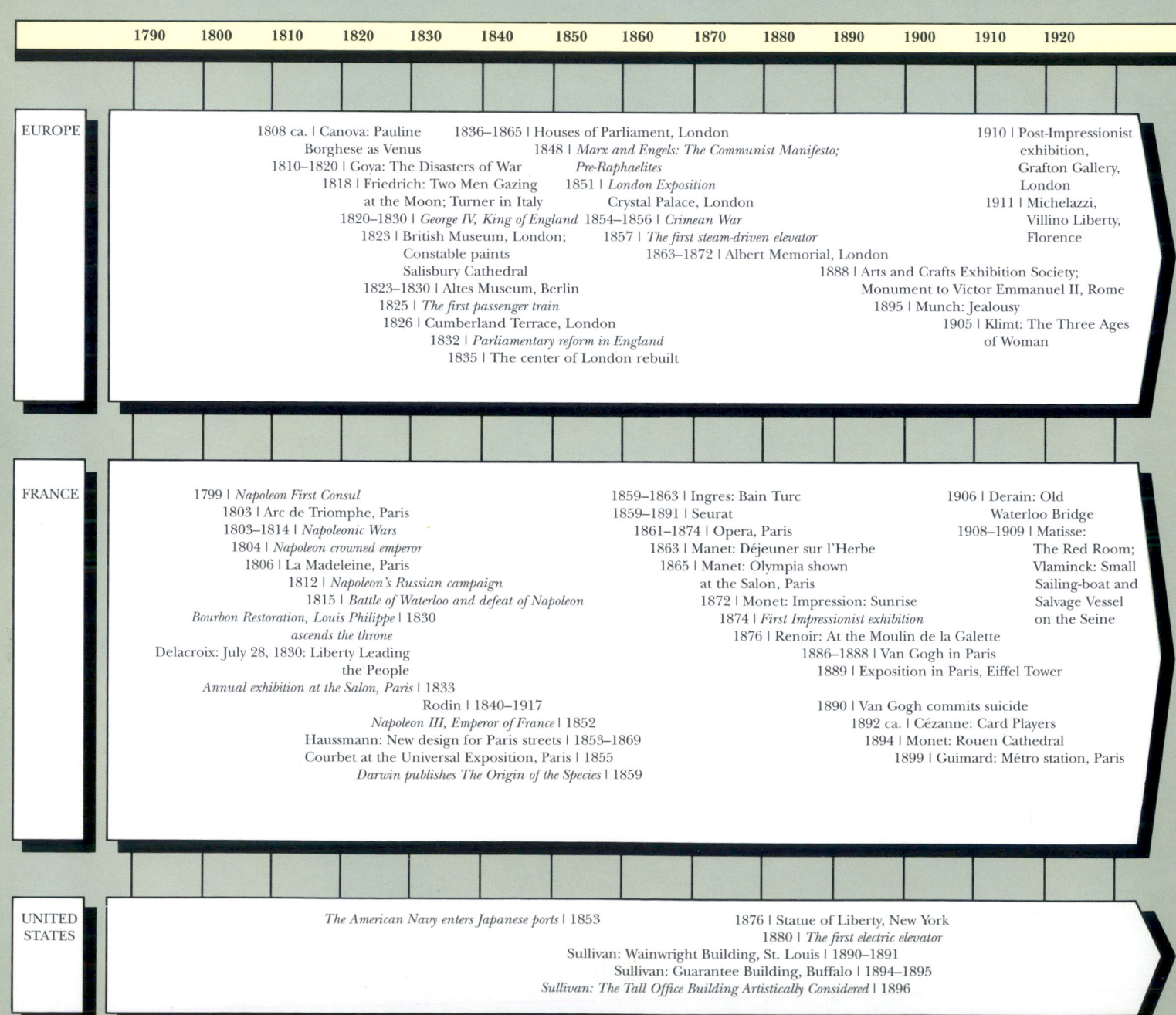

1790	1800	1810	1820	1830	1840	1850	1860	1870	1880	1890	1900	1910	1920

EUROPE

1808 ca. | Canova: Pauline Borghese as Venus
1810–1820 | Goya: The Disasters of War
1818 | Friedrich: Two Men Gazing at the Moon; *Turner in Italy*
1820–1830 | *George IV, King of England*
1823 | British Museum, London; Constable paints Salisbury Cathedral
1823–1830 | Altes Museum, Berlin
1825 | *The first passenger train*
1826 | Cumberland Terrace, London
1832 | *Parliamentary reform in England*
1835 | The center of London rebuilt

1836–1865 | Houses of Parliament, London
1848 | *Marx and Engels: The Communist Manifesto; Pre-Raphaelites*
1851 | *London Exposition* Crystal Palace, London
1854–1856 | *Crimean War*
1857 | *The first steam-driven elevator*
1863–1872 | Albert Memorial, London

1888 | Arts and Crafts Exhibition Society; Monument to Victor Emmanuel II, Rome
1895 | Munch: Jealousy
1905 | Klimt: The Three Ages of Woman

1910 | Post-Impressionist exhibition, Grafton Gallery, London
1911 | Michelazzi, Villino Liberty, Florence

FRANCE

1799 | *Napoleon First Consul*
1803 | Arc de Triomphe, Paris
1803–1814 | *Napoleonic Wars*
1804 | *Napoleon crowned emperor*
1806 | La Madeleine, Paris
1812 | *Napoleon's Russian campaign*
1815 | *Battle of Waterloo and defeat of Napoleon*
Bourbon Restoration, Louis Philippe | 1830 *ascends the throne*
Delacroix: July 28, 1830: Liberty Leading the People
Annual exhibition at the Salon, Paris | 1833
Rodin | 1840–1917
Napoleon III, Emperor of France | 1852
Haussmann: New design for Paris streets | 1853–1869
Courbet at the Universal Exposition, Paris | 1855
Darwin publishes The Origin of the Species | 1859

1859–1863 | Ingres: Bain Turc
1859–1891 | Seurat
1861–1874 | Opera, Paris
1863 | Manet: Déjeuner sur l'Herbe
1865 | Manet: Olympia shown at the Salon, Paris
1872 | Monet: Impression: Sunrise
1874 | *First Impressionist exhibition*
1876 | Renoir: At the Moulin de la Galette
1886–1888 | Van Gogh in Paris
1889 | Exposition in Paris, Eiffel Tower
1890 | Van Gogh commits suicide
1892 ca. | Cézanne: Card Players
1894 | Monet: Rouen Cathedral
1899 | Guimard: Métro station, Paris

1906 | Derain: Old Waterloo Bridge
1908–1909 | Matisse: The Red Room; Vlaminck: Small Sailing-boat and Salvage Vessel on the Seine

UNITED STATES

The American Navy enters Japanese ports | 1853
1876 | Statue of Liberty, New York
1880 | *The first electric elevator*
Sullivan: Wainwright Building, St. Louis | 1890–1891
Sullivan: Guarantee Building, Buffalo | 1894–1895
Sullivan: The Tall Office Building Artistically Considered | 1896

THE TERROR OF THE FRENCH REVOLUTION and the execution of Louis XVI (1793) inspired the nations of Europe to take up arms against the new regime. Very soon, however, they were faced with a far greater threat to their own survival. The rise to power of Napoleon Bonaparte (1769–1821) was meteoric. First as commander of the French armies (1796), then as first consul (1799), and ultimately as emperor (1804), Napoleon conquered much of Europe and created an empire on the scale of Ancient Rome. But ambition betrayed him. After his disastrous campaign in Russia (1812), he was finally defeated

CHAPTER 45

THE NAPOLEONIC EMPIRE

From Neoclassicism to Romanticism

by Wellington and Blücher at Waterloo (1815). The Napoleonic Wars caused a massive upheaval in Europe, exacerbating more fundamental changes under way as a result of the Industrial Revolution. Economically, socially, and politically, the old order began to break down. The rational ideals of the eighteenth century gave way to introspection and doubt as it became clear that the pursuit of order and harmony had failed to ensure stability. Emotion and instinct inspired the poetry of Byron and Keats, the stories of Edgar Allan Poe, the operas of Wagner, and the philosophies of Kant and Hegel. Change also inspired fear

1

and a developing gulf between those determined to preserve links with the past and those excited at the prospect of the new.

Napoleon

The self-proclaimed emperor imposed order on his dominion, centralizing administration and enforcing a new legal system, the *Code Napoléon*. He established Paris as his capital, and, like his Ancient Roman predecessors, exploited the potential of the arts to reinforce and consolidate power. The image of Republican Rome, adopted in previous decades as a visual expression of revolutionary ideals, was entirely inappropriate for the greatest empire Europe had seen since the time of Charlemagne. With triumphal arches and columns, processions, and trophies, Napoleon declared himself the legitimate heir to the Imperial Roman tradition. The cultural fruits of his conquest of Italy, including classical statues such as the *Laocoön*

1. Caspar David Friedrich, Tree with Crows. Louvre, Paris. Canvas. Ca. 1822. Arguably the leading German Romantic painter, Caspar David Friedrich (1774–1840) painted landscapes imbued with spiritual feeling to emphasize the power of nature.

2. Antonio Canova, Bust of Emperor Napoleon. Palazzo Pitti, Florence. Marble. Ca. 1810. Canova (1757–1822) was one of the many neoclassical artists employed by Napoleon to give visual expression to his power and prestige.

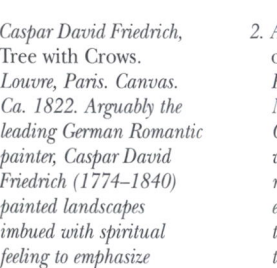

3. Charles Percier and Pierre-Léonard-François Fontaine, Arc de Triomphe du Carrousel. Paris. 1803–1836. Crowned by the four bronze horses from St. Mark's in Venice, this triumphal arch deliberately recalled the imperial power of Ancient Rome in style and decoration.

4. Claude Vignon and others, La Madeleine. Paris. 1806–1842. Neoclassicism had provided an image for the French monarchy of the ancien régime as well as for the rational idealism of the Revolution. It was now used as propaganda for Napoleon's power and prestige.

and the *Apollo Belvedere*, were paraded in a triumphal procession through Paris (1798). These two works held the place of honor in the new Musée Central des Arts (1800). The four bronze horses from St. Mark's Basilica in Venice were placed atop one of the two triumphal arches built by Napoleon in Paris, the *Arc de Triomphe du Carrousel*. Goudoin's *Colonne de la Grande Armée* in the Place Vendôme was modeled on Trajan's column in Rome and cast from the bronze of captured German and Austrian cannon.

The ambitious architectural projects realized by Napoleon in Paris included the church of La Madeleine, the Bourse, and the Palais Bourbon, all undertaken soon after his military triumphs at Austerlitz (1805) and Jena (1806). Classical in style and imperial in scale, Napoleon's patronage presented a clear and direct message to his subjects. Imperial portraits reinforced the nature of his power. Jacques-Louis David (see chapter 43), whose paintings had expressed the desire for moral purpose in late eighteenth-century France as well as the republican ideals of the Revolution, now turned his talents to the depiction of the emperor. Realistic and minutely detailed, David's portrait of Napoleon in his study showed him at work in the early hours of the morning, emphasizing the image of the emperor as the servant of his people. Antoine-Jean Gros's *Plague House at Jaffa* (1804), depicting a visit by Napoleon with the afflicted, implied the emperor's sympathy for those in suffering and his courage in the presence of the disease. (The real story may have been less flattering; so as avoid delaying his military campaign, Napoleon apparently ordered all the sick to be killed.) The enormous variety of Napoleonic portraits suggested his unbridled desire for self-glorification, a tendency invariably encountered among those who hold absolute power but that also testified

5

5. Malmaisons. *Library, Paris. Ca. 1810. Elegant and austere, the decorative scheme for Napoleon's library was based on the forms and motifs of Ancient Roman art.*

6

6. Jacques-Louis David, Napoleon in his Study. *Louvre, Paris. Canvas. 1812. David (1748–1825) carefully reproduced not only the facial features of the emperor but also his clothes and furniture.*

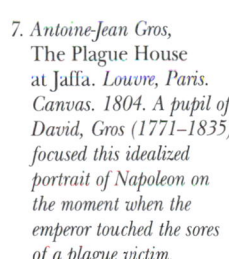

7

7. Antoine-Jean Gros, The Plague House at Jaffa. *Louvre, Paris. Canvas. 1804. A pupil of David, Gros (1771–1835) focused this idealized portrait of Napoleon on the moment when the emperor touched the sores of a plague victim.*

8

8. Canova, Pauline Borghese as Venus. *Galleria Borghese, Rome. Marble. 1808. Married to the Roman prince Camillo Borghese, Napoleon's sister chose Venus as a fitting image for her portrait by the neoclassical sculptor Canova.*

Francisco Goya y Lucientes (1746–1828) trained as a painter in his hometown of Zaragoza, Spain, and visited Rome (1770–1771) before moving to Madrid (1775). Appointed court painter (1786), he designed tapestry cartoons for the royal palaces (see chapter 39) and produced a number of portraits of King Charles IV and the royal family. Around 1792, however, Goya's paintings began undergoing a radical change. Serious illness and an association with the liberal reformist elements in Spanish society contributed to innovations in the style, content, and approach of his work. In fact, these last works greatly differ from the popular and traditional ones of his younger years. In 1794 he produced a series of paintings for the Academy that included depictions of the inmates of a lunatic asylum and a hospital for wounded soldiers. In a pair of powerful and dramatic canvases, Goya documented the events of May 2–3, 1808, when popular Spanish resistance to the French invasion sparked brutal reprisals and mass executions. But far from portraying the heroism of the resistance, Goya emphasized the violence of the events and the terror of the victims. In a subsequent series of private etchings, he explored the personal world of his imagination. The *Disasters of War* (1810–1813) gave visual expression to his own feelings of horror at the brutality and futility of armed conflict. His last works, done as murals for his house, were the so-called *Black Paintings*. Somber, savage, and often grotesque, Goya's interpretation of religious and mythological scenes emphasized the instinctive and emotive forces that motivate humanity to deeds beyond the bounds of reason. In 1792 Goya became deaf, and this greatly affected his state of mind. He was to remain imprisoned until his death in a tormenting silence.

9

9. Francisco Goya, Charles IV. *Prado, Madrid. Canvas. 1789. As the court artist in Spain, Goya painted portraits of the royal family and tapestry cartoons for the royal residences.*

10

11

10. Goya, May 2, 1808. *Prado, Madrid. Canvas. 1814.*

11. Goya, May 3, 1808. *Prado, Madrid. Canvas. 1814. Painted after Wellington had driven out the French occupying forces, Goya's dramatic record of the Spanish resistance to the French invasion was dramatically different from his earlier lighthearted court style.*

to his belief in the power of art as an instrument of propaganda.

Romanticism

Throughout Europe, Napoleon's conquests were reinforced by the installation of new monarchs. His brothers, Louis and Joseph, were made kings of Holland and Naples (1806), respectively; Joseph was also appointed king of Spain after Napoleon had forced the abdication of Charles IV (r. 1788–1808). At the Spanish court, Francisco Goya had produced a number of images for Charles IV and became the most requested portrait artist in Madrid. His early career and the style of his work had followed traditional paths; the latter was often lighthearted. But his response to the events of May 1808, in which a popular Spanish uprising against the French invasion was brutally suppressed, was certainly not traditional and anything but light. Rather than celebrate the heroism of the rebels, Goya's canvases brought the horror of the violence dramatically to life. His works from that point on reflected an increasing preoccupation with the instinctual and emotional forces that drive humanity to behavior beyond the limits of reason.

Goya was one of many artists whose works were a reaction to the ordered, rational vision of the neoclassicism. An attitude of mind rather than a single distinctive style, Romanticism emerged as a consciously modern movement that emphasized the subjective, the instinctual, and the emotional in literature, philosophy, and music as well as the visual arts. With its roots in the eighteenth century, the Romantic movement in art broke decisively with the classical desire for rules and revived an interest in the dramatic potential of color, composition, and form. It had an enormous influence on the development of landscape painting,

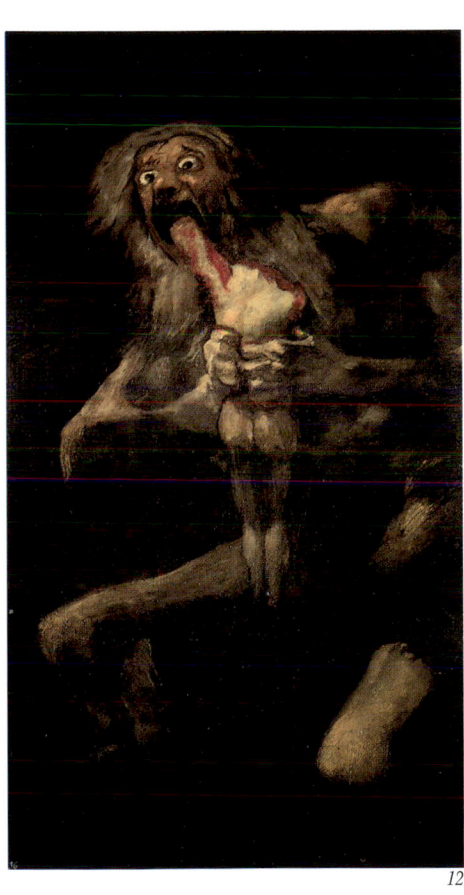

12

13. *Jean-Auguste-Dominique Ingres,* Apotheosis of Homer. *Louvre, Paris. Canvas. 1827. A pupil of David, Ingres (1780–1867) won the prestigious Prix de Rome (1801) and established himself as the leading neoclassical painter of his generation.*

13

14

12. *Goya,* Saturn Devouring One of His Children. *Prado, Madrid. Detached fresco on canvas. Ca. 1820–1823. The Romantics emphasized the power of instinct and emotion as motivations of human behavior—from sublime acts of love to savage acts of brutality— unrestrained by reason.*

14. *Théodore Géricault,* Wounded Cuirassier Leaving the Field. *Louvre, Paris. Canvas. 1814. Fascinated by the physical power of the horse, Géricault (1791–1824) exploited its potential to reinforce this image of defeat.*

THE SALON
AND OFFICIAL ART

The regular exhibition of works of art in France began in the seventeenth century as part of a program of state sponsorship. Participation in the Salon, originally restricted to members of the official Académie, was opened to all artists in 1791. The exposition became an annual event in 1833, held in the Grande Galerie of the Louvre until 1848. Its place in the French art world was of primary importance; for an artist, the inclusion of paint-

THE SALON AND OFFICIAL ART

ings in the exhibition was the equivalent of formal recognition. The introduction of a selection jury was initially intended as a way of limiting the enormous number of works submitted. The works of art admitted for display were those that adhered to the artistic canons of official art. And soon it became a means of perpetuating official taste.

Consisting largely of members of the École des Beaux-Arts, the jury imposed the strict orthodoxy of the establishment and resisted innovation. By the mid-nineteenth century, the number of works displayed at the Salon reached 5,000; audiences arrived at the rate of 10,000 per day. The importance and popularity of the event were reflected in the extensive critical debates that appeared in the newspapers and magazines of the time.

stimulating a desire to record the uncontrollable forces of nature. For the Romantic artist, storms, rocky crags, chasms, and torrents replaced the idyllic streams and meadows, blue skies, and calm lakes of the classical landscape painters.

The debate between neoclassicists and Romantics was perhaps most clearly drawn in France. The classical tradition was continued by artists like Jean-Auguste-Dominique Ingres (1780–1867), whose official state commissions included the *Apotheosis of Homer* for the ceiling of a room in the Louvre. Austere and heroic, Ingres's interpretation of this overtly classical theme demonstrated the influence

15

16

16. Delacroix, The Death of Sardanapalus. *Louvre, Paris. Canvas. 1827. Criticized for its riotous use of color, this painting typified the Romantic emphasis on extremes: brutality and apathy, black and white skin tones, violence and resistance.*

15. *Eugène Delacroix,* Women of Algeria in Their Apartment. *Louvre, Paris. Canvas. 1834. Evoking a very different atmosphere from that of Ingres's* Bain Turc, *this image captures the earthy exoticism of an Algerian harem.*

17

17. Delacroix, July 28, 1830: Liberty Leading the People. *Louvre, Paris. Canvas. 1830. In France, the Revolution of 1830 saw the overthrow of Charles X, the installation of the bourgeois monarch Louis-Philippe, and a dramatic increase in middle-class suffrage. This celebration dramatizes the popular support that helped bring the wealthier classes to power.*

of his teacher, David. The appearance in the fresco of such personalities as Raphael and Mozart reinforced the debt to antiquity in the development of European civilization. The women in his *Bain Turc* derived from Raphael's nudes and reflected the importance that Ingres and the later neoclassical painters placed on draftsmanship. Eugene Delacroix (1798–1863) and other Romantic artists conceived of painting in a very different way. His *Algerian Women* is a far more immediate and earthy depiction of the sensual atmosphere of a harem. In his *Death of Sardanapalus*, light, color, and movement are used to heighten the drama of battle.

Inspired by a scene from the works of Byron, the painting broke every traditional rule of order, decorum, and rational clarity, causing an uproar when it was exhibited at the Salon. Traditional religious art had not hesitated to depict extremes of human feeling to reinforce the faith of the viewer; now Romantic artists portrayed suffering and ecstasy, anguish and triumph, as expressions of the common human experience and their own personalities. The differences between the rational beliefs of the neoclassicists and the subjective world of the Romantics were summed up by the English artist and poet William Blake in the phrase, "Talent thinks but genius sees." This new approach placed a considerable onus on the artist to develop his originality and had major implications for the development of modern art.

Architecture and Nationalism

In Europe of the nineteenth century, the rising tide of nationalism—which ultimately led to the outbreak of the World War I—had its roots in the defeat of Napoleon and was reinforced by the new constitutional monarchies and republics that emerged in response to bourgeois demands for political

18. Ingres, Bain Turc. Louvre, Paris. Canvas. 1859. Idealized beauty, static poses, and rational composition were hallmarks of Ingres's neoclassical style.

20. Eduard Riedel and Georg Dollmann, Neuschwanstein Castle. Bavaria. Begun 1869. Inspired by medieval fairy tales, this castle for Ludwig II of Bavaria gave visual expression to the new interest in past cultures other than those of Greece and Rome.

18

19. Karl Friedrich Schinkel, Altes Museum. Berlin. 1823–1830. The architecture of Karl Friedrich Schinkel (1781-1841) was austere and neoclassical. His use of Ionic columns supporting an entablature emphasized this museum's debt to the Greek cultural tradition.

19

20

involvement. The growing importance of Prussia in European politics was given visual expression in the adoption of a pure Greek classical style for public monuments. Antiquity was also the inspiration for Georges Eugène Haussmann's reconstruction of the center of Paris (1853–1869) under Napoleon III; its regularized street plan, monumental new buildings, and grand vistas marked the restoration of the empire after the 1848 Revolution. In recently unified Italy, the image of the new state was inevitably inspired by Roman tradition. King Victor Emmanuel II (1820–1878), a leading figure in the unification campaign and the first ruler of the Italian state, was commemorated in a white marble monument of classical grandeur. The interest in historical styles, however, went beyond the ancient models promoted by neoclassicism. By the middle of the century, indigenous strains of Romanesque, Gothic, and other variations of medieval architecture in Germany, Holland, Austria, and France, as well as in Great Britain (see chapter 46), were providing direct visual links to their respective national cultures. Interest in medieval culture was an important element of Romanticism, stimulating a fascination for Gothic architectural fantasy. In France, the approach to Gothic was more archaeological, developed in the theories and medieval restorations of architect Eugène Emmanuel Viollet-le-Duc.

To more forward-looking minds in the latter part of the century, however, the architectural styles of both the Middle Ages and antiquity were too firmly rooted in the past and reinforced ties to outdated traditions. The pervasive historicism in nineteenth-century architecture finally triggered a reaction to the established order and the birth of modernism at the end of the century (see chapter 49).

21

22

23

21. Anonymous, Portrait of Napoleon III. *Museo del Risorgimento, Milan. Canvas. Nineteenth century.*

22. Giuseppe Sacconi, Monument to Victor Emmanuel II, interior detail. *Rome. 1865– 1877. Glorifying an ideal as well as an individual and with no apparent practical value, this commemorative monument was the nineteenth-century culmination of Ancient Roman tradition.*

23. Auguste-Frédéric Bartholdi, Statue of Liberty. *New York. Bronze. 1876; unveiled 1886. This colossal personification of the Ancient Roman concept of* libertas, *erected at the entrance to New York Harbor, was a gift to the United States by the people of France to mark the centennial of the Declaration of Independence (1776).*

THE BRITISH EMPIRE HAD BEEN FOUNDED on trade, but it soon extended political control in colonies all over the globe. With the Napoleonic Wars (1803–1815), Great Britain—ever aware of the narrow channel of water separating it from continental Europe—became economically dependent on its colonies. Victory over the French marked the beginning of a century of peace and unprecedented prosperity at home, as the impact of the Industrial Revolution was felt in the dramatic growth of manufacturing industries.

Middle-class demands for stronger representation in Parliament and the organs

CHAPTER 46

PAX BRITANNICA

British Art in the Nineteenth Century

of government were partially answered by parliamentary reform in 1832. The British constitutional monarchy thus avoided the violence of popular revolutions experienced elsewhere in Europe in 1848. With national confidence running high despite the disastrous handling of the Crimean War (1854–1856) and the Indian Mutiny (1857), Britain reinforced its wealth and power in the patronage of art and architecture on a grand scale. Unlike Napoleon, however, its great patrons did not look to imperial Rome for images of the new national prestige but developed new and distinctive solutions.

1

The Regency

The appointment of the prince of Wales as regent for the mentally ill George III (1811) had far-reaching implications for the visual appearance of London. The new regent used his power to ensure official approval of a plan to restore the center of London (1812–1827) devised by his architect, John Nash (1752–1835). The plans included development of a fashionable residential district called Regent's Park. Grand and ornate, Nash's classically inspired architecture set the tone for Regency London. The park was linked by a new road, Regent's Street, with Carlton House, the home of the regent and center of London social life. Exploiting the eighteenth-century principles of town planning developed in Bath (see chapter 42), Nash combined curved lines and straight lines in the design of streets and traffic circles, creating pronounced visual variety, ceremonial approaches, and triumphal perspectives.

After the defeat of Napoleon (1815) and the succession of the regent as George IV (r. 1820–1830), the urban restoration of central London was extended in two directions. To the west, Nash remodeled Buckingham House as a palace for the new king and opened a triumphal approach through St. James's Park, the Mall. To the east he designed an immense plaza, named Trafalgar Square to commemorate the British naval victory at Trafalgar (1805); at the center of the square a column was erected in honor of the victorious but mortally wounded commander, Admiral Horatio Nelson. The imperial theme was ultimately reinforced by two buildings around the square, one that would become the National Gallery and another that would serve as offices of colonial administration. The duke of Wellington, the other great

1. *John Nash,* Cumberland Terrace. *Regent's Park, London. 1826–1827. The grand and imposing style of new residential buildings in Regent's Park, designed by John Nash (1752–1835), reflected the current fashion for Greek culture.*

2. *Thomas Jogg,* Napoleon Omnipotent, or the Acme of Arrogance and Presumption. *1813. This cartoon was a typical British satire on Napoleon's bid for power in Europe. The words reflect the British conviction that God was on the side of Napoleon's enemies.*

2

3. *Antonio Canova,* Napoleon. *Apsley House, London. Marble. 1802–1810. The torso of this neoclassical statue of Napoleon by Canova (1757–1822) was taken directly from the Greek statue of the* Apollo Belvedere.

4. *Thomas Lawrence,* Wellington. *Apsley House, London. Canvas. 1814. One of the leading British artists of the nineteenth century, Sir Thomas Lawrence (1769–1830) was a great admirer of Reynolds, whom he succeeded as painter to the king.*

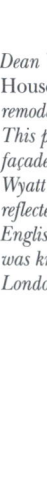

4

3

5. *Dean Wyatt,* Apsley House. *London. Façade remodeled 1828–1829. This plain but imposing façade by Benjamin Dean Wyatt (ca. 1755–1850) reflected established English taste. The house was known as No.1, London.*

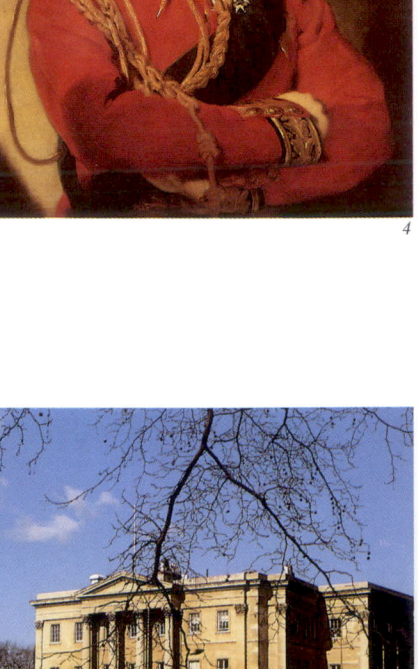

5

hero of the Napoleonic Wars, received Apsley House as a gift from the nation; the façade of the building was remodeled in the Palladian style established as the prime image of aristocratic power in eighteenth-century England. Also presented to Wellington was Antonio Canova's nude statue of Napoleon, commissioned by the emperor and purchased by the British government from France. This extraordinary gesture not only testified to the importance of Wellington's achievement but also to the power of art as political propaganda. The victory over Napoleon was celebrated in numerous official commissions, ranging from portraits of Nelson and Wellington to historical paintings commemorating the naval and military victories of the campaign in dramatic style.

Battle of Styles

The renewed interest in the culture of classical antiquity during the eighteenth century (see chapter 41) had given architects and patrons a wide range of stylistic choices, from the purity and austerity of Greek Doric to the elaborate and sumptuous extravagance of the Roman imperial Composite. Conveying more than aesthetic preferences, these choices also embodied identification with the particular cultural values they represented. The Ionic temple façade of the British Museum, for example, reinforced the role of Greek civilization as the foundation of Western culture. The architect John Soane, who had been appointed surveyor of the Bank of England (1788), combined Greek caryatids, Roman thermal windows, and Byzantine domes on pendentives in his design for the bank's new headquarters (finished 1818; largely demolished). The growing interest in medieval culture, evident throughout Europe (see chapter 45),

6

7

9. *Charles Barry* and *Augustus Welby Pugin*, Houses of Parliament. *London. 1836–1865. Massive scale and intricate detail are brought together in a distinctive image for the power of the British Empire.*

6. *Robert Smirke,* British Museum. *London. Begun 1823; south front finished 1847. This great ceremonial entrance was inspired by Greek religious architecture to create a temple of the Muses.*

7. *George Gilbert Scott,* Albert Memorial. *London. 1863–1872. Paid for by public subscription, this quasi-religious memorial to Queen Victoria's husband combined* the Italian Gothic form of a ciborium with a series of classically inspired reliefs depicting imperial and artistic themes.

8

8. *Augustus Welby Pugin,* House of Commons, interior. *Houses of Parliament, London. Opened 1852.*

9

assumed particular significance in Britain. In the wake of a Catholic revival, the architect Augustus Pugin and the critic John Ruskin affirmed the need to return to Gothic art as an affirmation of ethical-religious ideals. The range of stylistic choices was thereby widened considerably.

The issue of choices became especially poignant when the old Houses of Parliament were destroyed by fire (1834). Before the competition for a reconstruction plan was even announced, a committee of experts was appointed by the government to decide on the style of the new building. Declaring that a distinctive national style was required for this prestigious project, the committee settled on a choice of two variations of late Gothic that were both typically English, Tudor style and Perpendicular Gothic style. Britain thus became one of the few European countries to reject the classical style, with its moral and political overtones, as its image of state. The winning design, conceived by Pugin and Charles Barry, was also notable for its lack of a grand ceremonial entrance. Based on a functional and rationally ordered plan, the exterior structure bore little resemblance to that of any medieval building. But the intricate network of Gothic details, covering both the interior and exterior surfaces, conveyed a distinctly national, moral, Christian message.

By the late 1850s, the repertoire of ornamental motifs in Britain spanned the entire range of historical European styles. Public and private patronage on a huge scale throughout the country financed the construction of town halls, universities, churches, monuments, banks, hotels, and private houses that gave visual expression to the prosperity of the nation. Each was designed in a historical style that conveyed a deliberate message by association. In the far-flung British colonies, especially India, the architectural language of Western

10

11

10. *Frederick William Stevens,* Railway Station. *Bombay, India. 1887. Western European Romanesque and Gothic features were combined with details derived from the Indian Moghul tradition to provide a visual image for one of the great contributions to India by the British Raj—the railroad.*

11. *James Baillie Fraser,* View of Government House, Calcutta, India. *Guildhall Library, London. Aquatint. 1824. The neoclassical style of British imperial architecture promoted an image of grandeur and reinforced the supremacy of Western culture over Indian traditions.*

12. *Robert Martineau,* The Last Days in the Old Home. *Tate Gallery, London. Canvas. 1862. Sentimental and idealized, the theme and execution of this painting gave visual expression to the bourgeois morality of Victorian Britain.*

Europe reinforced British imperial rule. Despite the radical innovations brought by the Industrial Revolution (see chapter 49), the architectural expression of British power remained firmly rooted in tradition.

Portraiture

The grand, heroic ideals of neoclassicism that had dominated British painting in the eighteenth century now gave way to less formal expressions of power. The Industrial Revolution had brought radical technological and social changes in Britain that were recorded in images ranging from Joseph Mallord William Turner's recreation of the atmospheric effects of a steam engine driving through a storm, *Rain, Steam, Speed* (1844), to William Powell Frith's panoramas of middle-class Victorian life at the railroad station or at the races. The dramatic rise in bourgeois wealth in nineteenth-century Britain was reflected in a new approach to portraiture. Informality and spontaneity replaced formality and pose. In A.E. Emslie's *Dinner at Haddo House* (1884), for example, Lady Aberdeen presides over a dinner party attended by such leading political figures as William Gladstone and Lord Rosebury; only the back of the hostess is seen. The many informal portraits of Queen Victoria and Prince Albert with their children emphasized not only the continuity of the monarchy, but the family's identification with middle-class values, especially the virtues of domestic life. Sentimentality and morality pervaded Victorian Britain. The bold soldier and the chivalrous gentleman coming to the rescue of a defenseless woman were among the images created during this period to promote the ideology of imperialism but masked the unpleasant realities of civilian and military service overseas.

12

13

13. *William Powell Frith,* The Bridge of Love. *Victoria & Albert Museum, London. Canvas. 1852. This painting by William Powell Frith (1819–1909) illustrates a scene from* The Bride of Lammermoor *(1819) by Walter Scott.*

14

14. *James-Jacques-Joseph Tissot,* Frederick Gustavus Burnaby. *National Portrait Gallery, London. Canvas. 1870. Cocky and refined, the soldier portrayed by Tissot (1836–1902) conveys prevailing British confidence in the defense of a far-flung empire.*

Despite his posthumous fame, the English landscape painter John Constable (1776–1837) earned little recognition during his lifetime. His contribution to the landscape genre, however, was immense. Unlike his more successful contemporary, Turner, Constable never traveled abroad, concentrating his energies on recording the landscape of the south of England. The countryside around his native Suffolk village of East Bergholt provided material for

CONSTABLE

much of his work. His efforts to capture the ephemeral nature of the countryside were summed up in a letter to a friend: "I shall make laborious studies from Nature and I shall endeavor to get a pure and unaffected representation of the scenes that may employ me." Emphasizing the importance of open-air sketching, Constable used oils to record his

observations of the changes in nature from moment to moment. His habit of using tiny white flecks to convey the effects of light, however, was soundly criticized by the contemporary art establishment, who referred to them as his "snow." Aware that the spontaneity of a sketch is lost if the work is finished in the studio, he often tried to complete his pictures on site, an approach that was to become a key feature of the Impressionist movement.

Landscape

British landscape painting was well established by 1800, having been used both to reflect the nation's wealth and to express more poetic feelings about nature. During the course of the nineteenth century, this tradition developed in significant new ways. For some years, travel in Europe had been made hazardous by the Napoleonic Wars; in Britain, the concentration of landscape painters on their own surroundings reinforced strong feelings of local identity and insularity from the Continent. Reacting

15. John Constable,
Salisbury Cathedral.
*Victoria & Albert
Museum, London.
Canvas. 1820.
Constable's landscape
celebrates the grandeur
of English medieval
achievement. His friend,
Archbishop Fisher, appears
in the right-hand corner.*

15

17

16. Constable, Evening
in Dedham Vale.
*Victoria & Albert
Museum, London.
Canvas. Ca. 1802.*

16

17. Constable, Cottage
at Cornfield. *Victoria
& Albert Museum,
London. Canvas.
Exhibited at the Royal
Academy 1833. John
Constable (1776–1837)
was one of the leading
landscape painters in
nineteenth-century
Britain. His pictures
were even exhibited at
the Salon in Paris.*

to the idealized formulas of the classical landscape tradition, artists such as John Constable painted outdoors, using both watercolors and oils to capture the effects of light on trees, water, and fields. In his writings, Constable emphasized the importance of the sky and cloud formations as essential elements in landscape. Painting the scenery of his native Suffolk, of the south coast, and of the countryside around Salisbury, Constable conveyed his deep feeling for the harmonious beauty of nature and invariably included images of human activity: peasants in carts, farmhouses, and cathedrals.

Other artists gave more dramatic expression to the subjective, instinctive, and emotional aspects of human experience that characterized the Romantic movement. The poetry and painting of William Blake rejected the order and rationality of neoclassicism in favor of a spiritual, visionary approach that expressed the spirit of Christianity rather than its rules. Romantic painters traveled the mountains of Scotland and Wales in search of the drama in nature. In the landscapes of J.M.W. Turner, the presence of human figures reinforced a sense of powerlessness against the forces of nature. Turner went

so far as to have himself lashed to the mast of a boat to experience firsthand the beauty and terror of a storm at sea. Exploiting the atmospheric effects of light and color, Turner's rough technique appalled his critics but set a precedent for later experiments with artistic expression.

18

19

18. William Blake, Pietà. *Tate Gallery, London. Colored print. Ca. 1795. Intensely religious, the works of William Blake (1757–1827) reflected the intensity of his inner feelings. His comment that "talent thinks but genius sees" reinforced the Romantic view of art as an expression of personal experience.*

19. Blake, Oberon, Titania and Puck with Dancing Fates. *Tate Gallery, London. Watercolor. Ca. 1795.*

20

20. John Sell Cotman, The Shipwreck. *British Museum, London. Watercolor. Ca. 1823. Cotman (1782–1842) was one of many artists during this period who experimented with pictorial composition using flat blocks of watercolor. These sketches were the basis of a finished oil painting.*

The cultural traditions of Scotland and England are highly distinct. Never conquered by the Angles or Saxons, Scotland was not officially united with England until 1707 and to this day retains its own legal system. After the failed rebellion of 1745, led by Bonnie Prince Charlie, the kilt was banned and popular English opinion dismissed the Scots as barbarians.

That image, however, soon underwent a dramatic change. James Macpherson, a Scottish poet from the Highlands, claimed to have discovered a third-century epic poem in Gaelic on the life of the ancient king Fingal, purportedly written by his son, the legendary warrior Ossian. Macpherson, who had composed the poem himself, published the apocryphal work in 1761. The success of the book contributed to a new image for the Scots as the victims of cultural genocide and cultivated widespread interest in Scottish culture. The image was propagated by the Highland Society, founded by Macpherson himself around 1780, and by the emergence of clan tartans, the fabric designs of which reflected the uniforms of Scottish regiments.

Scotland and her traditions and culture became enormously popular, almost a fad, in the first half of the nineteenth century. We need only consider Napoleon, who decorated his library with scenes from the poems of Ossian. Felix Mendelssohn-Bartholdy wrote an overture titled *Fingal's Cave* (1830), and Queen Victoria was one of the many tourists who visited the cave itself, which is located on the island of Staffa. Victoria's contributions to the Romantic image of the Highlands included the construction of Balmoral Castle and her insistence that the staff wear specially designed Balmoral tartan.

21. J.M.W. Turner, The Music Party, Petworth. *British Museum, London. Bodycolor on blue paper. 1830. Trained as a watercolorist, Turner exploited the effects of color to create impressions rather than minutely detailed records.*

21

22. Turner, Snowstorm, Avalanche and Inundation, a Scene in the Upper Part of the Val d'Aosta. *Art Institute, Chicago. Canvas. 1837. Applying his exceptional talents to conveying the overwhelming power of nature, J.M.W. Turner (1775–1851) painted landscapes of remarkable intensity.*

23. Turner, Landscape with a River and a Bay in the Distance. *Louvre, Paris. Canvas. Ca. 1835–1840.*

24. Turner, Panorama of Florence. *Uffizi, Florence. Watercolor. Ca. 1819.*

22

23

24

THE SHIFT IN NINETEENTH-CENTURY Europe from a predominantly agricultural economy to an industrial economy led to a dramatic rise in urban population and to appalling living conditions for the new urban poor. The humanitarian idealism of the eighteenth century now gave way to increasingly strident demands for social and political reforms. This met with considerable opposition from established authority, determined not to relinquish its traditional privileges. Violent confrontation was inevitable. The year 1848 saw not only the publication of Karl Marx's *Communist Manifesto* but also rioting and rebellion in

CHAPTER 47

NEW HEROES FOR A NEW ERA

Realism, 1840–1880

France, Italy, Austria, and Germany. The French king was forced to abdicate in February, and a provisional socialist government instituted radical reforms, including a state job creation plan and universal male suffrage. These reforms were immediately repealed by the bourgeois republican majority elected to the Assembly in April, and the riots that ensued were ruthlessly suppressed. By 1852, France was once again under the authoritarian rule of an emperor, Napoleon III. The experience in France was exceptional in many respects; elsewhere in Europe, the call for reform was met by compromise solutions that ensured

1

417

middle-class participation in government but did little to alleviate the urban poverty engendered by the Industrial Revolution.

"Il faut être de son temps" (Daumier)

Dissatisfaction with the political establishment encouraged dissent at many levels and a growing interest in the issues of contemporary society. Urban and rural poverty, the rise of industry, the well-being of the bourgeoisie, and life in the slums, cafes, theaters, and boulevards of the modern city inspired the radical socialist theories of Marx and Pierre Proudhon and provided a new range of subject matter for the literary works of Émile Zola, Charles Baudelaire, and Charles Dickens. The same themes found visual expression in the development of the Realist movement in art. Baudelaire's exhortation to artists to take up the "heroism of modern life" was answered by a growing number of painters who rejected the styles, subjects, and conventions of the past. Honoré Daumier's affirmation, "*Il faut être de son temps*" ("One must be of one's own time"), reinforced the widening gulf between official art and that of the avant-garde. The Realist movement of the nineteenth century, which originated primarily in France, found followers elsewhere as well. The rejection of established standards took many forms. While some writers and painters conveyed explicitly socialist messages, others were less politically motivated. Far from being coherent or organized, the movement in general reflected a desire for self-expression in the context of modern society and a rejection of links with tradition.

Courbet

Arguably the major exponent of nineteenth-century Realism, Gustave Courbet (1819–1887) was among those who attempted to

1. *Édouard Manet*, Déjeuner sur l'Herbe. *Musée d'Orsay, Paris. Canvas. 1863. In rejecting the standards of the official art establishment, Manet (1832–1883) had a major influence on both the Realist movement and the development of Impressionism.*

2. *Jean-Louis-Ernest Meissonier*, The Barricade, June 1848. *Louvre, Paris. Canvas. 1850. Far from emphasizing the heroism of defeat, Meissonier (1815–1891) recorded the brutal realities of the suppression of the June 1848 Revolution.*

3. *Honoré Daumier*, Allegory of the Republic. *Musée d'Orsay, Paris. Canvas. 1848. Daumier's allegorical image of the Republic nurturing her children was never completed.*

4. *Gustave Courbet*, A Burial at Ornans. *Musée d'Orsay, Paris. Canvas. 1849–1850. Arguably the leading Realist of the nineteenth century, Courbet (1819–1877) painted many scenes of bourgeois and peasant life around the rural town of Ornans, consciously avoiding the grandeur of his Romantic contemporaries.*

use figurative art as a vehicle of socialist ideals. Typical of this innovative approach was his *A Burial at Ornans*, which he originally titled *Painting of Human Figures. Historical Record of a Burial at Ornans.* The composition, like the title, was deliberately informal. Painted on the grand scale of an historical epic, the picture was remarkable for its lack of heroic gestures or patronizing, moralistic overtones. On the contrary, it was an impartial view of people attending the burial of an unspecified corpse. But Courbet's pictorial honesty and careful avoidance of idealization was misinterpreted by contemporary viewers, who assumed that

he was ridiculing a solemn event. Similarly, his work entitled *Interior of My Studio, A Real Allegory Summing up Seven Years of My Life as an Artist* scrupulously avoided the grand references and classical settings traditionally associated with images of artists at work. The figures on the left portrayed various types associated with contemporary society: a Jew, a priest, a huntsman and his dogs, and a destitute woman with her child. To the right are portraits of his friends, including Baudelaire immersed in reading and the bearded socialist, Proudhon. Courbet adopted the term "Realism" from the critical reviews of a one-man show (1855), which

he staged outside the Paris World Exhibition to protest the official procedure of submitting paintings to a selection jury.

Labor

The central theme of contemporary political and cultural debate was labor. Attacking the age-old distinctions between rich and poor, the ordinary worker was now elevated to the level of hero. An appropriate subject for modern art, he provided images that could express both the social injustice of inequality and the moral virtue of physical work. Courbet's socialist beliefs were reflected

5

5. *Courbet,* Interior of My Studio, A Real Allegory Summing up Seven Years of My Life as an Artist. *Musée d'Orsay, Paris. Canvas. 1855.*

In this painting of the artist with his models and friends, Courbet emphasized his own interest in contemporary society and culture.

in his *Stonebreakers* (1851; believed destroyed during World War II), a depiction of two life-size figures engaged in backbreaking toil that was hailed by Proudhon as the first socialist painting. Jean-François Millet's paintings of French peasants at work reflected the extremes of rural poverty in a country where some three-quarters of the population still lived outside cities and towns. But Millet denied any political content in his works; his intention, beyond depicting the exhausting reality of field work, was to stress the timelessness and grandeur of human toil in a way that urban industrial themes, so essentially modern, could not.

The city provided an inexhaustible source of contemporary subjects. Prostitutes, laundresses, rag-pickers, beggars, drunkards, railway workers, and miners now appeared in literature and the visual arts as well as in numerous reports on the appalling social conditions of the urban poor in nineteenth-century Europe. Daumier's paintings and lithographs of Parisian life encompassed all classes, from the impoverished proletariat to the wealthy bourgeoisie. His caricatures ridiculed the posturing of politicians; at the other end of the social spectrum, his painting of a washerwoman carrying her load from the river represented an industry that

employed as much as a quarter of the labor force of Paris. Daumier's disenchanted look at a badly paid, overworked segment of the population expressed his own liberal ideas and reflected, more generally, the prominent new position of poverty and manual labor in the visual arts of the time.

Manet and the Bourgeoisie

Other artists chose to emphasize their identification with contemporary life through images of the urban bourgeoisie. Édouard Manet (1832–1883) deliberately violated the canons and conventions of the official art

6. *Daumier,*
The Washerwoman.
Musée d'Orsay, Paris.
Panel. Ca. 1863.
The laundry industry
provided an important
service for the Parisian
bourgeoisie and employed
large numbers of working-
class women. Daumier's
image of a washerwoman
carrying her bundle from
the river is an unidealized
portrait of urban manual
labor.

7. *Jean-François Millet,*
The Gleaners.
Musée d'Orsay, Paris.
Canvas. 1857.

8. *Millet,* Peasants
Carrying Brushwood.
Hermitage, St. Petersburg.
Canvas. Ca. 1858.
The life of French peasants
as recorded by Millet
emphasized the tedium,
arduousness, and
moral virtue of
agricultural labor.

world by translating the traditional subjects of the old masters into a modern idiom; he reinforced the modernity of his interpretations by choosing well-known themes. His groundbreaking *Déjeuner sur l'Herbe* (Luncheon on the Grass), for example, reinterpreted the theme of the *fête champêtre* ("country outing") as a contemporary bourgeois picnic. His *Olympia* consciously recalled Titian's *Venus of Urbino* in both subject matter and composition, but Manet's prostitute could in no way be mistaken for a classical sensual beauty. Indeed the artist consciously avoided any such references by emphasizing her

uninviting pose and cold stare, reinforced by the flatness of the image; the latter quality owed much to Manet's study of Japanese prints. Exhibited at the 1865 Salon, *Olympia* shocked and offended critics, who called it ugly and obscene. Picnics in the park, horse racing, outings at seaside resorts, and the other new leisure pursuits of the urban bourgeoisie afforded the Realist artists new opportunities to demonstrate their own modernism. The dramatic expansion of the railroads during the nineteenth century allowed cheap travel and stimulated the development of coastal towns as fashionable holiday resorts for the middle classes.

Relaxed and informal, Realist paintings of the beach and its facilities provided a marked contrast to the traditional image of the sea— as an expression of naval power or the Romantic forces of nature—and emphasized the modern pursuit of pleasure.

Realism and Portraiture

The impartiality and informality with which the Realists approached their depictions of working-class and bourgeois life was also evident in their portraits of friends and families. Having already raised the status of the laborer and the fallen woman to the

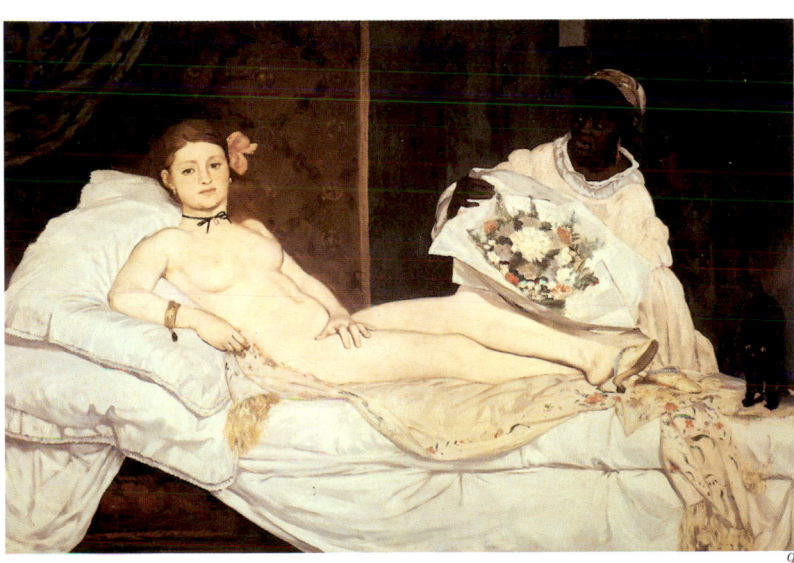

9

10

9. Manet, Olympia. Musée d'Orsay, Paris. Canvas. 1863. Presenting this traditional theme in a modern idiom, Manet launched a broadside attack on established standards of beauty.

10. Edgar Degas, L'Absinthe. Musée d'Orsay, Paris. Canvas. 1876. Images of the fallen woman were popular with Realist artists and writers, who saw her as a direct reflection of the effects of poverty on the urban poor.

11. Eugène Boudin, Bathers on the Beach at Trouville. Musée d'Orsay, Paris. Panel. 1864. Uninterested in specific events and unconcerned with individual portraits, Boudin (1824–1898) simply recorded the new leisured life of the urban bourgeoisie.

12. Winslow Homer, Croquet. Art Institute, Chicago. Canvas. 1866. Neither grand nor dramatic, this scene of middle-class leisure by the American painter Winslow Homer (1836–1910) reflected the changing attitude to art in the late nineteenth century.

11

12

Japan had deliberately closed its doors to foreign influence, resisting all attempts on the part of the West to engage in trade until the U.S. Navy broke the blockade in 1853. *Japonisme* was a term used to describe the fad for Japanese items in Europe and America in the second half of the nineteenth century. By 1866, European and American markets were flooded with Japanese prints, tea, bamboo furniture, lacquerware, ceramics, and fans (see chapter 40). Some shops specialized in extravagant and costly furnishings, like Tiffany's in New York and Liberty's in London, and imported Japanese craftsmen to design goods for them. In these same years, Gilbert and Sullivan were inspired to write their operetta, *The Mikado* (1885), and Giacomo Puccini his *Madame Butterfly* (1904). The appearance of Japanese products and cultural artifacts in the West inevitably affected the styles and themes of the visual arts as well. Manet's portrait of Émile Zola included items imported from Japan on the writer's desk and a Japanese print on the wall. Realist, Impressionist, and Post-Impressionist painters of the late nineteenth century all found inspiration in the distinctive style of Japanese prints. Manet and Toulouse-Lautrec adopted their black, sinuous outlines. Both Toulouse-Lautrec and Gauguin exploited the flat blocks of decorative color used in Japanese prints, albeit with different results. Matisse was one of a number of artists influenced by their patterned surfaces. Degas collected Japanese woodblock prints, whose subject matter influenced his many paintings of courtesans at their dressing tables. Van Gogh was deeply impressed by Japanese landscapes; his trip to Arles, he said, was a search for a natural setting like that of Japan.

13

13. Manet, Servante de Bocks. *Musée d'Orsay, Paris. Canvas. 1878. The free brushwork of Manet's later paintings signaled the emergence of Impressionist technique (see chapter 48).*

14. Manet, Zola. *Musée d'Orsay, Paris. Canvas. 1868. The French naturalist writer Émile Zola (1840–1902) was closely associated with the Realist movement. In such novels as L'Assommoir (1877), Nana (1880), and Germinal (1885), he addressed many of the same modern urban themes as the Realist painters.*

14

level of art, they now attempted to demythologize the political and cultural elite. In a portrait of Proudhon with his children, Courbet avoided any association with the lifestyle of the ruling class. The subject is portrayed at work, in a casual pose; his proletarian clothes reinforce Proudhon's identification with the plight of the oppressed working classes. All evidence of praise or veneration is absent as well from Manet's portrait of Zola, which emphasizes the writer's participation in contemporary society and culture by the appearance on his wall of Manet's *Olympia* and images of Japanese fashion.

The Pre-Raphaelites

While not, strictly speaking, part of the Realist movement, the British artists of the Pre-Raphaelite Brotherhood (established 1848) also reacted against official standards and conventions. Founded by Holman Hunt, John Everett Millais, Dante Gabriel Rossetti, and others, the group attacked what they regarded as frivolity in contemporary art. Although the themes of their painting were often historical or religious, the Pre-Raphaelites distinguished themselves from academic tradition by their concern with naturalistic

representation and correct detail. Hunt, for example, traveled to the Holy Land several times to paint the real settings for his biblical scenes. Associated with the Arts and Crafts Movement (see chapter 49), the Pre-Raphaelites were an important influence on the development of Art Nouveau and Symbolism.

Landscape

French landscape painters also questioned the validity of established tradition, drawing inspiration from the seventeenth-century Dutch school as well as contemporary

15. Courbet, Proudhon and his Children. *Musée du Petit Palais, Paris. Canvas. 1865. Careful attention to detail reflected Courbet's desire to create a true-to-life image of his friend, the left-wing philosopher Proudhon, at work in a family setting.*

15

16. James McNeill Whistler, Arrangement in Grey and Black, a Portrait of the Artist's Mother. *Musée d'Orsay, Paris. Canvas. 1871. Not strictly part of the Realist movement, the American painter James McNeill Whistler (1834–1903) worked in Paris and was much influenced by the new emphasis on contemporary life.*

16

17. John Everett Millais, Ophelia. *Tate Gallery, London. Canvas. 1852. The Pre-Raphaelites consciously broke away from the official standards of the British artistic establishment and reinforced the reality of their scenes with minute attention to both historical and natural detail.*

17

English painters like Constable, whose *Haywain* was exhibited in Paris in 1824. Rather than travel to Italy like their predecessors, many in the decade of the 1830s settled along the Channel coast or in villages located in or near the Forest of Fontainebleau. At Barbizon, for example, a colony of artists was formed that included painters of the caliber of Camille Corot, Charles-François Daubigny, and Théodore Rousseau. Reacting against the formal rules of classical landscape formulated by Poussin and Lorrain in the seventeenth century, the Barbizon school sought to capture the fleeting effects of nature, the play of outdoor light, and the changing seasons, using bright colors and loose brushwork. But the spontaneity of their informal open-air sketches was lost when the works were finished in the studio according to official Salon requirements. Their recognition that the original sketch was a truer likeness than the finished painting was a major step in the development of modern art.

The new approach to landscape painting and the Realist movement in general had a direct and vital influence on the emergence of Impressionism in the late 1860s (see chapter 48).

18. *Charles-François Daubigny,* The Harvest. *Musée d'Orsay, Paris. Canvas. 1851. The French rural landscape provided a range of subject matter for the Barbizon artists, including Charles-François Daubigny (1817–1878).*

19. *Jean-Baptiste Camille Corot,* The Bridge at Nantes. *Musée d'Orsay, Paris. Canvas. Ca. 1868. Recording the effects of light on landscape, Corot (1796–1875) was an important influence on the development of Impressionism.*

19

18

20

20. *Théodore Rousseau,* Normandy Market Place. *Hermitage, St. Petersburg. Canvas. Ca. 1830. This ordinary marketplace was typical of the contemporary scenes chosen by Théodore Rousseau (1812–1867).*

THE CAFÉ GUERBOIS IN PARIS WAS THE meeting place for a group of young artists during the 1860s who were united in their desire to explore new approaches to artistic style, subject matter, and technique. Like the Realist painters, with whom they had close connections, they rejected the Romantic, historical, and imaginative themes of the artistic establishment in favor of the objective recording of contemporary life. Although Édouard Manet was a member of the Café Guerbois group and had a fundamental influence on its development, it was the contributions of the others, notably Claude

CHAPTER 48

ARTISTIC FREEDOM

Impressionism and Post-Impressionism

Monet, Pierre Auguste Renoir, Camille Pissarro, Edgar Degas, and Paul Cézanne, that created the style known as Impressionism, a major turning point in the history of Western art.

Impressionism

The Impressionists rejected the traditional concept of formal composition, preferring to paint what they actually saw. The structure of their pictures depended entirely on their choice of view, as they attempted to capture a fleeting impression of the scene before them. The idea of painting outdoors was

1

not new. During the 1820s, colonies of artists had been established in the countryside around Paris with the aim of recording the momentary effects of nature, the play of light, and seasonal changes. But these paintings were sketches and only a part of the process of creating finished, large-scale studio works that could be submitted to the Salon for exhibition. The Impressionists, on the other hand, saw such "sketches" as more accurate reflections of reality than the finished pieces. Painting on small canvases, without preparatory drawings, they used a light palette and applied their colors with loose, spontaneous brushstrokes.

The concept evolved during the course of the 1860s, and the Impressionist style was fully established by Monet and Renoir while they were working together at La Grenouillière outside Paris.

The First Impressionist Exhibition

In 1874, Monet was instrumental in organizing an independent exhibition with more than 200 works by 30 artists, including Renoir, Cézanne, Degas, Pissarro, and Alfred Sisley. A conscious challenge to the authority of the Salon and academic art, the exhibition marked the beginning of a new relationship between art and the public. The term "Impressionism" was borrowed from the title of Monet's *Impression: Sunrise* by the art critic Leroy for his review of the exhibition; the label stuck. The first exhibition was unsuccessful, but later ones (1876, 1877, 1879, 1880, 1881, 1882, 1886), along with the efforts of art dealers such as Paul Durand-Ruel, established a market for the works, which by 1890 commanded high prices.

Monet and Renoir

Although the artists found themselves grouped together under the heading

1. *Claude Monet,* Impression: Sunrise. *Musée Marmottan, Paris. Canvas. 1872. Exhibited at the first Impressionist exhibition in 1874, this painting typified Monet's interest in the effects of light and provided a name for the fledgling movement.*

2. *Monet,* Poppies. *Musée d'Orsay, Paris. Canvas. 1873. Rejecting outlines and solidity, Monet (1840–1926) attempted to capture his fleeting impressions of light and color.*

3. *Camille Pissarro,* Entry to the Village. *Musée d'Orsay, Paris. Canvas. 1870. The simple, uncontrived landscapes of Camille Pissarro (1831–1903), who also participated in the first Impressionist exhibition, reflected the aims of the group.*

4. *Auguste Renoir,* Claude Monet at his Easel. *Musée d'Orsay, Paris. Canvas. 1875. Recognizing the significance of their innovations, the Impressionists frequently recorded each other at work.*

"Impressionists," their unity was solely one of purpose. As individuals, they each pursued separate interests and creative visions. Impressionism was not based on any specific theory; on the contrary, they avoided any comparison with the academic art world. Monet, while not poor, cultivated the bohemian image of a petit bourgeois with his scruffy clothes and untidy beard. Both Monet and Renoir concentrated on scenes of lower middle-class life but avoided its depressing aspects. Their artistic radicalism had no parallels in political ideology; they loved sunshine, pretty women, and the pursuit of leisure.

This was reinforced by their choice of La Grenouillière, a restaurant and bathing spot on the Seine that had become popular with the petit bourgeoisie since the expansion of the railroad had made the countryside accessible to the less well-to-do. But Renoir's petit bourgeoisie also enjoyed city life, drinking, and flirting at bistros like the Moulin de la Galette in the Montmartre section of Paris. With its low rents, plentiful prostitutes for models, and cheap places of entertainment, Montmartre was the ideal location for this new generation of artists. Their separation from the conventional

respectability of the École des Beaux-Arts on the left bank was reinforced by the fact that it was located on the other side of the Seine.

Degas and Toulouse-Lautrec

Unlike Monet and Renoir, both Degas and Toulouse-Lautrec came from wealthy, aristocratic families. While very much a part of the Café Guerbois group, Degas remained a figurative artist. Rejecting typical academic subjects, he concentrated on the leisure pursuits of the upper middle classes, in particular the opera and racetrack.

5. Renoir, Jeanne Samary. *Pushkin Museum, Moscow. Canvas. 1877. Renoir's skill at capturing the elusive effects of light and color were well suited to the portrayal of people. This quick glimpse contains all the freshness of the sitter without creating a formal image.*

6. Renoir, La Grenouillière. *Hermitage, St. Petersburg. Canvas. 1868. Working together at this riverside restaurant popular with the petit bourgeoisie, Renoir (1841–1919) and Monet developed the basic ideas of the Impressionist movement.*

6

7. Renoir, At the Moulin de la Galette. *Musée d'Orsay, Paris. Canvas. 1876. Renoir's happy and relaxed scenes of bourgeois entertainment were not intended to express the social inequalities evident in nineteenth-century Paris.*

5

7

But Degas also responded to the growing social awareness that characterized the Realist movement. His images of ironers, working in the steamy back rooms of the laundry trade, were the other side of the coin to Renoir's scenes of bourgeois entertainment.

Toulouse-Lautrec was never truly part of the Impressionist group and concentrated on the night haunts of prostitutes and the seamy side of Montmartre café life. Deeply influenced by Japanese prints, his lithographic advertisements for café entertainment exploited the effects of sinuous contour and solid blocks of color.

New Directions

By the early 1880s, the Impressionists had reached a crisis point. They had achieved their immediate aim of formulating a new approach to style in defiance of the official art world, but their individual differences were becoming prominent. Reevaluating his concepts of line and form, Renoir traveled to Italy to study classical and High Renaissance art. Pissarro joined Georges Seurat in his experiments with the rationalization of color (see below). Degas developed his interest in female nudes. Monet concentrated on the effects of light

on form, painting a series of canvases that recorded the changing effects of light on particular objects. He continued in this direction until his death in 1926; his later works took on an increasingly subjective character, as he had minimal contact with the new developments in contemporary art.

Cézanne

After his early association with the Impressionists, Cézanne abandoned the Parisian art scene and retreated to the hills of Provence to explore the representation of three-dimensional space on the flat

8

9

10. *Degas*, The Ironers. *Musée d'Orsay, Paris. Canvas. Ca. 1884. Attractive, flirtatious, and with a reputation for heavy drinking, these ironers had specifically sexual connotations in late nineteenth-century Paris.*

11. *Henri de Toulouse-Lautrec*, Woman Drinking. *Musée Toulouse-Lautrec, Albi. Paper. 1889. Women and drink were recurrent themes in the work of Toulouse-Lautrec (1864–1901). The cafés of Montmartre provided a marked contrast to his aristocratic background.*

8. *Edgar Degas*, Four Ballerinas Preparing in the Wings. *Museum of Modern Art, Moscow. Canvas. Ca. 1897. Degas (1834–1917) was fascinated by the arduous training that lay behind the apparently effortless performances of ballerinas.*

9. *Degas*, Jockeys. *Musée d'Orsay, Paris. Canvas. 1877–1880. Degas never abandoned the classical principles of draftsmanship; his studies of horses and jockeys illustrated the importance he attached to the representation of form.*

10

11

surface of a canvas. Modulating tones to create a sense of depth and applying thinned paint in solid blocks, he created loosely defined scenes that all but dissolved into patchworks of color. Cézanne's emphasis on two-dimensionality set a precedent later taken up by the inventors of Cubism (see chapter 50).

Post-Impressionsm

The generation of artists that followed the Impressionists is commonly grouped under the generic heading of Post-Impressionism. The term was coined by the critic Roger Fry for a 1910 exhibition at the Grafton Galleries in London that featured the works of Cézanne, Vincent van Gogh, and Paul Gauguin. But labels may be misleading: today Cézanne is generally seen in a class of his own, while Seurat is often counted among the Post-Impressionists. In fact, these painters had little in common other than a desire to exploit certain aspects of Impressionism. Rejecting the bourgeois pettiness on both banks of the Seine, they went in search of environments that would better suit their own interests and temperaments. Seurat experimented with color in Paris; Van Gogh evolved a distinctive style of brushwork in the southern French town of Arles; Gauguin finally rejected modern civilization altogether and moved to Tahiti.

Seurat and Neo-Impressionism

Seurat's investigations into the use of color were stimulated by contemporary scientific research. After reading a number of treatises on the subject, he considered writing his own manifesto on color and optics. Based on his belief that colors mixed by the eye are more intense than those mixed by the artist, he developed a technique intended to

12

14. *Georges Seurat,* The Circus. *Musée d'Orsay, Paris. Canvas. 1891. Seurat (1859–1891) was the prime force behind the development of Neo-Impressionism. His experiments in color separation would prove highly influential.*

13

12. *Monet,* Rouen Cathedral, *Full Sunlight. Musée d'Orsay, Paris. Canvas. 1894.*

13. *Monet,* Rouen Cathedral, *Morning Light. Musée d'Orsay, Paris. Canvas. 1894. Monet's interest in the effects of light came to dominate his later works. By painting the same scene at different times of day, he was able to record its changes while showing little concern with the object itself.*

14

rationalize the Impressionist method: applying primary and secondary colors in dots over the canvas based on strict scientific criteria, and juxtaposing complementary colors, like orange with blue or red with green, to intensify their effects. Seurat was soon joined by other painters, notably Pissarro, whose style became variously known as Neo-Impressionism, Pointillism, or Divisionism. Seurat's later paintings explored the emotive effects of color and line; red and yellow were believed to promote happiness, blue sadness; depressing downward vertical lines were contrasted with spirit-lifting upward diagonals.

Van Gogh

Van Gogh arrived in Paris in 1886, the year of the last Impressionist exhibition, and the effect on his style was dramatic. Dropping the somber mood and dark colors of his earlier works, he adopted the brighter Impressionist palette, experimented with the scientific Neo-Impressionist approach to color, and was deeply influenced by the fashion for Japanese art. Leaving Paris in search of an environment more similar to that illustrated in Japanese prints, he moved to Arles in February 1888, where his delight in the freshness of the southern spring found

expression in numerous paintings of blossoms and flowers. Van Gogh worked exceptionally fast. He used color for expressive purposes rather than for description and further reinforced the emotive content of his works with vigorous brushwork. Egocentric and profoundly neurotic, he produced canvas after canvas that reflected a highly personalized view of the world. His loneliness and desire to be part of an artistic community led him to invite Gauguin to Arles. Gauguin arrived in October 1888, but the tensions between the two artists contributed to a major nervous breakdown for Van Gogh two months later;

15

16

17

15. *Paul Cézanne*, Plateau with Houses and Trees. *Pushkin Museum, Moscow. Canvas. 1882–1885. Cézanne (1839–1906) participated in the first Impressionist exhibition but left Paris to develop his own approach. His paintings reflected a desire to make Impressionism into a more solid and timeless style.*

16. *Cézanne*, Bathers. *Pushkin Museum, Moscow. Canvas. 1892–1894. Cézanne experimented with contrasting poses in his studies of bathers. These works were a powerful influence on later artists, especially Picasso.*

18

17. *Cézanne*, Bridge on a Pond. *Pushkin Museum, Moscow. Canvas. 1888–1890. Patchworks of color, Cézanne's landscapes verged on the abstract.*

18. *Cézanne*, Card Players. *Musée d'Orsay, Paris. Canvas. 1890–1892*

another breakdown in May 1889 was followed by a period of hospitalization.

Van Gogh's mental confusion found expression in a series of frenzied, delirious works characterized by swirling brushstrokes and dramatic use of color. He moved to Auvers in May 1890 to be under the care of Dr. Paul Gachet, but committed suicide that July. It is impossible to separate Van Gogh's mental problems from his art; the concept of art as an expression of personality, unrestricted by rules and conventions, had important implications for the development of twentieth-century painting.

Gauguin

Gauguin's passion for painting led him to abandon his career as a stockbroker in 1883 and concentrate exclusively on his art. Some of his works had already been exhibited at the Impressionist shows. Seeking to escape what he regarded as the corruption of modern urban life, he left Paris in 1888 and sought spiritual truth in the peasant culture of Brittany. Working with a group of artists at Pont-Aven, he sought to represent the world of his imagination and the battle between the forces of good and evil. Quickly abandoning any pretense of naturalism, he developed a two-dimensional style influenced by the outlined blocks of flat color found in Japanese prints and medieval stained glass. Like Van Gogh, he used colors for their emotive associations rather than for their descriptive qualities. Gauguin's visit with Van Gogh at Arles encouraged his desire to paint exclusively from the imagination. His quasi-abstract and symbolic approach to representation was intended to suggest mental images rather than a record of visual experiences. Gauguin's decision to leave France for the South Pacific in 1891 was a final break with what he called "the disease of civilization" and the artificiality and

19

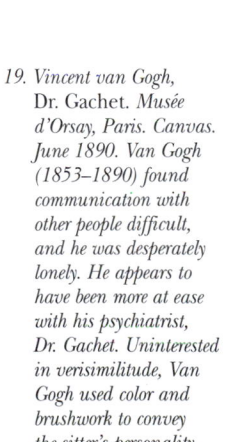

19. *Vincent van Gogh,* Dr. Gachet. *Musée d'Orsay, Paris. Canvas. June 1890. Van Gogh (1853–1890) found communication with other people difficult, and he was desperately lonely. He appears to have been more at ease with his psychiatrist, Dr. Gachet. Uninterested in verisimilitude, Van Gogh used color and brushwork to convey the sitter's personality.*

20. *Van Gogh,* Lilac. *Hermitage, St. Petersburg. Canvas. 1888. The son of a Dutch Protestant pastor, Van Gogh considered a life in the clergy and later worked in the depressed coal-mining areas of Belgium. He was largely self-taught as an artist; his paintings can be understood as the expression of a profoundly disturbed personality.*

20

21. *Van Gogh,* Van Gogh's Bedroom in Arles. *Rijksmuseum, Amsterdam. Canvas. 1888. After a short stay in Paris, Van Gogh moved south to Arles, where his pictures increasingly reflected his highly personalized view of the world.*

21

convention associated with it. Apart from a short trip to Paris in 1895, he remained in the Pacific Islands until his death in 1903, finding inspiration in the native art and religion of Tahiti.

The avant-garde community in Paris during the 1880s and 1890s was small but extremely vociferous. Poets, writers, musicians, and critics publicized their new ideas in manifestos and small magazines. Artists established an independent Salon (1884) without a jury, in direct contravention of the elitism practiced by the official art world. Although they were united in defiance of tradition and the cultural establishment, the bewildering variety of their responses reflected the communal belief in individual expression.

Symbolism

Uninspired by the Realist concern for everyday life, artists and writers of the Symbolist movement expressed a shared perception of the lack of imagination in contemporary culture. In the literary realm, this conviction inspired Joris Karl Huysmans's novel *À Rebours* (1884), whose hero isolated himself in an apartment and surrounded himself with objects chosen to satisfy his exotic tastes and provoke his sensual imagination. Symbolist art aimed at stimulating the imagination, enriching classical and religious themes with esoteric visual clues and subtle mysteries. Influenced by the sensual curving forms of Art Nouveau (see chapter 49), painters such as Edvard Munch and Gustave Klimt produced images heavily loaded with symbolic meaning that appealed suggestively to the imagination and had little in common with the real world.

The Fauves

At the beginning of the twentieth century, young artists in Paris were presented with a

22

23

22. *Paul Gauguin*, La Belle Angèle. *Musée d'Orsay, Paris. Canvas. 1889. Gauguin (1848–1903) had an immeasurable influence on the development of modern art. This portrait of the wife of a prominent citizen of Pont-Aven was refused by the sitter when Gauguin offered it to her as a present. Degas bought it instead.*

23. *Gauguin*, Rave Te Hiti Aamu. *Hermitage, St. Petersburg. Canvas. 1898. Entitled* Presence of the Evil Demon, *this picture was one of a series that explored religious beliefs in the native culture of Tahiti.*

24. *Gauguin*, Arearea. *Musée d'Orsay, Paris. Canvas. 1892. Gauguin moved to Tahiti to escape what he called the "disease of civilization." This peaceful image of Pacific life, entitled* Happiness, *reflected the simplicity of his new existence.*

25. *Gustave Moreau*, Orpheus. *Musée d'Orsay, Paris. Canvas. 1865. Exquisite, precious, and deliberately suggestive, this painting by Gustave Moreau (1826–1898) was an early example of Symbolism, an artistic and literary movement that emerged in reaction to the contemporaneity of Realism.*

24

25

RODIN

The major innovations in late nineteenth-century art were not limited to painting. The contribution of Auguste Rodin (1840–1917) to the development and evolution of new sculptural techniques and interpretations was considerable. Revitalizing the process of modeling in clay, Rodin created bronzes that were very different from the highly finished works that were normally accepted by the Salon. By the end of the century, his style had become so intentionally loose that it was possible to see clearly the marks left by his fingers and tools as well as the lumps of clay added to enhance the expressive effect.

Rodin's choice of subject matter was invariably traditional, relying on religious, historical, and literary themes to express the full range of human emotion, from torment and anguish to joy and glory. The scheme for his most prestigious commission, the *Gates of Hell* for the École des Arts Décoratifs in Paris (1880), was inspired by Dante's *Inferno*. This work, however, was to remain unfinished.

His iconic statue of *The Thinker*, originally intended for the tympanum of the doors as a substitute for the traditional figure of Christ, represented Dante as a creative force. Inscribed on the door of the school there was to appear a quotation from the *Inferno*: "Abandon all hope, ye who enter"—a curious choice for an educational establishment! Rodin's *Burghers of Calais* conveys emotions very different from this last work. Gaunt but dignified after their prolonged siege by the English army (1347), these figures show their anguish in gestures and poses, though preserving intact their dignity. Once again, Rodin's ability and impressive skill in portraying emotion in human form is quite evident.

ARTISTIC FREEDOM

26

27

26. Auguste Rodin, The Thinker. *Musée Rodin, Paris. Bronze. 1880.*

27. Rodin, The Burghers of Calais. *Westminster Gardens, London. Bronze. 1884–1886.*

28

29

28. Gustave Klimt, The Three Ages of Woman. *Galleria d'Arte Moderna, Rome. Canvas. 1905. The three ages of man was a traditional image in Western art. This variation by Gustave Klimt (1862–1918) emphasized the decorative and spiritual potential of the theme.*

29. Edvard Munch, Jealousy. *Historical Museum, Bergen. Canvas. 1895. The Norwegian painter Edvard Munch (1863–1944) developed a distorted and highly expressive style. His use of red was intended to signify sexual love.*

variety of stylistic options. This in itself was a startling change from the situation fifty years earlier. In evolving his own personal style, Henri Matisse experimented with the ideas of the Impressionists, Cézanne, Van Gogh, Seurat, and Gauguin. After moving to the town of Collioure in southern France (1905), Matisse and André Derain painted canvases whose subject matter recalled that of the Impressionists—landscapes, still lifes, nudes, and portraits of family and friends—but whose interpretation was markedly different. Adopting the Neo-Impressionist concept of color separation, Cézanne's pictorial structure, Gauguin's decorative use of color, and Van Gogh's expressive and instinctive response to his subject matter, their new style synthesized the major advances in art realized over the previous forty years.

At the Salon d'Automne in 1905, Matisse and Derain were joined by Maurice de Vlaminck and others in exhibiting their works in a room that also contained a traditional academic statue. The contrast in styles was captured in a phrase that gave the group its name: "Donatello among the wild beasts (*fauves*)." No longer tied to any convention or academic tradition, art was free to develop in new directions.

30

30. Henri Matisse, Landscape at Collioure. *Hermitage, St. Petersburg. Canvas. 1906. The principal exponent of the Fauvist movement, Matisse (1869–1954) experimented with the use of pure colors to create violent and distorted patterns in essentially two-dimensional compositions.*

32

31

31. André Derain, Old Waterloo Bridge. *Thyssen-Bornemisza Museum, Madrid. Canvas. 1906. Under the influence of the Neo-Impressionists, Matisse and Derain (1880–1954) juxtaposed colors for maximum visual impact rather than for their descriptive value.*

32. Maurice de Vlaminck, Small Sailing-boat and Salvage Vessel on the Seine. *Thyssen Collection, Amsterdam. Canvas. 1908–1909. One of the original fauves, Vlaminck (1876–1958) was deeply influenced by Cézanne's use of blocks of color to add depth and volume in his scenes.*

THE INDUSTRIAL REVOLUTION WAS INDEED a revolution, bringing a sweeping transformation of Western civilization. The capitalist demand for increased productivity led to the invention of more efficient, power-driven machinery that caused massive economic and social upheaval, radically altering the collective worldview. Sophisticated new machines and processes replaced simple tools and manual labor in the manufacture of basic goods. Major improvements in transportation and communication dramatically altered the perception of time and distance, with far-reaching effects on the conduct of daily life.

CHAPTER 49

THE CHALLENGE OF NEW MATERIALS

Architecture and the Industrial Revolution

Advances in medical care caused a decline in the death rate, and a massive population explosion fueled economic expansion. Industry replaced agriculture as the basis of economic wealth, and an increasing majority of the population became concentrated in urban areas. Cities underwent a period of tumultuous expansion. Between 1801 and 1901, the population of London grew from 1,000,000 to 6,500,000; the increase was even more spectacular in New York, where the number of residents rose from 33,000 to 3,500,000 over the same period. These changes found visual expression in the development of a new range of building

1

types; factories, warehouses, commercial offices, and railway stations became prominent images—and symbols—of the modern industrial age.

New Materials

Although iron had been used for centuries to strengthen masonry structures, it was only after 1750 that improved methods of production gave it sufficient tensile strength to be used as a building material in its own right. The pioneering work on the use of coke to replace charcoal for smelting ore was done in 1740s in the foundry of Abraham Darby at Coalbrookdale, in the central English county of Shropshire; it was here that the elements for the first iron bridge were cast. The span was modest in length (about 98 feet, or 32 meters) but highly important in structural innovation. The development of cheaper and more efficient methods of refining cast iron into steel soon led to the construction of much longer spans. In London, the enormous hall designed by Joseph Paxton for the Great Exhibition of 1851 exploited the potential of prefabricated units of glass in iron frames to cover a large area quickly, cheaply, and efficiently. Among the buildings erected for the Paris Exhibition of 1889 were those with the widest span and the greatest height ever constructed: Victor Contamin's Galérie des Machines, whose arches spanned 368 feet (112 meters), and the Eiffel Tower, rising 984 feet (300 meters). In the artistic circles of Paris, however, these technical achievements were regarded as expensive acts of folly and triumphs of bad taste. Iron was cheap, strong, and fireproof; but in a society in which tradition reigned supreme, it was considered too modern to be aesthetically acceptable. Thus, while widely used in prestigious architectural projects, it was invariably encased in stone. These

1. *Claude Monet*, Gare Saint-Lazare. *Musée d'Orsay, Paris. Canvas. 1877. The railroad station provided a modern subject for painters like Monet, who questioned traditional values in art.*

4. Eiffel Tower. *Paris. 1889. The tallest structure of its time, the Eiffel Tower was not superseded until the construction of the Empire State Building in New York City (1930–1932).*

2. *Gustave-Alexandre Eiffel*, Viaduct Over the Truyère. *Garabit. 1884.*

2

3. *Joseph Paxton*, Crystal Palace. *London. 1851. The combination of iron and glass was developed in greenhouses to contain collections of exotic plants popular in nineteenth-century Britain. Cheap and effective, the method was exploited by Joseph Paxton (1803–1865) in the sprawling Crystal Palace for the Great Exhibition of 1851.*

3

4

restrictions did not extend to the industrial and commercial building types, in which the practical advantages of iron far outweighed its lack of aesthetic appeal.

The Railroad Station

Perhaps more than any other building type, the railroad station symbolized the dawn of the new industrial age. The railroad developed in England, initially for the purpose of transporting coal. Soon, however, its potential for transporting other commercial and industrial goods—as well as people—was recognized. The first passenger train (1825) inaugurated a massive expansion of the railroad network. By 1848, more than 5,000 miles (8,000 km) of railway had been built in Britain. In addition to stimulating major technological advances in bridge construction and tunneling, this brought a boom in the construction of stations. The solid brick and stone façade of St. Pancras Station in London declared its respectability by adhering to the cultural conventions of the period and by using forms and details derived from the styles of the past. Behind the façade, however, the shed exploited new materials for practical advantage; exposed iron girders provided uninterrupted cover to the platforms below. The contrast between the façade and the station proper reflected the cultural gulf between engineering and architecture in the nineteenth century. Covering an area far greater than that of the medieval cathedral, the urban railroad station was a conspicuous working symbol of the dramatic changes brought by the Industrial Revolution.

The Arts and Crafts Movement

Dissatisfaction with the effects of the machine on the quality of design was widespread among the cultural elite. Also

5. *George Gilbert Scott*, St. Pancras Station, façade. *London. 1868–1874. The Midland Grand Hotel, designed by George Gilbert Scott (1811–1878), formed the façade of St. Pancras Station in London.*

His attitude toward the new materials and building types of the Industrial Revolution was typical of the cultural elite of Victorian England.

7. *Currier and Ives*, The "Lightning Express." *Museum of the City of New York, New York. Print. 1875. Today speed is something we take for granted. When the first railroad engines were developed, some believed that moving so fast could seriously damage the human metabolism.*

6. *Barlow and Ordish*, St. Pancras Station, railroad shed. *London. 1863–1865. The great art theorist John Ruskin put railroad stations in the same category as rat holes and wasp nests.*

6

8. *Howlett*, Isambard Kingdom Brunel. *Victoria & Albert Museum, London. Photograph. 1857. Arguably the greatest engineer of the nineteenth century, Brunel (1806–1859) was employed by the Great Western Railway to construct not only its track from London to Bristol, but tunnels, bridges, and stations as well. This portrait presented him in front of the chains of his record-breaking steamship, the Great Eastern.*

8

5

7

disturbing to some were its effects on the quality of daily life. William Morris (1834–1896), a socialist thinker from a prosperous middle-class family, sought to revive the methods of the medieval craftsman, whose work was not subject to the standardization and dehumanization of machines. Morris's thinking provided the ideological foundation for the Arts and Crafts movement (formally constituted in 1888 as the Arts and Crafts Exhibition Society) and inspired the formation of art and design societies for the promotion of craftsmanship. Morris's commercial firm (Morris, Marshall, Faulkner & Co.) established a distinctive

and influential style in the decorative arts. In the design of his own house, Morris rejected the prevailing taste for historical grandeur in favor of traditional features of vernacular English architecture. This so-called Domestic Revival Style, also promoted by such architects as Richard Norman Shaw and C.F.A. Voysey, was a deliberate contrast to the ostentation that characterized the houses of many wealthy industrialists. The same desire to humanize industrial society can be seen in worker housing projects of the time whose layouts recalled those of a typical English village; the projects were commissioned by wealthy entrepreneurs

motivated by a philanthropic spirit, such as George Cadbury at Bournville, near Birmingham. Although retrogressive in many ways, the Arts and Crafts movement marked a change from the eclecticism of the nineteenth century. Morris's ideas were an important influence in early twentieth-century German architecture and the evolution of modernism (see chapter 50).

Art Nouveau

Art Nouveau, which took its name from a gallery shop opened (1895) in Paris by Samuel Bing, developed the decorative

9

10

9. Morris, Marshall, Faulkner & Co., Green Dining Room. *Victoria & Albert Museum, London. 1866–1868. With wallpaper designed by William Morris and stained-glass windows and other details designed by the Pre-Raphaelite artist Edward Burne-Jones, this interior illustrates the close links between the Pre-Raphaelite and Arts and Crafts movements.*

11

10. Philip Webb, The Red House. *Bexleyheath. 1859. Local building materials and traditional vernacular forms provided a distinctive and unassertive image for philanthropic middle-class intellectuals like William Morris, who commissioned Philip Webb (1831–1915) to design his home.*

11. Victor Horta, Tassel House, *interior. Brussels. 1892. Designed by the Belgian architect Victor Horta (1861–1947), this early Art Nouveau interior illustrates the potential of iron as a decorative material. It is significant in this context that the patron of the house was an engineer.*

potential of Arts and Crafts design while largely ignoring its socialist ideals. A craze throughout Europe and America (1890–1910), it was known in Germany as *Jugendstil*, in Italy as *Stile Liberty*, and in Austria as *Sezessionstil* (after the *Sezession* group, which broke away from the Viennese artistic establishment in 1897). Sinuous and slender, its characteristically asymmetrical curves were a rejection of traditional ornament formality. The style took on distinct regional variations: floral motifs in Belgium and France, and more linear patterns in Austria and the designs of Charles Rennie Mackintosh in Scotland.

Art Nouveau found its highest expression in architecture and the decorative arts. The interior of the Tassel House in Brussels, designed by the Belgian architect Victor Horta, exploited the decorative potential of iron in fluid organic patterns that were repeated on the inlaid floors and painted walls. Such visual unity was typical of Art Nouveau designers, who applied their new style to the whole range of interior furnishings, even including cutlery. Horta's ideas influenced another Belgian architect, Henri Van de Velde, who designed the interior of Samuel Bing's gallery. In France, the style was popularized by Hector Guimard, whose Paris Métro stations illustrated how far Art Nouveau designers had moved away from tradition. Ornamental and frivolous, the style was soon adopted for the great department stores opening in cities across Europe and America, providing a highly decorative image for commercial success.

Development of the Skyscraper

Increasing demand for office space and competition for land in the booming commercial cities of the United States forced architects and engineers to address the problems associated with extreme vertical

12

12. Giovanni Michelazzi, Villino Liberty. Florence. 1911. Elegant and modern, Art Nouveau was popular for domestic architecture and interior decoration.

13. René Lalique, Belt buckle. Victoria & Albert Museum, London. Silver and gold. Ca. 1897. Asymmetrical, sinuous, and floral, this decorative belt buckle by the French jewelry designer and glassmaker René Lalique (1860–1945) was typical of Art Nouveau style.

13

construction. The invention of the steam elevator, first installed in New York in 1857, was followed in 1880 by that of the electric elevator, thereby solving the practical problem of access. But traditional building techniques, based on brick or rock, continued to restrict height. Borrowing a technique pioneered in factory design, architects of the Chicago school experimented with the replacement of load-bearing walls with steel frames. This method proved successful and was soon imitated elsewhere. Like the Gothic masons of the twelfth century, the American architects not only recognized the potential of a skeleton frame for increasing window area, but reinforced their achievement by maximizing vertical thrust. In reality, despite their structural innovations, the early skyscrapers conformed to traditional masonry design by stressing the horizontal divisions between floors. The Chicago architect Louis Henry Sullivan broke decisively with ornate horizontal divisions in his design for the Wainwright Building in St. Louis; unadorned vertical pilasters and heavy corner piers provided visual reassurance only, masking the actual structure beneath. Unfettered by centuries of tradition, the United States took the lead in devising solutions for the realization of new building types demanded by the Industrial Revolution. The skyscraper soon became the prime image of U.S. economic wealth and power.

14

14. Currier and Ives, New York and Brooklyn. *Museum of the City of New York, New York. Print. 1875. Celebrating the commercial and industrial success of* the United States, this print included the new Brooklyn Bridge (begun 1870). Its span of 1,595 feet (486 meters) was a major technical achievement.

In his essay *The Tall Office Building Artistically Considered* (1896), the American architect Louis Henry Sullivan (1856–1924), a founder of the influential Chicago school, described the process he followed in designing a skyscraper. The title itself was novel.

In England, the birthplace of the Industrial Revolution, commercial buildings were not accorded the status of art; Sullivan's approach reflected more the modern attitude in the United States. According to his plan, the tall office building was divided into five basic levels, distinguished by function. Below ground were the boiler and engine rooms, where heat and light were generated for the building. At ground level, rental space for stores and banks required especially easy access and plentiful light. The next story, immediately above ground level, was designated for large rooms with staircases for easy access. The fourth level, according to his basic plan, comprised the many floors devoted to office space. In fact, Sullivan likened it to a honeycomb. The fifth level, at the top, was an attic. In his essay, Sullivan then discussed and analyzed how these divisions affect and influence the design of the façade. The entrances, he explained, should immediately grab the eye's attention; the block of office tiers should be articulated according to window units, thereby defining the interior organization to the outside viewer.

Sullivan's innovative solutions to the problems of commercial building design on the basis of functional requirements were enormously influential to later generations in the development of modern architecture, despite the fact that his importance and reputation as an architect during the last phase of his career was diminished.

THE CHALLENGE OF NEW MATERIALS

16. Sullivan, Wainwright Building. *St. Louis, Missouri. 1890–1891. Vertical elements dominated and reinforced the height of this landmark building.*

15. Louis Henry Sullivan, Guarantee Building. *Buffalo, New York. 1894–1895. Classically inspired arches and piers, resting on a podium and crowned by a cornice, provided a new solution for the decoration of large commercial buildings.*

17. Henry Hobson Richardson, Marshall Field Warehouse. *Chicago, Illinois. 1885–1887. After training at the École des Beaux-Arts in Paris, Henry Hobson Richardson (1836–1886) set up a lucrative architectural practice in New York.*

15

17

THE TWENTIETH CENTURY

New discoveries led to the most radical changes history had ever seen. In art the new century began, in the wake of the earlier experiments in avant-garde painting, under the aegis of a great adventure: a break with traditional values of beauty, color, shape, and space. Paris became the main point of reference, where artists flocked from all over the world. The first Cubist experiments had already been heralded by a Picasso painting considered scandalous: Les Demoiselles d'Avignon. *Colors were aggressive and violent: some artists* (such as Matisse and Derain) were significantly called fauves, *that is,* "*beasts.*" *Primitive art attracted attention because of its essentiality and exoticism, and it fascinated Picasso, Matisse, Modigliani, and others. The challenge of the new era was also manifested in architecture that at the end of the last century had seen the first daring skyscrapers, the first buildings constructed with industrial materials such as steel or glass and then even reinforced concrete. The industrial era launched the myth of the machine,* motion, and speed. The revolutions and wars that involved the entire globe did not interrupt this exceptional sequence of experiments and research of many artistic and cultural movements. And finally, after World War II, art in many ways began to reflect the doubts and contradictions of modern civilization. But we are at the threshold of our own era, and perhaps it is still too early to make an impartial assessment.

| 1880 | 1900 | 1905 | 1910 | 1915 | 1920 | 1925 | 1930 | 1935 | 1940 | 1945 | 1950 | 1955 | 1960 | 1965 |

EUROPE

1884 ca. | Gaudí: La Sagrada Familia, Barcelona
1892 | *Reinforced concrete invented*
1896 | Kandinsky in Munich
1898 | *Madame Curie discovers radium*
1899 | *Marconi invents wireless telegraph*
1900 | *Freud: The Interpretation of Dreams*
Gaudí: Parc Guell, Barcelona
Brancusi in Paris | 1904
The "Brücke" established | 1905
in Dresden; the "Fauves"   1906 | Picasso: Portrait of Gertrude Stein
exhibition in Paris   1907 | Picasso: Les Demoiselles d'Avignon
(Matisse, Vlaminck,   1908 | Loos: Ornament and Crime
Derain)   1908–1914 | Picasso and Braque
Marinetti: Futurist Manifesto | 1909   together
Behrens: AEG Turbinenfabrik,
Berlin
Kandinsky: Concerning the Spiritual | 1910
in Art; Modigliani in Paris;   1911 | The term "Cubism" is coined;
Kandinsky: first abstract   Mondrian in Paris
watercolor   1911–1914 | Gropius and Meyer: Fagus
factory, Alfeld-an-der Leine
Picasso: Still Life with Chair Caning; | 1912
Balla: Young Girl Running   1912 ca. | Bec_____Mind
on a Balcony; Carrà: Gallery, Mil____   191_ _____o White Field;
World _____
Sant'Elia: Manifesto of Futurist Arch___ ___ ___
Malevic establishes Suprematist Movement; | 1915
Gropius appointed director of Ar___ ___
Wein___   1917 | *Russian Revolution;* De Stijl journal;
Picasso: scenery for Diaghilev's
Ballets Russes
___ | Morandi: Metaphysical Still Life

1920 | Ernst exhibition, Cologne;
El Lissitskij: design
for the Lenin Tribune
1922 | *Le Corbusier: A Contemporary City;*
Mussolini comes to power;
De Chirico: Disturbing Muses;
Matisse: Odalisque
1923 | Klee: Still Life with Dice
1924 | *Breton: Surrealist Manifesto;*
Rietveld: Schroeder House,
Utrecht
1925 | *Bauhaus moved to Dessau*
1926 | *Kandinsky: Point and Line to Plane*
1932 ca. | Dali: Birth of Liquid Desires
1933 | *Hitler closes the Bauhaus*
1934 | Picasso: engravings for
Ovid's Metamorphoses;
Arp: Concretions;
Chagall: To My Wife
1936 | *Surrealist Exhibition*
1937 | Picasso: Guernica

1939–1945 | *World War II*
1945 | *Fronte Nuovo per le Arti in Italia*
1947 | *Marshall Plan;*
Pollock: The Enchanted Forest
1948 | Le Corbusier: private housing
complex (Unité d'Habitation),
Marseille
1949 | Ensor dies
1949 ca. | Moore: Family Group

1952 | *Start of the Cold War*

1955–1959 | Nervi
and Ponti:
Pirelli
Building,
Milan

1956 | Nolde dies

UNITED STATES

1898–1976 | Calder
1903 | *Wright brothers, first airplane flight*
1905 | *Einstein publishes his Theory of Relativity*
1906 | *F.L. Wright: The Art and Craft of the Machine*
1909 | F.L. Wright: Robie House, Chicago
1920 | *Prohibition passed*
1922 | *Competition for the Chicago Tribune Tower*
1926 | Brancusi in the USA
Van Alen: Chrysler Building, New York | 1926–1930
First International Exhibition of Modern Architecture in New York | 1932

F.L. Wright shows Plans for Broadacre City | 1935
Mies van der Rohe in the USA | 1938
United Nations Building, New York | 1948
Abstract Painting and Sculpture Exhibition, | 1951
birth of "action painting"

Pop Art | 1960 ca.

John F. Kennedy assassinated | 1963

THE INDUSTRIAL REVOLUTION HAD fundamentally challenged the old order. At the beginning of the new century, accepted truths in every area of human thought and endeavor were openly questioned. The call for social and political reform that had led to the formation of left-wing parties now directly threatened the established structures of authority, as demonstrated by the events of the Russian Revolution (1917). In the realm of science, the new spirit of inquiry dramatically increased human understanding and control of the physical world. Within a few years of the turn of the century, Marie Curie

CHAPTER 50

INNOVATION AND ABSTRACTION

Art for a New Century

discovered radium (1898), Einstein proposed his theory of Relativity (1905), Freud published his *Interpretation of Dreams* (1900), and Amundsen reached the South Pole (1911). Marconi's invention of wireless telegraphy (1895) enabled direct communication between Europe and the United States, and the first powered flight by the Wright brothers (1903) inaugurated a new era in transportation.

In the arts, the avant-garde movements of the nineteenth century also had questioned traditionally accepted rules and standards. Now all ties to the past were cut, and radical new solutions were sought to give visual

1

The discovery of the native cultures of Africa, Oceania, and America (see chapters 12 and 35) by Europeans was chiefly motivated by a desire to extend economic, religious, and political hegemony.

Portuguese seamen looking for a route to the East had begun to explore the west coast of Africa during the fifteenth century, but it was not until Captain James Cook's voyages to the South Seas (1769–1779) that Europe was brought into contact with the civilizations of Oceania. As Western traders exploited these cultures, tribal artifacts slowly found their way into European collections. Exhibited at the world fairs of the nineteenth century, they were not considered art in the traditional Western sense but provided a visible expression of colonial power.

This was also true of the ethnographic museums founded in cities like Berlin (1856), Dresden (1875), and Paris (1878). The cult objects were rarely decorative; their function was invariably associated with the rituals and religions of native societies.

The scope of tribal art is enormous, ranging from the monolithic stone images of Easter Island and the totem poles of North America to portable African masks and statuettes, many of which were deliberately intended to evoke terror.

The objects were made from a wide variety of materials, including ivory, brass, wood, and stone; some included materials less common in the European sculptural tradition, such as nails, fibers, and feathers.

It was these smaller objects from different cultures that found their way into the museums of all Europe and had such a vital impact on the development of modern art.

1. *Pablo Picasso*, Les Demoiselles d'Avignon (detail). *Museum of Modern Art, New York. Canvas. 1907. This violently fragmented brothel scene is commonly regarded as the first Cubist painting, radically altering the course of art history.*

2. *Emil Nolde*, Dancing Around the Golden Calf. *Neue Pinakothek, Munich. Canvas. 1910. The violent use of color and form by the German Expressionist Emil Nolde (1867–1956) was intended to convey spiritual intensity.*

3. *Ernest Ludwig Kirchner*, Fränzi in a Carved Chair. *Thyssen-Bornemisza Museum, Madrid. Canvas. 1910. The features of this portrait by Ernest Ludwig Kirchner (1880–1938) were directly influenced by his study of African masks.*

expression to the spirit of modernism. The nine years from 1905 to 1914 were exceptionally fertile in the history of art. The extraordinary variety of ideas and styles that emerged during this period cannot be reduced to categories. Well aware of having entered a new century, the artists of the time strove to be modern and original. Change itself became a motivating force; innovation became the paramount goal. Some artists went so far as to backdate their works to make them appear more original. Well recognizing their debt to the pioneers of the nineteenth century, they decisively challenged the traditional concepts of beauty, the representation of form and space, the use of color, and the choice of subject matter, delving ever more deeply into the realms of emotion, intellect, and abstraction.

The Inspiration of Tribal Art

One of the major influences on the innovative artists of the early 1900s was the art of African (see chapter 12), Oceanic, and other so-called "primitive" cultures. Perceived as instinctive creations unbound by formal rules or constraints, the works they encountered lacked any patina of what the dominant Western culture called "civilization." African masks were far removed from the refined and polished sculptures of Ancient Greece, and they could hardly be called "beautiful" according to the accepted Western standards of the time. For the dissident avant-garde, however, who were in the process of deliberately abandoning traditional criteria of beauty, their appeal was obvious. Tribal art had an important influence on the German Expressionist painters; Emil Nolde, for example, used its expressive forms to enforce the emotional power of his religious paintings. The energy and intensity of tribal sculpture also inspired the members of

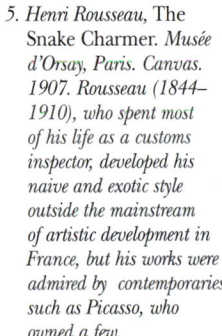

4. James Ensor, The Masks. *Musée Royale des Beaux-Arts, Brussels. Canvas. 1892. A precursor of the Expressionist movement, the Belgian painter James Ensor (1860–1949) exploited more traditional Western masks with disturbing effect.*

5. Henri Rousseau, The Snake Charmer. *Musée d'Orsay, Paris. Canvas. 1907. Rousseau (1844–1910), who spent most of his life as a customs inspector, developed his naive and exotic style outside the mainstream of artistic development in France, but his works were admired by contemporaries such as Picasso, who owned a few.*

6. Henri Matisse, The Red Room. *Hermitage, St. Petersburg. Canvas. 1908–1909. By his own admission, Matisse (1869–1954) was inspired by Eastern art, especially Persian miniatures. His lyrical style was characterized by the use of flat blocks of color, curved outlines, and simplified forms.*

7. Amedeo Modigliani, Head of a Woman. *Musée d'Art Moderne, Paris. Stone. 1910. Influenced by his study of African tribal art, Amedeo Modigliani (1884–1920) developed simplified formal outlines in both his paintings and sculptures.*

Die Brücke (The Bridge), a group of German Expressionist painters founded in Dresden (1905) by Ernest Kirchner, Erich Heckel, Karl Schmidt-Rottluff, and Fritz Bleyl. The group's manifesto declared radical opposition to traditional values and a desire to express their innermost feelings and fears about contemporary society. Harsh and aggressive, the paintings and woodcuts of *Die Brücke* well reflected the aims of the group.

Paris was a crucible of new ideas and initiatives. The official outcry that greeted the 1905 exhibition of works by Henri Matisse, André Derain, and Maurice Vlaminck earned them the label *fauves* (wild beasts). The aggressive use of color that united these artists was loathed by some and promptly imitated by others (see chapter 48). Never an organized group, the *fauves* soon separated to pursue their individual interests. In the later paintings of Matisse, traditional concepts of space were subordinated to his love of color and patterned surfaces. Posthumous exhibitions of paintings by Paul Gauguin (1906) and Paul Cézanne (1907), two of the leading pioneers of the nineteenth century, provided further inspiration. Above all, the new anti-establishment fashion for tribal art inspired painters such as Matisse and Pablo Picasso to study the ethnographic collections in the museums of Paris and to assemble their own collections of masks and other objects.

Drinking Gasoline and Spitting Fire

It was in this exciting and creative atmosphere that Picasso produced what is generally regarded as the first Cubist painting, *Les Demoiselles d'Avignon* (1907). It was as if Picasso had "drunk gasoline and spat fire," said Georges Braque, emphasizing the painting's radical departure from tradition. The five female figures were

8

9

11

10

8. *Picasso,* Gertrude Stein. *Metropolitan Museum of Art, New York. Canvas. 1906. The American writer Gertrude Stein was one of the leading figures of the cultural avant-garde movement in early twentieth-century Paris, to which Picasso (1881–1973) became attached after his arrival from Spain (1904).*

9. *Picasso*, Les Demoiselles d'Avignon. *Museum of Modern Art, New York. Canvas. 1907.*

10. *Picasso,* Lady with a Fan. Hermitage, *St. Petersburg. Canvas. 1908. Picasso's play with strong geometric forms made no attempt to capture traditional concepts of beauty.*

11. *Picasso,* Ambrose Vollard. Pushkin *Museum, Moscow. Canvas. 1910. Picasso and Braque exploited angular facets and muted colors to create a new relationship between the three-dimensional subject and its representation on a flat canvas.*

reduced to basic geometric shapes, and the depiction of their faces was directly inspired by forms of Iberian sculpture and African masks. The distribution of the basic features of the human body on the surface of the canvas reflected, in its crude aggressiveness, an entirely new approach to pictorial representation. From 1908 to 1914, Picasso and Braque worked together in close collaboration, executing still lifes and portraits in which they developed the essential elements of a distinctive Cubist style. Dramatically altering the traditional relationship between the three-dimensional world and its representation on a canvas,

Cubist art decisively rejected the illusion of space as a necessary element of pictorial imagery. But neither Picasso nor Braque was prepared to explain their invention, arguably the most radical and influential artistic movement of the twentieth century. Fundamentally elitist and reactionary, this highly conceptual style of painting was intended to be understood only by the initiated.

Cubism

One of the key influences in the efforts of Picasso and Braque to represent three-

dimensional forms on a flat surface no doubt was the method of Cézanne: simplifying natural forms into a patchwork of colors in which space becomes solidified. In contrast to the *fauves*, Picasso and Braque avoided violent contrasts in color, developing a preference for more monotone images. By about 1910, their images dissolved into fragmented series of facets that lost all connection with the three-dimensional object, now presented parallel to the picture plane. The Spanish Cubist Juan Gris came to define this stage as Analytical Cubism. The image was no longer a representation, an expression, or even a symbol of a still life

12. Georges Braque, Duet for Flute*. Private collection, Milan. Canvas. 1911. Although Braque and Picasso approached complete abstraction, neither of them disassociated their images entirely from the tangible world.*

13

12

13. Picasso, Still Life with Chair Caning*. Musée Picasso, Paris. Canvas. 1912. Wrapped in a rope frame and including a piece of printed oilcloth, this still life questioned the traditional content of a painting.*

14. Picasso, Guitar*. Private collection, Paris. Metal. 1914. Experimenting with the use of solid materials applied to the canvas, Picasso narrowed the traditional gap between sculpture and painting.*

14

or a person; it was now an object in its own right. Just at the point that Picasso and Braque reached the level of abstraction, however, they retreated, reinforcing the relationship between the image and the real world by incorporating stenciled letters, or later, such objects as a newspaper, sheet music, and even a biscuit. In his first collage, *Still Life with Chair Caning* (1912), Picasso used a piece of oilcloth printed with caning. Works of this kind were no longer called "paintings," but *tableaux-objets* ("object pictures").

Picasso's Cubist sculptures also revolutionized the traditional approaches to subject matter, materials, and method. Influenced by the combinations of materials used in African art, his compositions included string, bits of old wood, sheet metal—indeed anything he found lying around that piqued his creative impulse. But the new sculptural style was most clearly reflected by a radical change in the creative process itself. Rather than model or carve in the traditional method, Picasso now worked with the tools of the blacksmith and metalworker for pounding and punching. The conceptual and intellectual content of the piece thus took precedence over the handiwork of the craftsman.

The term "Cubist" was first applied to the works of a group of artists exhibited in Paris in 1911, all of them inspired by the radical ideas of Picasso and Braque. The two originators, however, remained aloof from the movement and declined to take part in this or any subsequent Cubist exhibitions that disseminated the style throughout Europe, Russia, and the United States. Other painters, such as Robert Delaunay, Fernand Léger, and Marcel Duchamp, conducted important experiments with the use of color, attempting in their works to arouse what the poet, writer, and critic Guillaume Apollinaire called "pure aesthetic pleasure." Apollinaire

15. *Juan Gris,* The Man from Touraine. *Museum of Modern Art, New York. Canvas. 1918. The Spanish painter Juan Gris (1887–1927) exploited the use of the curve in his Analytical Cubist works.*

16. *Fernand Léger,* The Steps. *Kunsthaus, Zurich. Canvas. 1913. Inspired by fauve painters like Matisse, Fernand Léger (1881–1955) exploited the emotional content of color. His Orphic Cubism came close to complete abstraction.*

17. *Robert Delaunay,* Champ de Mars, La Tour Rouge. *Art Institute, Chicago. Canvas. 1911. Delaunay (1885–1941) combined the Cubist ideas of Picasso and Braque with his own use of color.*

himself coined the term "Orphism" to define the style of this group.

Innovation in Architecture

Architects also responded to the challenge of the new era. While the prestigious commissions of the establishment remained stubbornly conservative in their choice of historical styles and traditional materials, a new generation of designers developed modern and innovative solutions. These took many forms. In Barcelona, Antoni Gaudí combined the sinuous forms of Art Nouveau with elements of Spanish medieval and Arabic architecture, adding features from his own fertile imagination. Asymmetrical and amorphous, his designs exploited the structural and decorative potential of the curve to create distinctive and supremely original buildings. Elsewhere, the desire to develop a style that reflected the new industrial age became paramount. In *The Art and Craft of the Machine* (1901), the American architect Frank Lloyd Wright foresaw the day when railroad engines and steamships would take the place of art; in parallel, his own designs for residential buildings challenged established models in domestic architecture. The open plan of his Robie House (Chicago, 1909) was based on functional requirements rather than custom. Simplifying the essential features of the building and avoiding unnecessary decoration, Wright's design was indisputably modern, giving visual expression to his dream of a new industrial democratic society unfettered by the traditions of the past. Wright encouraged other architects to follow his example and exploit the potential of new industrial materials, iron and concrete. The latter had been used to dramatic effect in monumental Roman architecture, but the technique of concrete manufacture itself had been lost during the Middle Ages.

19

18. *Antoni Gaudí*,
La Sagrada Familia.
Barcelona. begun 1884.
Arguably the most
innovative architect
of the early twentieth
century, Antoni Gaudí
(1852–1928) designed
a series of radically
modern buildings for his
hometown of Barcelona.

19. *Gaudí*, Parc Guell.
Barcelona. 1900–1914.
The organic, amorphous,
and fantastic forms in
Gaudí's architecture
exploited the decorative
and structural
possibilities of the curve
beyond the wildest dreams
of other Art Nouveau
designers.

18

It was rediscovered in the eighteenth century, only now the material was strengthened by reinforcing iron mesh (1861) and later steel (1892). While concrete had the virtues of being inexpensive, fireproof, and water-resistant, it was, like iron, considered inappropriate for the prestigious architectural projects of the establishment. That status, however, would be radically altered by the growing cult of the machine.

The Cult of the Machine

The exaltation of the machine, central to the works of Wright in the United States, was echoed in Europe. As the fashion for Art Nouveau began to wane, a new movement developed in reaction to its curved forms and decorative emphasis. Viennese architects took the lead in the development of a more linear style. In his essay, *Ornament and Crime* (1908), Adolf Loos stressed the need to reject what he regarded as superfluous detail. Like Wright, Loos had worked with Louis Sullivan in Chicago; his American experience was reflected in the conviction that beauty is directly related to functionality. If the machines of the new industrial age had no need for ornament or aesthetic proportion in order to function at maximum efficiency, then neither did architecture.

This radical proposition found fertile ground in Germany and the recently formed Deutscher Werkbund (1907). Founded to promote quality in industrial design, the institution was the result of a collaboration between Friedrich Naumann, a socialist politician, and Hermann Muthesius, an architect with strong views on the value of the new machine aesthetic. Muthesius engineered the appointments of like-minded architects to head schools of arts and crafts in Germany, and his aims were encouraged by new industrial patrons. One of his

20. *Frank Lloyd Wright,* Robie House. *Chicago, Illinois. 1909. The American architect Frank Lloyd Wright (1869–1959) admitted the influence of Froebel building blocks on the spatial complexity of his works.*

21. *Walter Gropius and Adolf Meyer,* Fagus factory. *Alfeld-an-der-Leine. 1911–1914. The use of a steel-frame structure with recessed piers allowed Walter Gropius (1883–1969) and his partner, Adolf Meyer (1881–1929), to wrap a glass curtain wall around the corners of the building.*

22. *Peter Behrens,* AEG turbine factory. *Berlin. 1909. With its steel columns and an industrial logo in the pediment, this design by Peter Behrens (1868–1940) created a modern Parthenon to glorify the new religion of industry.*

protégés, Peter Behrens, was employed by AEG (the *Allgemeine Elektrizitats-Gesellschaft*) as an architect and artistic advisor, designing everything from factories and showrooms to electrical equipment and publicity material. From his studio in Berlin, Behrens—undoubtedly one of the most significant figures in prewar design—enlisted the talents of Walter Gropius, Ludwig Mies van der Rohe, and Le Corbusier, three of the greatest architects of the twentieth century. Gropius's belief in the machine aesthetic, standardization, functionalism, and socialist ideals led him to write a pamphlet (1910) on worker housing in which he proposed

solutions that would combine low-cost and quality design. The same principles inspired his innovative design of the Fagus factory, developed in collaboration with Adolf Meyer, in which the steel, glass, and brick structure was reduced to a functional minimum. These ideas, explored more fully after the war, would form the basis of modern architecture.

Futurism

The cult of the machine achieved its highest expression in the work of a group of Italian artists united under the banner of Futurism.

As its name implies, this movement revolted against the standards and ideals of the past. In the first *Futurist Manifesto* (1909), Filippo Tommaso Marinetti celebrated the new industrial age, the beauty of speed, the love of danger, and the unbridled power of factories, shipyards, railroad engines, and airplanes; he declared that he was more excited by a racing car than by a classical Greek statue like *Winged Victory of Samothrace*. The painters of the group—Umberto Boccioni, Carlo Carrà, Luigi Russolo, Gino Severini, and Giacomo Balla—were later joined by an architect, Antonio Sant'Elia, whose manifesto, *Futurist*

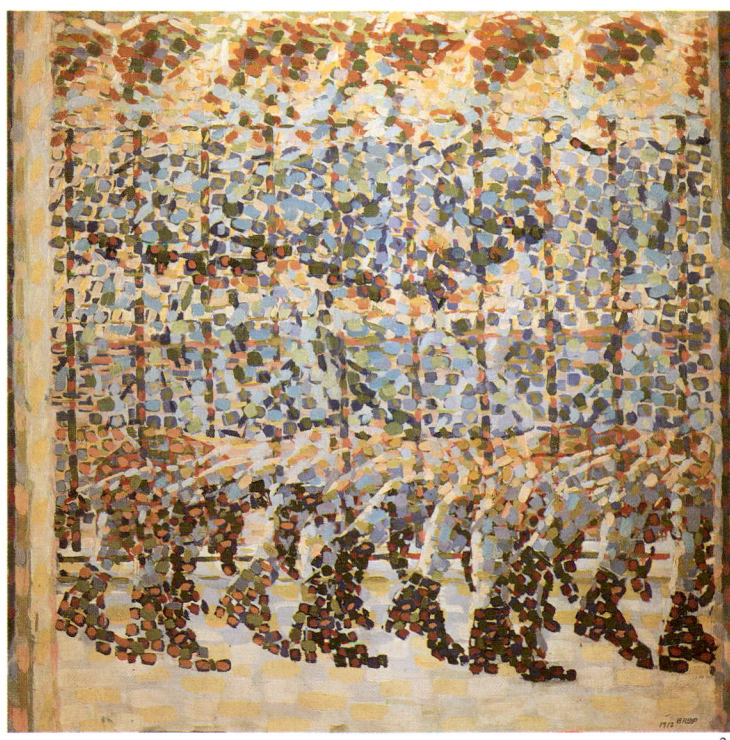

24

23. *Antonio Sant'Elia,* Design for an airport. *Museo Civico, Como. 1914. According to the Futurist architect Antonio Sant'Elia (1888–1916), the important buildings of the new age were hotels, railroad stations, and airports, which had superseded the cathedrals of the past.*

24. *Giacomo Balla,* A Girl Runs Along the Balcony. *Galleria d'Arte Moderna, Milan. Canvas. 1912. Influenced by Neo-Impressionist theories on the division of colors, Giacomo Balla (1871–1958) exploited the techniques of action photography to create this Futurist image of movement.*

25. *Umberto Boccioni,* States of Mind I: The Farewells. *Private collection, New York. Canvas. 1911. Umberto Boccioni (1882–1916) combined urban imagery and confusion to give visual expression to the Futurist belief in change.*

26. *Carlo Carrà,* La Galleria, Milan. *Mattioli Collection, Milan. Canvas. 1912. Influenced by the innovative Cubist styles of Picasso and Braque, Carlo Carrà (1881–1966) exploited the technique in his Futurist compositions that celebrated modern urban life.*

25

26

Architecture (1914), included designs for offices, apartment blocks, factories, and an aircraft hangar. Sant'Elia was convinced that the staircase was now obsolete, superseded by the elevator. Adapting Cubist techniques, the Futurist artists gave visual expression in their paintings and sculptures to the dynamism and roar of modern urban life. Marinetti was a brilliant publicist, and Futurism, an essentially patriotic Italian movement, had a considerable influence on Parisian artists such as Léger, Delaunay, and Raymond Duchamp-Villon. Its anarchic ideals contributed directly to the birth of Dada (see chapter 51) and had notable similarities with the experiments of the Russian avant-gardists.

Abstract Art

In developing the principles of Cubism, Picasso and Braque had been careful to avoid total abstraction and had consciously maintained links, however tenuous, with the objects of the exterior world. Other artists, however, pushed the innovations of Picasso and Braque to their extreme. If the works of Léger and Delaunay came close to abstraction, those of Wassily Kandinsky, Kasimir Malevitch, and Piet Mondrian realized a truly nonrepresentational, nonobjective, nonfigurative style. Kandinsky was a Russian academic who abandoned his university career to study painting and moved to Munich (1896). In his early works, he experimented with the *fauve* use of color. Transfixed by the beauty of one of these paintings lying on its side, Kandinsky recognized that it was irrelevant to continue representing objects of the exterior world. He articulated the theoretical framework of his ideas in a treatise entitled *Concerning the Spiritual in Art* (1910), in which he affirmed that the primary objective of art is to express

28

27

27. *Raymond Duchamp-Villon,* The Great Horse. *Art Institute, Chicago. Bronze. 1914. The Horses series by sculptor Raymond Duchamp-Villon (1876–1918) was influenced by both Cubist and Futurist ideas.*

28. *Piet Mondrian,* The Grey Tree. *Gemeentesmuseum, The Hague. Canvas. 1914. In the years prior to World War I, Piet Mondrian (1872–1944) developed an increasingly abstract style in his studies of trees and other objects, which evolved into purely geometric patterns. Mondrian was a founding member of the Dutch De Stijl group, whose ideas were enormously influential after the war.*

29. *Piet Mondrian,* Composition No. 6. *Gemeentesmuseum, The Hague. Canvas. 1914.*

29

the artist's deepest feelings. This belief was shared by three other German Expressionist painters: Franz Marc, August Macke, and Paul Klee, with whom Kandinsky founded a group called *Der Blaue Reiter* (The Blue Rider) in Munich (1911). Convinced that society was becoming increasingly greedy, materialistic, and corrupt, they escaped into the world of pure imagination. Kandinsky's belief that colors, forms, and lines could be used to stimulate the senses owed much to the theories of the philosopher Rudolf Steiner, who was also living in Munich. Likening colors to sounds, Kandinsky gave musical titles to two series of paintings,

Compositions and Improvisations, which reinforced their nonobjective content.

In Russia, the urge to escape from the objective world into abstraction was evident in the works of Malevitch and others. The innovative works of the Parisian avant-garde had been exhibited in Russia, and enthusiastic patrons had begun to collect works by Picasso, Matisse, and others. These paintings also encouraged Russian artists to experiment with abstraction. Like Kandinsky, Malevitch rejected the objective world, proposing pure geometric forms to affirm his belief in the superiority of the human intellect over nature. His first Suprematist

painting, *Black on White* (1913), was simply a black square on a white background. His later *White on White* (ca. 1918) marked the point of arrival in the search for pure abstraction.

The outbreak of World War I (1914) signaled the end of an era. The intensely creative atmosphere of the prewar years rapidly dissolved, as artists and their public in Paris, Berlin, and Munich were swept into the hostilities. The center of artistic life moved to the neutral countries of Western Europe. With the development of *De Stijl* in the Netherlands and of Dada in Switzerland, the search for new means

INNOVATION AND ABSTRACTION

30. Wassily Kandinsky, Composition. *Pushkin Museum, Moscow. Watercolor and ink on paper. 1915. The leading figure in the Blaue Reiter group, Wassily Kandinsky (1866–1944) developed a truly nonrepresentational abstract style. Never intended as pretty or decorative, Kandinsky's paintings expressed his spiritual and intellectual ideas.*

31. August Macke, Woman on a Divan. *Thyssen-Bornemisza Museum, Madrid. Watercolor. 1914. A member of the Blaue Reiter, August Macke (1887–1914) exploited the expressive potential of color in figurative compositions.*

30

31

of expression continued. The results would form the basis of a new conception of art in the cultural panorama of the postwar era.

PAUL KLEE

Paul Klee (1879–1940) was born in Switzerland and moved to Munich to study art in 1898. This important cultural center was a focus of progressive, avant-garde ideas, and it was here that Klee came into contact with Kandinsky, Marc, and Macke. He participated with them in the *Blaue Reiter* exhibitions of 1911–1912 and pursued his own experiments in abstract art. In France, he had come into contact with the exciting new work of Cézanne, the Post-Impressionists, and the *fauves.*

The diaries and letters of a trip to Italy record his amazement at the effects of light and color. But it was his trip to North Africa with Macke in 1914 that most influenced Klee's work. Fascinated by the problem of reproducing the brilliant Tunisian atmosphere, he experimented with watercolor to record the emotive effects of color in quasi-abstract patterns. For him, the subconscious revealed itself through color, line, and the act of creation. He experimented with automatic drawing and described painting as "taking a line for a walk." His pictures were characterized by carefully planned, naive imagery contrasted with a subtle and complex use of color. After serving in the German army during World War I, he joined the Bauhaus staff, where his teachings were a formative influence on the development of the Bauhaus style (see chapter 51).

32. Paul Klee, Scheidung Abends. *Klee Foundation, Berne. Watercolor on paper. 1922.*

32

33. Klee, Green Bell Tower As Center. *Klee Foundation, Berne. Watercolor on gesso. 1917.*

33

34. Klee, Small Picture of Pine Tree. *Kunstmuseum, Basle. Oil on canvas. 1922.*

34

WORLD WAR I CAME AS A PROFOUND economic, political, and social shock to the nations of Europe. The Treaty of Versailles, drawn up in a spirit of vindictiveness, demanded huge reparations from Germany, which it could not pay. Massive inflation followed, sowing the seeds of the next world war. The balance of power shifted from a financially and spiritually devastated Europe to the United States, whose booming postwar economy was bringing unprecedented prosperity to its citizens. The Russian Revolution (1917) and execution of Tsar Nicholas II had made the ruling classes of the West only too aware of

CHAPTER 51

THE AFTERMATH OF THE GREAT WAR

Art Between the Wars

the fragility of their claim to power in the face of organized mass opposition. Socialist movements were forcibly repressed and countered by increasingly vociferous right-wing nationalist groups.

If upholding tradition was the primary concern of the establishment, attacking them was now fundamental to left-wing opposition. A perceived association between left-wing ideology, moral laxity, and the threat of revolution lay behind Prohibition in the United States (1920) and the banning of the full text of D.H. Lawrence's *Lady Chatterley's Lover* in England (1928). The radical ideas that had challenged traditions in art and

architecture before the war were now more directly identified with political dissent.

Constructivism

In Russia, the revolution had established a new regime vehemently opposed to the bourgeois and capitalist values of the West. The ideology was visually reinforced by official support for modern art. Wassily Kandinsky and Kasimir Malevitch, two of the leading figures in the development of abstract art (see chapter 50), were appointed to key positions in new art schools. Both continued their experiments with abstraction.

Malevitch explored new possibilities in the use of color and three-dimensional geometric forms. His theories were an important influence on El Lissitzky, whose dynamic *Proun* series (1919) featured asymmetrical groupings of planes and masses along diagonals. Vladimir Tatlin, the founder of Constructivism, exploited the dynamic effects of diagonals in his design for a monument to the Third International; intertwined steel spirals enclosed three congress halls, in the shape of a cube, a pyramid, and a cylinder. The use of technically advanced materials and abstract design, without any reference to tradition,

gave visual expression to the spirit of the revolution. As an artist in the service of the socialist state, Tatlin also produced paper patterns for clothing and designs for a more efficient stove. It was this practical and utilitarian application of abstract art that formed the basis of Constructivism.

As the idealistic fervor of the revolution dissolved into the prosaic need for industrialization and economic reform, modern abstract art was rejected in favor of a more naturalistic style capable of providing effective, easily intelligible propaganda for the state. Kandinsky and El Lissitzky were forced to leave Russia

2

1. Pablo Picasso, The Race. *Private collection. Canvas. 1922.*

2. El Lissitzky, Project for the Tribune of Lenin. *Tretjakov Gallery, Moscow. Paper. 1920. Abstract design and industrial materials in this Constructivist design by El Lissitzky (1890–1941) gave visual expression to the radically new political regime in Russia.*

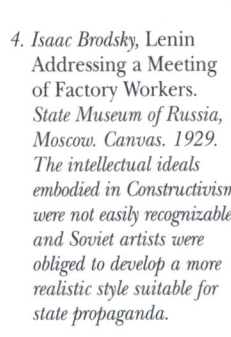

3

3. Georg Grosz, Twilight. *Thyssen-Bornemisza Museum, Lugano. Watercolor. 1922. Neue Sachlichkeit artists like Georg Grosz (1893–1959) drew on the traditions of German Expressionist paintings to create images that reinforced their disgust for contemporary German society.*

4

4. Isaac Brodsky, Lenin Addressing a Meeting of Factory Workers. *State Museum of Russia, Moscow. Canvas. 1929. The intellectual ideals embodied in Constructivism were not easily recognizable, and Soviet artists were obliged to develop a more realistic style suitable for state propaganda.*

and moved to Germany, where their ideas stimulated exciting new developments.

De Stijl

With war raging in France and Germany, the center of artistic innovation shifted to the neutral countries. In the Netherlands, the magazine *De Stijl* (*The Style,* 1917) was founded by Theo van Doesburg, Piet Mondrian, Gerrit Rietveld, Pieter Oud, Cornelius van Eesteren, Bart van der Leck, and Georges Vantongerloo. These painters, sculptors, architects, and graphic designers promoted a new style of abstract art based on the purity of horizontal and vertical lines combined with black, white, and the three primary colors. Mondrian had developed his ideas in Paris before the war from what he understood as the logical consequences of Cubism. Translating these ideas into three dimensions, *De Stijl* architects exploited the potential of Frank Lloyd Wright's experiments in informal planning, further breaking down the traditional barriers between internal and external space. Rietveld's design for the Schroeder House in Utrecht (1924), for example, abandoned the concept of wall enclosures, replacing them with a series of intersecting planes supported by metal elements painted in the *De Stijl* colors: red, yellow, and blue. The harmony, balance, and formality of *De Stijl* reflected a desire for order in a world of chaos. But the rigidity of its rules ultimately led to its demise. In 1924, Mondrian resigned from the group over the introduction of diagonals in the designs of Van Doesburg, influenced by El Lissitzky.

Dada

If *De Stijl* artists escaped into the puritan world of rules, the other major art movement of the period found refuge in the opposite

5

7

7. *Gerrit Rietveld,* Schroeder House. *Utrecht. 1924. The De Stijl architects, including Gerrit Rietveld (1888–1964), created three-dimensional versions of Mondrian's paintings.*

6

5. *Piet Mondrian,* Composition. *National Museum, Belgrade. Canvas. 1929. The purity of De Stijl was embodied in abstract works by Piet Mondrian (1827–1944), composed of straight lines and primary colors.*

6. *Marcel Duchamp,* Fountain. *Galleria Schwarz, Milan. Replica (1964) from lost original (1917). Dada was against everything, including itself. Marcel Duchamp (1887–1968) attached artistic value to everyday objects, even a urinal.*

direction. Dada was born in Switzerland, which during the war was a haven not only for political exiles like Lenin, but also for a group of artists and poets who met for literary evenings at the Cabaret Voltaire in Zurich (1916). Antiwar, antinationalist, and antitraditional, Dada was against everything—including itself. Even the name was nonsense. The Rumanian writer Tristan Tzara punctuated his unintelligible songs with screams and sobs. Marcel Duchamp questioned the very meaning of art by elevating everyday objects to the status of sculpture, called "ready mades." One of these was a snow shovel carrying the inscription, "In advance of a broken arm." The Dada poet wrote nonsense verse by cutting out words from the newspaper, shuffling the pieces, and removing them one by one. The cutout sculptures of Hans Arp were similarly haphazard, arranged according to chance. Anarchic and spontaneous, the Dada movement made an explicit comment on the futility of war.

Aftermath of the War

The declaration of peace encouraged many of the Dada artists to leave Zurich for France and Germany, where they continued their revolt against the establishment. In Cologne, the German painter Max Ernst put on an exhibition (1920) that visitors entered through a public lavatory. The Berlin Dada artists responded more directly to the chaos of postwar Germany with a satirical verve that was explicitly socialist. Profoundly affected by his experience in the trenches, Georg Grosz savagely attacked the bourgeois values of German society and the corruption and incompetence of those who directed the war. Grosz was a leading figure in the left-wing German movement called *Neue Sachlichkeit* (New Objectivity). His detached, satiric images of daily life stressed the realities

8. *Hans Arp*, Concretion. *Musée d'Art Moderne, Paris. Marble. 1934. Inspired by the forms of the natural world, the sculptures of Hans Arp (1887–1966) fused reality and the imagination into a higher, surreal dimension.*

8

9. *Salvador Dalí*, The Birth of Liquid Desires. *Guggenheim Collection, Venice. Canvas. 1931–1932. Using sexual and religious imagery to shock bourgeois complacency, Salvador Dalí (1904–1989) was a leading figure in the Surrealist movement.*

10. *Yves Tanguy*, The Sun in Its Case. *Guggenheim Collection, Venice. Canvas. 1937. Disturbing and inexplicable, this image by Yves Tanguy (1900–1955) exploited the unnerving effects of the concept of infinity.*

11. *Paul Delvaux*, Dawn. *Guggenheim Collection, Venice. Canvas. 1937. These female figures merging into fantastic, unnatural vegetation were deliberately designed to disturb.*

9

10

of inflation and depression in postwar Germany and provided a stark contrast to the intellectualism of abstract art.

Surrealism

Under the influence of André Breton, the Paris Dada group developed into a more theoretical and overtly left-wing movement: Surrealism. Less anarchic than Dada, Surrealism mounted a more systematic attack on the values of bourgeois society. Breton's *Manifesto of Surrealism* (1924) emphasized the importance of the subconscious mind. In this and other works he acknowledged debts not only to Freud's research into dreams, but also to the nineteenth-century poetry of Comte de Lautréamont, who wrote: "As beautiful as the chance meeting on a dissecting table between a sewing-machine and an umbrella." The phrase became the Surrealist motto. Surrealism extended the long tradition of fantasy in art, ranging from medieval images of hell to the metaphysical paintings of the Italian artist Giorgio de Chirico. Its goal was to fuse dreams and reality into a higher, "surreal" dimension. Surrealist art was deliberately intended to disturb, disconcert, and shock. At the Surrealist Exhibition of 1938, visitors were greeted with hysterical laughter recorded in lunatic asylums. Salvador Dalí, the most famous and influential Surrealist painter, exploited the shock effect of sexual images, distorted religious themes, and dreamscapes. Others, critical of abstraction, imitated Lautréamont's poetry by juxtaposing seemingly unrelated but recognizable objects in relationships inspired by the subconscious. The use of precise, carefully painted, factual details reinforced the reality of the Surreal world. René Magritte, for his part, achieved a disturbing effect by distorting proportions, by combining incongruous objects, or by reversing images—as in the case of a

11

12. *Giorgio de Chirico,* Unquiet Muse. *Private collection, Milan. Canvas. 1922. The leading Italian Metaphysical artist, Giorgio de Chirico (1888–1978) created dreamlike images of people and architecture that were distinctly ominous. His works were influential in the development of Surrealism.*

13. *Joan Miró,* Dutch Interior. *Museum of Modern Art, New York. Canvas. 1928. Automatic drawing, a means of expressing the subconscious mind on paper, gave rise to strange, biomorphic forms in the work of Joan Miró (1893–1983) and others.*

14. *Max Ernst,* The Toilette of the Bride. *Guggenheim Collection, Venice. Canvas. 1940. The fantasy, eroticism, and distortion inherent in the works of Max Ernst (1891–1976) were reinforced by his careful attention to detail.*

12

13

14

mermaid whose upper body was that of a fish, attached to human legs. One of the most disconcerting Surrealist images was Meret Oppenheim's *Luncheon in Fur* (1936), consisting of a fur-covered cup, saucer, and spoon. Joan Miró and Yves Tanguy experimented with automatic drawing as a means expressing the subconscious mind on paper and with fantastic, often disturbing biomorphic figures. Disseminated through exhibitions in Paris, New York, and elsewhere, the Surrealist movement was immensely influential, providing a new language of artistic expression that has inspired,

amused, and revolted its public and its followers.

Other Directions

While highly important, Surrealism was by no means the only artistic style extant during the period between the wars. On the contrary, variety in the arts reflected the diversity of responses to the political and social issues of the time. Many abstract artists found employment in the socialist environment of the Bauhaus (see below). Other artists pursued more individual paths. Two of the leading prewar painters, Matisse

and Braque, avoided association with left-wing politics. Matisse's domestic interiors emphasized bourgeois comfort, reflecting his belief that art should avoid depressing themes. The Italian Giorgio Morandi produced subtle and uncomplicated still lifes that combined abstract space with real objects, such as bottles found in a junkyard. The Rumanian sculptor Constantin Brancusi, inspired by a range of non-Western traditions, emphasized formal simplicity in works of highly finished bronze, wood, and marble. Simple, pure, and abstract, his sculptures reflected his belief that art should be joyful rather than enigmatic or disturbing.

16

16. Henri Matisse, Odalisque in Red Pantaloons. Musée d'Art Moderne, Paris. Canvas. 1922. Apparently unaffected by the crises of the postwar world, Henri Matisse (1869–1954) explored themes of luxury and pleasure.

17

15. Marc Chagall, To My Wife. Musée d'Art Moderne, Paris. Canvas. 1933–1934. Containing many of his favorite

images, this work by the Russian naive artist Marc Chagall (1887–1985) was dedicated to his wife and steeped in Jewish tradition.

15

17. Giorgio Morandi, Metaphysical Still Life. Private collection, Milan. Canvas. 1919. Simple, identifiable objects formed the basis of the metaphysical still lifes by Giorgio Morandi (1890–1964); his subtle use of color reinforced their quasi-abstract quality.

18. Constantin Brancusi, Maiastra. Guggenheim Collection, Venice. Canvas. 1912. Constantin Brancusi (1876–1957) studied with Rodin before developing his talent for expressing deep spiritual feelings in abstract sculptural forms.

18

Picasso

Picasso abandoned his single-minded exploration of Cubist techniques after 1914. Remaining outside the major postwar movements, he experimented with different styles and produced works of remarkable variety and versatility. Above all, he returned to the human figure. His scene designs for Serge Diaghilev's *Russian Ballet* (1917) were followed by a series of realistic portraits. A new interest in classical antiquity led him to study the figure styles of neoclassical painters, especially Poussin and Ingres, and to produce a series of etchings for Ovid's *Metamorphoses* (1934). He also continued to experiment with Cubism, developing an interest in the use of the curve. For a brief period he came under the influence of the Surrealists, even exhibiting at some of their shows. In 1928 he returned to sculpture, which he had avoided since 1914; his use of welded steel to create imaginative forms was widely influential.

The Bauhaus

The desire to reform art education and to enlist artists from elitist academies into the service of industry had its roots in the prewar Deutscher Werkbund. That organization, whose goal was to improve the quality of industrial design, was now explicitly dedicated to the socialist cause. Walter Gropius, who had been appointed head of the Weimar School of Art in 1915, reopened the school after the war, renaming it the Bauhaus. Its manifesto declared his intention of educating a new generation of artist-craftsmen to build, decorate, and furnish the architecture of an industrial, socialist future. Deliberately associating itself with modern abstract ideas, the school attracted talents from the major movements to its staff. El Lissitzky's Constructivism was an important

20. *Picasso*, Pipes of Pan. *Musée Picasso, Paris. Canvas. 1923. The exploration of solid human forms and classical themes played an important part in Picasso's postwar paintings.*

21. *Picasso*, Atelier of the Modiste. *Musée Picasso, Paris. Canvas. 1926. Picasso's later Cubist works continued his prewar experiments in the representation of three-dimensional forms on a flat canvas.*

19. *Picasso*, Paul as Pierrot. *Musée Picasso, Paris. Canvas. 1924. Combining naturalistic forms and flat planes of color, this painting represented one of the many directions taken by Pablo Picasso (1881–1973) in his postwar search for a new style.*

461

influence on both Laszló Moholy-Nagy and the *De Stijl* theorist Theo van Doesburg. Kandinsky taught at the Bauhaus after leaving Russia, along with Paul Klee, Lionel Feininger, and Hannes Meyer. Under Meyer's influence as head of the architecture department and later as Gropius's successor, the Bauhaus became more closely associated with the socialist aims of *Neue Sachlichkeit*. In 1925 the Bauhaus moved from Weimar to Dessau, and Gropius's design for the new complex gave visual expression to the school's ideals. Unornamented concrete, glass, and steel promoted the industrial machine aesthetic and denied all links with the past.

Bauhaus design stressed economy, efficiency, and high quality, standards that were also applied to furniture design, interior decoration, and, above all, low-cost housing. The ideas advanced by Walter Gropius in his pamphlet, *How Can We Build Cheaper, Better, More Attractive Homes*, led to commissions for the design of housing developments in Dessau and Berlin. In these buildings, following his principle, beauty was embodied in functionality. Standardization, prefabrication, modern materials, and strict avoidance of historical ornament imposed the logical and impersonal

standards of industrial design on the human environment.

Le Corbusier

In France, Le Corbusier pursued a similar course. His treatises on architecture and town planning presented radical solutions to the problem of urban design in the new machine age. His book *Une Ville Contemporaine* (1922) attempts to rationalize the problem of traffic congestion, taking into account the effects of road and vehicle types. He also recognized the need to increase residential density with high-rise

22

24

22. *Paul Klee,* Still Life with Dice. *Thyssen-Bornemisza Museum, Madrid. Paper. 1923. Paul Klee (1879–1940) was associated with Kandinsky and the Blaue Reiter Expressionist group in prewar Munich. He later taught art and weaving at the Bauhaus (1921–1930), where he experimented with line and color.*

23

23. *Laszló Moholy-Nagy,* Yellow Cross. *Galleria d'Arte Moderna, Rome. Paper. 1922. The Hungarian painter Moholy-Nagy (1895–1946) was one of the leading abstract artists on the Bauhaus faculty. After the school was closed by Hitler, he opened a new Bauhaus in Chicago (1937).*

24. *Wassily Kandinsky,* Above. *Guggenheim Collection, Venice. Canvas. 1929. Exploiting the expressive potential of abstract art, Wassily Kandinsky (1866–1944) developed a more rigid, formal style after the war.*

blocks toward city centers, with green spaces relegated to the suburbs. Le Corbusier's ideas were immensely influential in the rebuilding of Europe after the devastation of World War II (see chapter 52). His deep commitment to the ethic of standardization was reflected in his *Vers une architecture* (1923), which compared the Parthenon and its repetitive columns with images of modern uniformity, such as factories, automobiles, and airplanes. By reducing and simplifying the component parts of a house to a human scale, he developed the concept of a house as a "machine for living in."

ART EDUCATION AND THE BAUHAUS

When Walter Gropius reopened the Weimar School of Art after World War I (1919), he renamed it the Bauhaus. The word derived from *Bauhutte*, the term for the masons' lodgings in a medieval cathedral. Gropius and his colleagues, whose goal was to train a generation of craftspeople who would create the cathedrals of the new industrial age, planned an innovative three-stage system of art education. The students first took a preliminary course designed to clear their minds of traditional prejudices. Introduced to abstract ideas and the socialist creed of the Bauhaus, they were encouraged to experiment with a wide range of design concepts, while giving the staff an opportunity to assess their potential. Successful students proceeded to the second stage, in which they learned a craft such as weaving, pottery, metalwork, or woodwork. The final stage was rigorous training in industrial design. The program was a revolutionary approach to art education, devoid of any contact with tradition and administered by a faculty that was fully committed to the principles of modernism. The Bauhaus, eager to promote its ideas, published works by many of its teachers. One of them, Kandinsky's *Point to Line and Plane* (1926), has since become a standard text for the teaching of modern art.

THE AFTERMATH OF THE GREAT WAR

25. Walter Gropius, Bauhaus complex (detail). Dessau. 1925–1926. The techniques, materials, and industrial design of the new Bauhause complex gave visual expression to the school's modernist principles.

25

26

26. Diagram of the Bauhaus complex. Dessau. 1925–1926.

27. Plan of the Bauhaus complex. Dessau. 1925–1926.

27

The International Style

The idea of creating a single style for modern architecture had evolved in the Deutscher Werkbund before the war. Inspired by Socialist and antinationalist ideals, the concept was further explored at the Bauhaus and directly implied by the title of Le Corbusier's *Vers une architecture*. Both had a major influence on the formation of the *Congrès Internationaux d'Architecture Moderne* (CIAM, 1928), which stressed the radical idea that governments had a moral obligation to provide low-cost housing. The term "International Style" was coined by the American critics and historians Henry-Russell Hitchcock and Philip Johnson in their catalog for the first International Exhibition of Modern Architecture, held in New York (1932). Tracing the development of the style to the early years of the century, it included seminal works by Rietveld, Gropius, and Le Corbusier. Above all, it introduced the new industrial, socialist style into the capitalist culture of the United States.

Attitudes to Modern Ideas

Notwithstanding the historical and cultural importance of the modern movements in art and architecture, it is often forgotten that they held little appeal during the period between the wars. Le Corbusier's villas were designed for the intellectual avant-garde, while the most prestigious buildings were invariably commissioned in traditional styles. The design competition for the Chicago Tribune Tower (1922) attracted entries from all over the world, including ones from the Bauhaus architects. But their modern industrial style was decisively rejected by the panel of city politicians and journalists, who opted instead for a project embellished with Gothic detail. When Brancusi brought one of his sculptures

28

28. Le Corbusier, Villa Savoye. Poissy. 1929–1930. Charles Edouard Jeanneret, known as Le Corbusier (1887-1965), was arguably the greatest architect of the twentieth century. His style was based on five basic points (1926): pilotis (stilts) to raise the house off the ground; a roof garden for private external space; a skeleton structure, which permitted a more flexible, interchangeable plan; a free façade; and standardized ribbon windows.

29. Ludwig Mies van der Rohe, Project for a brick country house. 1922. Informal interior planning was a hallmark of the architectural designs of Mies van der Rohe (1886–1969).

30. Mies van der Rohe, Tugendhat House, interior. Brno. 1930.

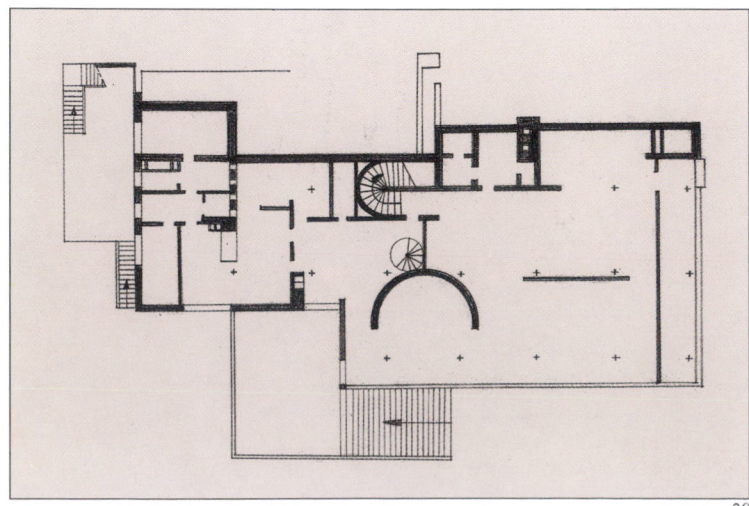

29

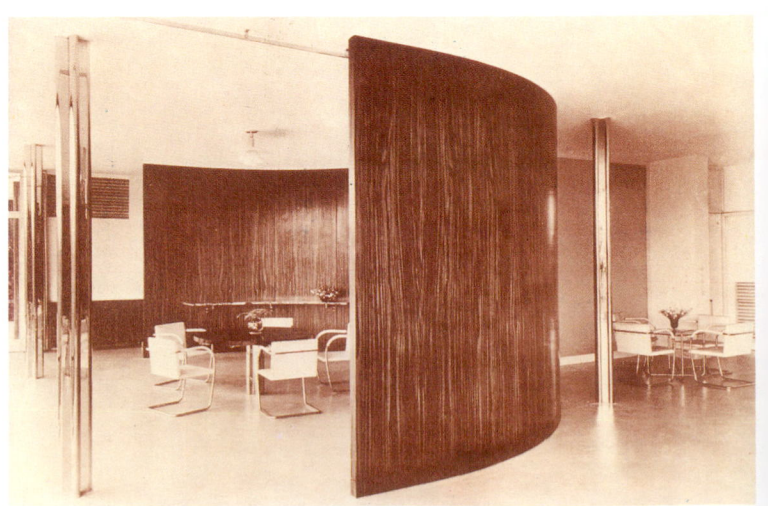

30

to the United States for an exhibition (1926), customs officials identified it as spare pieces of industrial metal rather than a work of art, and therefore subject to import duty; the ensuing court case highlighted the gulf between the establishment and the avant-garde.

During the same period, however, a distinctive modern style did emerge to provide an image for commercial success in Europe as well as the United States. Art Deco, now often called Art Moderne, exploited the exotic appeal of non-European cultures. The discovery of Tutankhamen's tomb in 1922 provided a rich new source

of motifs. Stylish and luxurious, Art Deco found its most prominent expression in the new palaces of popular entertainment, such as movie theaters, music halls, and ballrooms, where its glamour encouraged escape from the drab realities of everyday life.

The architect Frank Lloyd Wright, meanwhile, remained deliberately outside the orthodoxy of the modern movement but followed a different path from that of the Art Deco designers. In both his utopian town-planning projects, such as *Broadacre City* (first exhibited 1935), and his private commissions, Wright

refuted the idea of imposing standardized solutions on what he regarded as the unique requirements of each building and its natural environment. His house design (1936) for the millionaire Edgar Kaufmann in Bear Run, Pennsylvania, exploited the potential of reinforced concrete to balance cantilevered slabs over a waterfall, suspending the living room and main terrace above it. The Kaufmann house, now an icon of modern architecture, epitomized Wright's conviction that the style of a particular building should be organically unified with its natural surroundings.

31

32

33

31. *Frank Lloyd Wright,* Falling Water. *Bear Run, Pennsylvania. 1936. Indisputably modern, the architectural designs of Frank Lloyd Wright (1869–1959) blurred traditional concepts of exterior and interior space. He remained deliberately outside the orthodoxy of the modern movement, preferring to experiment with his own distinctive ideas.*

32. *William van Alen,* Chrysler Building. *New York City. 1926–1930. Glamorous and commercial, Art Deco provided a modern image for architecture between the wars without the political idealism of the International Style.*

33. *Giovanni Guerrini, Enzo Bruno La Padula, and Mario Romano,* Palazzo della Civiltà del Lavoro. *EUR, Rome. 1942. Modern and rational, Mussolini's architecture nevertheless evoked the past glory of Roman civilization.*

Art and Repression

In the Soviet Union, Italy, and Germany, a more dramatic reaction to the modern movements gave visual expression to political change. As revolutionary idealism in the USSR degenerated under Stalin's repressive regime, Constructivism and modern design were decisively rejected in favor of a simplified but recognizably neoclassical style for state architecture. In Italy, where Mussolini seized power in 1922, architects were critical of both traditional eclectic styles and the anti-historicism of the modern movement. Consciously emulating his imperial predecessors, Mussolini embarked on a massive renewal of the city of Rome, opening a ceremonial approach to St. Peter's (Via della Conciliazione) and commissioning his own forum, the *Esposizione Universale di Roma* (EUR). Designed for an international exhibition in 1942, the buildings of EUR were remarkable for their severe and austere application of modern rationalization to an essentially classical style. In Germany, meanwhile, the attitude of Hitler's government to modern socialist art and architecture was openly hostile. His appointment as chancellor in 1933 was rapidly followed by the closing of the Bauhaus. Hitler instituted a housing program that deliberately revived the traditional pitched roof, a feature carefully avoided by the Bauhaus architects. But the ultimate visual expression of the power of the Third Reich was Albert Speer's architectural plan for the city of Berlin. Massive neoclassical buildings and a grand triumphal boulevard declared Hitler's intention to revive the empire of Ancient Rome. With the closing of the Bauhaus, the persecution of Jews and left-wing activists, and finally the German conquest of France, modern painters, sculptors, and architects took refuge in the United States, setting the scene for dramatic changes after the war.

34

34. Picasso, Guernica. *Casón del Buen Retiro, Madrid. Canvas. 1937. This allegorical image of violence and brutality was inspired by the Fascist bombing of the Basque town of Guernica during the Spanish Civil War. The work was exhibited in the Spanish Pavilion of the 1937 International Exhibition as a public denunciation of Franco's attack on Republican Spain.*

CHAPTER 52

MODERNISM REVISITED

Art and Architecture from 1945 to the Present Day

EUROPE EMERGED FROM WORLD WAR II physically, economically, and politically devastated. Its position at the center of world power, already eroded by World War I, was now decisively broken. The United States and Soviet Union became the dominant figures on the world scene. The League of Nations in Geneva, which had failed in its missions of disarmament and peacekeeping, was replaced by the United Nations in New York. The European colonial empires in Africa and Asia were dismembered, as the former territories of Great Britain, France, Belgium, the Netherlands, and Italy were granted independence. The liberation of

Eastern Europe by the Red Army during the war led to long-term Soviet domination. The United States reinforced its economic and political links with Western Europe through the Marshall Aid Plan (1947) and NATO (1949). Deepening mistrust between the two superpowers resulted in the Cold War, the McCarthy "witch hunt" to root out Communists in the United States (1952–1954), and the construction of the Berlin Wall (1961).

The war also had important ramifications on a cultural level. Nazi and Fascist persecutions forced many of the leading intellectual and artistic figures of prewar Europe to emigrate to the United States.

1

The physicists Einstein and Fermi and the composers Schönberg, Stravinsky, and Bartók were joined by a large proportion of the painters, sculptors, and architects of the modern movement. Gropius, Mies van der Rohe, and Moholy-Nagy crossed the Atlantic after Hitler's closure of the Bauhaus (1933); the fall of France (1940) encouraged Léger, Chagall, Mondrian, Ernst, Dalí, and Tanguy to follow.

A New Image for America

The International Style had been developed by Gropius, Le Corbusier, and the other designers associated with the Bauhaus in prewar Europe as an architectural language appropriate to the new century. Uniformity, standardization, and, above all, the use of modern industrial materials and techniques expressed their belief in a new future. Explicitly socialist, the International Style was not popular with the establishment in either Europe or the United States, which tended to prefer architectural themes more closely linked with history and tradition. But Hitler's overt hostility gave the modern movement a new status in American eyes. Symbolizing freedom from oppression, the International Style was now wholeheartedly embraced as an expression of America's new power in the postwar world. Perhaps most significant in that regard was the United Nations Headquarters building (1948) in New York. The Bauhaus émigrés were given key academic positions; Gropius was appointed chairman of the Architecture Department at Harvard Graduate School. Mies van der Rohe went into private practice and soon established himself as the leading architect of the postwar consumer society. The United States emerged from the war relatively unscathed, and the nation's economy was in full boom. Commercial profits, which had doubled between 1940 and 1945, now

2

3. *Henry Moore,* Family Group. *Private collection. Bronze. 1948–1949. The English sculptor Henry Moore (1898–1986) experimented with both abstract and figural forms and their spatial relationships in solid, monumental works of bronze, stone, and wood.*

4. *Francis Bacon,* Second Version of "Painting 1946." *Museum Ludwig, Cologne. Canvas. 1971. Bizarre and disturbing, the works of the Irish-born painter Francis Bacon (1909–1992) exploit metamorphosis as a means of emphasizing victimization and imprisonment.*

1. *Le Corbusier,* Notre-Dame-du-Haut. *Ronchamp. 1951–1955. Le Corbusier (1887–1965) based the design for this church on his Modulor system, which related the proportions of the human body to the geometric principle of the Golden Section, believed by medieval and later theorists to have mystical properties.*

2. *Ben Shahn,* Albert Einstein and Other Immigrants. *New Jersey Community Center, Roosevelt Homestead. Canvas. 1937–1938. Born in Lithuania, Ben Shahn (1898–1969) moved to the United States in 1906 and developed his social realist style in large murals and smaller paintings. This one celebrated the arrival in America of the victims of Hitler's persecutions.*

3

4

financed the construction of modern skyscrapers. Dropping its socialist ideology, the International Style produced impersonal images that reinforced the ideals of corporate efficiency with steel skeleton structures, glass curtain walls, and standardized units. Imposing order on chaos, Mies van der Rohe promoted his purist concept of beauty with the phrase, "Less is more." The importance of conformity was reflected in the proliferation throughout America of Miesian glass boxes as images of commercial power, designed by firms such as Skidmore, Owings & Merrill. Not restricted to commercial architecture, the same uniform style was applied to political

and academic institutions as well as to residential buildings for every level of society.

Postwar Europe

The situation on the other side of the Atlantic was very different. With limited funds at their disposal, European governments faced the task of rebuilding cities devastated by aerial bombings and ground fighting. The consequences of the war, therefore, forced the realization of one of the ideals promoted by the International Style: the construction of low-cost housing by the state. Modern high-rise blocks and urban-planning projects

radically changed the face of cities throughout Europe.

The only major prewar architect remaining in Europe, Le Corbusier now had a chance to put the socialist ideals of the International Style into practice, an opportunity denied to the Bauhaus architects in the United States. But Le Corbusier abandoned many of the stylistic features of his earlier works, rejecting geometrical purity as his primary concern in favor of textural quality. This new emphasis led him to employ "primary" construction materials such as rough concrete (*béton brut*) and to add elements such as the sun break (*brise-soleil*). These features were incorporated

5. Ludwig Mies van der Rohe, Seagram Building. New York City. 1954–1958. The Bauhaus émigré Mies van der Rohe (1886–1969) became one of the leading exponents of the postwar International Style and its application to the images of commercial success in the thriving cities of the United States.

6. Frank Lloyd Wright, Guggenheim Museum. New York City. 1949–1959.

5

6

Established as one of the leading architects of the modern movement before World War II, Le Corbusier had relatively few opportunities to put his radical ideas into practice. They remained largely theoretical and formed the basis of his books, *Une Ville Contemporaine* (1922) and *Vers une architecture* (1923). Ironically it was the destruction caused by the war that prompted European governments to commission large-scale, low-cost housing projects, one of the shared ideals

LE CORBUSIER

of the International Style architects. The low-cost residential block, which Le Corbusier called l'*Unité d'Habitation*, embodied the socialist ideals of his prewar town-planning projects and had an enormous influence on postwar European architecture. Many of his later buildings, notably the church of Notre-Dame-du-Haut, were governed by a system he called Mod-

ulor and based on the Golden Section, a geometric proportion long believed to have mystical implications. In an effort to find a standardized unit that was "a harmonious measure to the human scale," Le Corbusier related the Golden Section to the proportions of the human body. In this way he sought to combine both the spiritual and physical aspects of humanity, a radical change from the mathematical purity of the International Style.

in his designs for low-cost housing projects like the Unité d'Habitation in Marseilles (1948). The enormous visual variety in Le Corbusier's postwar architecture was markedly different from the uniformity of the International Style.

His design for the church of Notre-Dame-du-Haut (1951–1955) in Ronchamp, France, criticized as irrational by supporters of his purist prewar buildings, was an attempt to convey the dual aspect of Christianity, combining a bold concrete exterior with a spiritual interior. It was a far cry from the Miesian glass boxes of postwar American design.

7

7. *Le Corbusier,* Unité d'Habitation, detail of roof. *Marseilles. 1948. Le Corbusier described his low-cost residential blocks as "vertical garden cities." This one contained 337 apartments arranged around interior shopping arcades. Other amenities included a nursery, kindergarten, gymnasium, restaurant, and rooftop swimming pool.*

8

8. *Alexander Calder,* Useless Machine. *UNESCO Building, Paris. The sculptor Alexander Calder (1898–1976) was one of the few American artists to develop a distinctly modern style. His associations in Paris with Miró, Léger, Arp, and Mondrian were highly influential in his work.*

9. *Pier Luigi Nervi and Gio Ponti,* Pirelli Building. *Milan. 1955–1959. Sleek and professional, the design of this skyscraper by the Italian engineer Pier Luigi Nervi (1891–1979) and the architect Gio Ponti (1897–1979) avoided the simple Miesian box so popular in postwar America.*

9

Abstract Expressionism

From the rational abstract painters of the Bauhaus to the emotionally charged Surrealists, the artists who fled Hitler's Europe brought the United States into direct contact with the wide range of styles associated with modern art. The impact was considerable, but America was not Europe, and its artists felt the need to visually reaffirm the nation's preeminence and their own identities. They were also eminently aware of their freedom from the constraints of European cultural tradition. Influenced by the expressive abstraction of Kandinsky, the formal abstraction of Mondrian, the use of color pioneered by Matisse, and the psychological automatism urged by the Surrealists, Abstract Expressionism developed as an innovative and distinctively American contribution to modern art. The term did not refer to a homogeneous or cohesive movement. It was coined by critics to cover a variety of personal styles that emerged in the late 1940s and came together in an exhibition called Abstract Painting and Sculpture in America, held at New York's Museum of Modern Art in 1951.

The Abstract Expressionists are generally divided into two groups, corresponding to distinct creative approaches: the *action painters* (Jackson Pollock, Willem de Kooning, Franz Kline, and others); and the *color-field painters* (Mark Rothko, Barnett Newman, Clyfford Still, Adolph Gottlieb, and others). The term "action painting" was officially born in 1952, when the critic Harold Rosenberg defined it as a "material-to-material" encounter between paint and canvas. The artist was no longer attempting to convey a mental image in picture form; the subject of art became the act of painting itself. This startlingly innovative approach was best exemplified by the work of Pollock. As seen in films that captured him in action, Pollock involved his whole body in the unpremeditated, spontaneous act of creation;

10

11

12

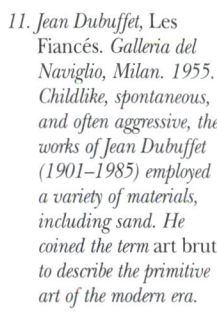

13

10. Jackson Pollock, The Enchanted Forest. *Guggenheim Collection, Venice. Canvas. 1947. One of the leading figures of the postwar Abstract Expressionist movement in the United States, Jackson Pollock (1912–1956) deliberately overwhelmed the viewer with oversized, highly distinctive images without a focal point.*

11. Jean Dubuffet, Les Fiancés. *Galleria del Naviglio, Milan. 1955. Childlike, spontaneous, and often aggressive, the works of Jean Dubuffet (1901–1985) employed a variety of materials, including sand. He coined the term* art brut *to describe the primitive art of the modern era.*

12. Willem de Kooning, Two Women on a Wharf. *Private collection, United States. Canvas. 1949. Willem de Kooning (born 1904) was an important figure in the "action" wing of Abstract Expressionism. His work was never completely nonobjective, and he maintained an abiding interest in the human form.*

13. Alberto Giacometti, Dog. *Thyssen-Bornemisza Museum, Lugano. Bronze. 1951 (cast 1957). Alberto Giacometti (1901–1966) developed a highly personal style characterized by elongated forms that appear tragic, isolated, and lonely.*

abandoning traditional brush-and-palette methods entirely, he preferred to drip, splash, or pour his paint onto a canvas placed on the floor.

Rothko, on the other hand, one of the founders of color-field painting, believed that abstract art was capable of evoking strong emotional responses in the viewer. Following that principle, he painted on a vast scale to engage the spectator and used large blocks of color to convey his own deep feelings. According to Rothko, if any viewers broke down and cried in front of one of his paintings, he would know the work was successful.

American sculptors also responded to the creative atmosphere of the postwar era. Loosely associated with the Abstract Expressionists, David Smith designed a series of stainless steel sculptures, titled *Cubi*, designed to exploit the expressive potential of basic geometric forms; the works were intended for open-air display, enabling the colors of the surrounding environment to be reflected in their surfaces.

Pop Art

Considering the elitist and highly personalized character of Abstract Expressionism,

emphasizing the artist's own emotions, subconscious impulses, and act of creation, a reaction was inevitable. Several artists thus began to reassert the importance of the real world. The compositions of Robert Rauschenberg, assembled from discarded everyday objects, and Jasper Johns's painted images of the American flag both conferred the status of art on the ordinary and familiar. The works of these artists, inspired as they were by Dada, came to be called neo-Dadaist. They were a direct prelude to the birth of Pop Art, which emerged toward the end of the 1950s in the affluent consumer culture of the United States, with exponents in Great

14. *Andy Warhol*, Marilyn Diptych. *Tate Gallery, London. Canvas. 1962. After working for the American magazine* Glamour, *Andy Warhol (1930–1987) became a painter, printer, filmmaker, writer, and celebrity. His identification with the consumer and media culture of contemporary urban society was reflected in his choice of subject matter.*

14

Britain, where the austerity of the postwar years had given way to an economic boom, and in Italy.

Debunking traditional concepts of good and bad taste, Pop Art was deliberately anti-intellectual. It gave visual expression to the impersonal, mass-media, urban world of advertising, movies, and television. Arguably the first Pop picture was produced by a British artist. Richard Hamilton's tiny collage *Just What Is It That Makes Today's Homes So Different, So Appealing?* (1956) was initially misinterpreted as a criticism of consumer society. But Hamilton, who offered the first definition of Pop Art, declared that it should appeal to a mass audience, especially the young, and emphasized its qualities of impermanence, gimmickry, and glamour. If Britain was excited by its new affluence, the United States was less so. American Pop emphasized the banal with images like Claes Oldenburg's *Giant Hamburger* (1962). Andy Warhol, the celebrity icon of American Pop Art, was trained as an advertising designer; his photographic silk-screens translated the uniformity of a mass-market, mass-media society into repetitive images of everything from Marilyn Monroe and soup cans to car accidents and the ultimate symbol of American culture, the Coke bottle. If art could be used for advertising, then advertising was art.

From Minimalism to Photo-Realism

The prosperous 1960s were also a period of discontent and disillusionment for the United States. An overconfident nation launched into the Vietnam War (1963–1975), and the consequences would prove disastrous. The assassination of President John Kennedy (1963) shocked the entire world; many in America said it marked the end of an age of innocence. Youth culture escaped into drugs and sex. Many artists escaped into the purist

15. *Jasper Johns,* Zero Through Nine. *Tate Gallery, London. Canvas. 1961. Much as the Dadaists had done, Jasper Johns (born 1930) conferred the status of art on familiar, everyday objects. The American flag was a favorite subject.*

16. *Arman,* Venus of the Shaving Brushes. *Tate Gallery, London. Mixed media. 1969.*

17. *Robert Rauschenberg,* Almanac. *Tate Gallery, London. Canvas. 1962. The neo-Dadaist works of the American artist Robert Rauschenberg (born 1925) were a direct prelude to the development of Pop Art.*

realms of Minimal Art and Conceptual Art. A new creative concept was born, emphasizing the value of the idea rather than the artist's personality or skill as a craftsman. The work thus became an object or combination of objects arranged for the purpose of making a statement through space, volume, texture, material, color, or light, even if its meaning was not always clear. An exhibition in Paris by the French artist Yves Klein consisted of nothing more an empty gallery, painted white. Other artists developed their own statements, no less distinctive or mystifying. Carl Andre arranged ordinary bricks on the floor. Christo created a number of variations on his theme of "packaged" objects, extending his idea to the point of covering part of the Australian coastline in plastic sheeting. Joseph Beuys and Allan Kaprow were among several artists who explored the concept of performance art, or "happenings," extending the concept of art as an immediate expression of the artist's ideas. At the other end of the spectrum, American painters like Chuck Close and Richard Estes and the sculptor Duane Hanson gave a new meaning to realism with their Photo-Realist, or Super-Realist, images of urban America.

Without the advantage of hindsight, it is difficult to categorize or judge the enormous variety of postwar artistic production. The task is made even harder if one considers that in contemporary art, unlike that of the past, originality itself is regarded as the true sign of merit. Yet contemporary art is at the center of a sometimes violent polemic, extensively and vigorously criticized by the viewing public. Pollock's drip paintings are regularly dismissed on the grounds that a child could have done them. The use of public funds by the Tate Gallery in London to buy Carl Andre's *Bricks* raised a public outcry that threatened the museum's function of acquiring works by modern artists. Contemporary art, widely condemned as self-indulgent and unnecessary, is similarly

19

19. Emilio Vedova, Travels in Italy. *Ca' Pesaro, Venice. Emilio Vedova (born 1919) was one of the leading artists of the New Art Front, a group of largely abstractionist painters founded in Italy after World War II.*

20. Alberto Burri, Large Sack. *Galleria d'Arte Moderna, Rome. Alberto Burri (1915–1995) exploited the textures of crudely sewn sacks and paint to convey the dislocation and horror of war.*

18. Joseph Beuys, Four Blackboards. *Tate Gallery, London. Chalk on board. 1972. The German artist Joseph Beuys (1921–1986) was a leading exponent of modern performance art.*

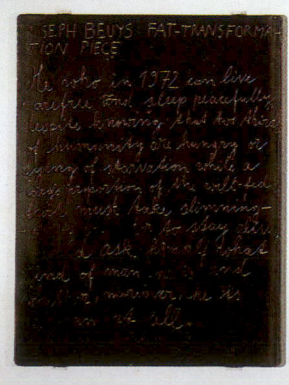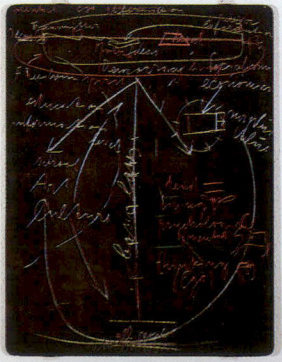

18

criticized for restricting its message to the initiated. Museums, therefore, have begun efforts to educate the public regarding its validity and "meaning." Today as in the eighteenth century, however, artistic taste is still the distinguishing mark of the elite connoisseur.

New Directions in Architecture

According to widely held opinion, the modern movement in architecture appears to have failed in key respects. The ideals of its creators have often proved both unworkable and unpopular in practice. At a functional level, heavy increases in the price of oil during the 1970s compromised the efficiency of the glass skyscraper. In postwar Europe, the failure to establish or enforce building standards in low-cost housing projects has had serious and sometimes disastrous consequences, from leaky apartment roofs to the collapse of tower blocks. At a social level, the uniform and impersonal housing projects originally intended to improve the quality of life for the poor and working classes have been blamed for everything from stress-related illnesses to violence and drug use.

The failures have been hardly less conspicuous at the visual level. Earlier in the century, architects such as Frank Lloyd Wright and Le Corbusier questioned the formal purity and orthodoxy of the International Style and forged distinctive new approaches to building design. In subsequent decades, the criticism became more widespread. In the United States as in Europe, architects began to think more seriously about the effects of their designs on those people most closely associated with the finished buildings: the users. Uniformity began to give way to individuality, and the Miesian glass box was superseded by a variety of shapes and forms. The categorical rejection of tradition was also cast into doubt, as many modern institutions

20

21

21. Giancarlo de Carlo, University Residences. Urbino. 1962–1966. New and informal ideas on the design of residential buildings emerged during the 1960s, as architects like the Italian Giancarlo de Carlo (born 1919) reacted to the orthodoxy of the modern movement.

22. Robert Venturi, John Rauch, and Denise Scott Brown, Gordon WU Hall, Butler College. Princeton, New Jersey. 1983. In his books Complexity and Contradiction in Architecture (1966) and Learning from Las Vegas (1972), Robert Venturi (born 1925) made a significant contribution to the development of a modern style that incorporates both tradition and innovation.

22

were recognized as having roots in the past. In the latter decades of the century, a new generation of architects, the Post-Modernists, began to reuse styles and motifs from historical prototypes to restore color, texture, decoration, and traditional composition to their designs. Foremost among these were Robert Venturi, Michael Graves, and Philip Johnson, whose buildings revived such classical details as pediments and the occasional column and capital. The Chinese-American architect I.M. Pei has brought a typically elegant, restrained style—if ever original and context-driven—to his prestigious commissions throughout the world. At the turn of the millennium, the term "neomodernism" began to be used for new building complexes in the United States and Europe, a movement led by Frank Gehry. In architecture, as in the other visual arts, the only certainty for the future would be a continuing cycle of innovation and revision in the postindustrial world.

23

24

25

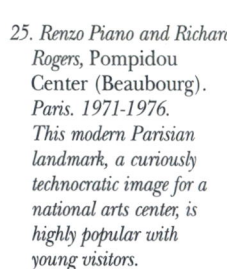

26

23. I.M. Pei, East Building. *National Gallery of Art, Washington, D.C. 1978. Stark and austere, the design of this building makes a comment on the almost religious role of art in modern society.*

24. Arata Isozaki, Tsukuba Civic Center. *Japan. 1980–1983. Isozaki (born 1931) and other modern Japanese architects have returned to the exploration of national traditions. In this complex, Isozaki deliberately blurred the distinction between human architecture and nature.*

25. Renzo Piano and Richard Rogers, Pompidou Center (Beaubourg). *Paris. 1971-1976. This modern Parisian landmark, a curiously technocratic image for a national arts center, is highly popular with young visitors.*

26. Philip Johnson and John Burgee, AT&T Building. *New York City. 1978–1982. Experimenting with traditional and highly recognizable architectural forms, Philip Johnson (born 1906) has rejected uniformity and developed a wide variety of solutions to the commercial office block.*

Whether displayed in public or appreciated in private, art has given visual expression to the ideals and values of the ruling elite for most of its history. Although modern art originated as a deliberate statement of opposition to established authorities, both aesthetic and political, it now is all too often put to the same purpose.

Only a half-century ago, state museums avoided association with the modern movements in architecture, painting, and sculpture. But this has changed.

Ieoh Ming Pei's glass pyramid at the Louvre in Paris (1989), for example, provides a dramatic contrast with the classicism of the museum's buildings.

The opening of museums and art galleries throughout the United States and Europe suggests that this building type is as essential to the cities and towns of today as the church was to the villages of the Middle Ages.

Squares and other public spaces celebrate their modernity with contemporary sculpture. Collecting and displaying works remains a reaffirmation of tradition and of art itself.

At the same time, the sense of what is good remains elusive to the general public, and the attitude of many modern artists toward the public is deeply ambiguous.

Contemporary architects, painters, and sculptors seem to shroud the meaning of their works in intellectual deep mysteries.

Understanding and appreciating modern art thus requires more than simple visual recognition, and the message is often incomprehensible to most people.

Like the eighteenth-century concept of taste, the ability to understand modern art is only reserved for the cultural elite.

MODERNISM REVISITED

27. Roy Lichtenstein, *That's the Way. Private collection. The American artist Roy Lichtenstein (1923-1997) was one of the signature stylists of American Pop Art.*

GLOSSARY

A

Abacus The upper part of the classic *capital* that serves to connect the column to the architectural element, *architrave* or *arch* that it supports.

Abbey A community of religious, mainly of the Benedictine Order, ruled by an abbot or abbess. The group of buildings that houses the monks or nuns is also known as the abbey. During the Middle Ages the complete abbey comprised the courtyard, *cloister*, porch, *basilica*, baptistry, *cells*, refectory, stables, *scriptorium*, abbot's residence, pilgrims' hospice and other buildings.

Abbey Church The church of a religious community ruled by an abbot.

Acanthus The decorative element of the *Corinthian capital*, inspired by the large, spiny, deeply scored leaves of *acanthus mollis*, a common herbaceous plant in the Mediterranean region.

Acropolis In Greek *acropolis* means "the top of the city." In artistic-architectural language it signifies the group of, mainly religious, buildings that were built at the highest point in the ancient cities.

Agora In Ancient Greek cities this was the main square, the site of public assemblies, the market and where people met to discuss public and private matters. It was generally a porticoed rectangle, flanked by the most important public and religious buildings.

Allegory The method of expressing ideas or concepts through figures or symbols.

Altar In pagan worship, the tumulus or structure on which sacrifices and offerings to the gods were made. In Christian churches, the table-structure used during the celebration of mass.

Altarpiece Also known as *ancona* (if it is architecturally square), is the rectangular, sometimes cusped panel above the *altar*. Always depicting a religious subject, the altarpiece is usually painted, but it may be made of other materials such as hammered or enameled metal, carved wood or marble sculpted in bas-relief.

Ambulatory In Romanesque and Gothic churches, the aisle around the *choir* from which chapels arranged in a ray going outward open.

Amphitheater Ancient Roman theater of oval or elliptical *plan* created by joining two ancient theaters. Used for gladiatorial games, mock naval battles and public events, the central arena was surrounded by tiered seating for the spectators.

Anubis Egyptian god of the Dead, usually depicted as a man with the head of a jackal.

Apse A semicircular, polygonal or lobed *plan* structure covered by a cupola that concludes one or both ends of the *nave* of Ancient Roman *basilicas;* the apse housed the tribune where the magistrates sat. In Christian churches it is generally situated at the end of the presbytery: it is the end of the central nave, behind the *altar* and where the *choir* is located.

Arch A curved architectural structure built into a wall or supported by piers, columns or *pillars*. The shaped bricks or stones from which it is made are called *wedges;* the central and highest wedge that closes and bears the weight of the arch is the *keystone*. The *intrados* is the inner, concave surface of the arch; the outer, convex surface is the *extrados*. The *archivolt* is the usually ornamental band that surrounds the front face of the arch, highlighting its structure. The *imposts* are the structures from which the arch springs. The distance between the two ends of the arch is the *chord* or the *span*. There are various types of arches:

- round headed;
- flat or segmented—if the chord is smaller than the diameter;
- pointed, ogee or lancet arch;
- trefoil, with three lobes;
- Moorish, horseshoe;
- rampant, if the piers are of different heights; typical of gothic architecture, it serves as a buttress to resolve the vertical pressure of the weight of the vault.

Architrave Also known as *epistilium*, a horizontal architectural element that rests on two piers, *pillars* or columns. It is the lower part of the *entablature* that rests on the *abacus*.

Art Nouveau Movement that developed in Europe in the late nineteenth and early twentieth centuries. It spread rapidly through Europe via great international exhibitions and concerned mainly architecture and the decorative arts. In Italy it was known as *Stile Floreale* or *Liberty*, in Great Britain as *Modern Style; Modernism* in Spain; *Velde Stile* in Belgium; *Sezessionstil* in Austria and *Jugendstil* in Germany. Art Nouveau was born as a reaction to eclecticism, sterile reproductions of historical styles and mainly the deterioration in tastes due to the growing popularity of industrial and mechanical goods.

B

Balustrade A row of balusters (small contoured columns) or short pillars resting on a quadrangular base and topped by a rail. In the early Christian *basilica* it delimits the *choir* area and can also be found as a divider among the presbytery, chapels along the central nave and the *ambulatory*. It can also be used as an open parapet along a balcony, terrace, roof of a building or staircase.

Baroque The Portuguese word *barrôco* originally meant an irregularly shaped pearl. Then, in the eighteenth century, it came to mean "bizarre" or "unequal" and was applied to paintings to define those pictures in which the traditional rules of perspective were not respected and everything was shown according to the artist's whim. Over time the adjective has been used to describe aspects of seventeenth- as well as sixteenth- and eighteenth-century art, and even Hellenistic and Art Nouveau artworks. Currently, when used as a noun, "baroque" mainly indicates the stylistic movement that developed in Rome starting from the third decade of the seventeenth century, with specific reference to the works of Bernini, Borromini and Pietro da Cortona, and is characterized by the abandonment of harmonious Renaissance proportions in favor of a more emotional relationship with the viewer.

Basilica In Ancient Rome this type of building was used for public occasions such as administering justice, or for trade. Rectangular in *plan*, sometimes with apses on the shorter sides, the pagan basilica was divided by columns or *pillars* into three (or even five) *naves*, the central one of which had windows and the highest ceilings. The Roman model was the basis of the early Christian basilica in which the naves end at three-quarters of the length of the building, and the transept separates the area of the worshipers from the part reserved for the clergy, thus creating a cross-shaped plan. In front of the basilica was the four-sided portico that was often reduced to a single porch that ran along the entire front of the façade: the *narthex*.

Buttress A masonry structure that reinforces a building by balancing the weight of an arch from the outside.

C

Cameo A picture carved into semiprecious stones or gemstones of two or more layers of color achieved by relief carving the lighter layer and leaving the darker as the background, or vice versa.

Canopy Traditionally, the term is used to describe a covering known since antiquity consisting in a cloth stretched over four or more vertical supports to shelter persons or things. Used in religious ceremonies or rituals during the Gothic period, they were often made of stone to decorate the bishop's throne and the *altar* and to crown and protect statuary or niches.

Canvas Coarse linen or cotton cloth stretched on a frame that is prepared with glues and to be used as a painting surface.

Capital The top portion of a column. There are three types of classical columns, according to the architectural *order*:

- *Doric* consisting of three annulets (rings), an *echinus* and an *abacus*;
- *Ionic* consisting of an *astragal* (contoured element), an *echinus* decorated with egg-and-dart molding, *volutes* on the front and rear faces and an *abacus*;
- *Corinthian* consisting of an *abacus, fleuron, volutes* and stylized *acanthus* leaves.

Capitals from the ancient Eastern civilizations as well as those in Byzantine, Romanesque and Gothic structures are very different from classical ones. Some are highly simplified, (such as the plain, Romanesque *dado* capital), while others are decorated with figures, scenes or plant motifs.

Cartoon Preparatory drawing on heavy paper used by painters to transfer the design to a wall, panel, glass or other surface. It is the same size as the project and is generally done on squared paper to facilitate transfer. The contours are pierced, charcoal dust is spread over them, and the marks are then transferred to the surface to be painted. This technique is called *pouncing*.

Caryatid Carved female figures used to support *corbels*, *architraves*, etc.

Casting The procedures for making a bronze sculpture starting from a plaster model. In the *lost wax* technique, a wax "negative" of the model is made around a core of refractory material. The wax model is then covered with refractory material as well, thus forming a mold; little holes are left in this outer covering. When it is heated, the wax melts and drips out. It is then buried to give the outer shell greater strength and the molten bronze is poured into it. The *sand casting* method requires covering the plaster model with refractory material and sand; then it is surrounded by a metal flask. The plaster model is then destroyed, a refractory core is put inside and the molten bronze is poured.

Catacomb Underground early Christian cemeteries comprising a tight network of *ambulacra* (galleries) on several levels with niches and recesses known as *cubicolae* that contained the tombs of martyrs and where religious services were held. The *cubicolae* got air and light from cylindrical holes that opened onto the land (generally the countryside) above.

Cathedral The church in which the bishop officiates at services. The name comes from *cathedra*, the lavish wooden, marble or ivory chair used by the bishop during services, and generally located in the church *choir*.

Cavea Latin translation of the Greek word *koilon*, the tiered semicircular seating space in ancient theaters. In the Roman theaters, the word also indicated the underground chambers where wild beasts were kept.

Cave Painting Paintings that primitive people made on cave walls starting in the Paleolithic era.

Cell The sleeping rooms of monks and nuns in religious monasteries and convents.

Cella The inner, closed room in ancient temples where the statue of the divinity stood and was worshiped. For the Romans it was also the place where food and wine were stored, and hence it is any small room of a house.

Ceramic The word has its root in the Ancient Greek *kéramos* (clay). It is used to describe all wares made from clay mixtures that are modeled and shaped either mechanically or by hand and then fired in hot kilns; usually they are decorated with glazes or paints.

Chaitya   A Buddhist shrine carved into rock. A chaitya consists of a rectangular room that culminates in a semicircular *apse* in which there is a small *stupa*.

Chapel   A small, consecrated place of worship, sometimes used to bury the dead; it can be an independent building or part of a complex architectural structure (palace, castle, cemetery or church). The many chapels in Gothic churches that open onto the *ambulatory* are known as radial chapels.

Chapter   The meeting of the members of a religious community; the meaning has been extended to the room in the cathedral or monastery where the meetings were held. In convents and monasteries, the chapter room opens onto a large *cloister*.

Chia   A Chinese word for a ritual bronze tripod used to hold and heat beverages for libations.

Chiaroscuro   A monochrome (one color) painting or drawing in which the shape of the subject is created through light and dark shadings.

Choir   The portion of the *apse* behind the *altar* with stalls for the *schola cantorum*, and by extension, the apse itself.

Cistercian   From the Latin *cistercium*, which corresponds to the French *Citeaux*, and means everything that has to do with the Cistercian monastic order (strict Cluniacs) founded by Robert de Molesme.

Clay (terracotta, earthenware)   In the strict sense, one of the categories of architectural ceramics, including bricks and tiles that are fired at 2732°F (1500°C) and 1832°F (1000°C), respectively. In the broad sense the term is applied to a type of porous pottery ware that may or may not be colored and is generally uncoated. *Glazed* refers to a terracotta that is covered with a lead-based paint known as *glaze*. The word is sometimes used as a synonym for ceramic. Ceramics, be they modeled manually or mechanically, are generally baked in kilns; among the native populations of Africa, Oceania, and South America they are baked outdoors. The items are placed one on top of the other, covered with dry branches, and then a fire is lit. This technique, however, does not make it possible to reach high temperatures, for even firing. In Asia,

the kilns are long and tilted so that the items can be arranged according to the various temperature levels that develop within. In China and Japan, since the earliest times, the ceramicists used vertical kilns that permitted accurate control of the temperature for firing various types of wares.

Cloister   The inner courtyard of a monastery or convent, sometimes annexed to the *cathedral*, surrounded by a portico and *loggia*; often there is a well in the middle.

Codex   From the Latin *codicem* (writing tablet), originally a set of wooden panels for writing. Later, the term was applied to manuscripts of unbound pages. The pages were generally made of parchment (sheep vellum) as opposed to papyrus. From the first to fourth centuries C.E. the codex gradually replaced the *scroll*.

Coffered   A ceiling with even, decorated "boxes" created by the intersection of the beams. During the classical and mainly Roman periods they were made of stone; the coffers, also known as *lacunars*, were revived during the Renaissance.

Concrete   A mixture of gravel or mortar used in constructing buildings or roads.

Corbel vault   Also known as the Mayan vault, a ceiling structure which, starting from two parallel walls, rises obliquely to form a more or less pointed *arch*; the structural stones are slightly staggered with respect to each other.

Cornice   In architecture, the horizontal projecting, molded member that crowns the element (e.g. door, window, etc.). In classical architecture it is the uppermost part of the *entablature*.

Cornucopia   A horn-shaped vessel overflowing with fruit and flowers; a symbol of abundance.

Crypt   For the Greeks and then for the Romans it was a secret, underground place for religious or funerary purposes. In the Christian *basilica* it is the underground chamber with a vaulted ceiling that contains the remains of the martyr over which the church is built. The columns of the crypt support the floor of the presbytery, the part of the church reserved for the officiating clergyman, and thus it is raised with respect to the central *nave*.

Cubism   Intellectual painting movement that developed in Paris in around 1907

with works by Georges Braque and Pablo Picasso who, according to some critics, had a tendency to "reduce everything to cubes."

Curia   In the Roman Catholic Church, the organizations, persons, and offices that assist the pope and bishops in governing and administrating the Church. By extension, the bishop's residence.

D

Decoration   The complex of paintings, sculptures, and architectural elements that embellish and decorate a building.

Diptych   A double tablet used in antiquity, generally of carved ivory and coated with wax to enable it to be used for writing; diptychs were generally given as gifts for special and happy occasions. The term is also used for a religious painting, the two parts of which are joined by a hinge.

Divisionism   Also known as Pointillism, a painting movement that spread through France and Italy during the late-nineteenth century; the technique did not mix colors, but applied them pure to the canvas in small dots.

Dome   Curved roof of a building, set on a circular or polygonal base around its own axis. It may be perfectly round, ellipsoidal or elongated.

E

Earthenware   Any object or artwork made of clay, terracotta.

Echinus   In architecture, a flat, ring shaped element between the column and *abacus* on the *Doric* and *Ionic capital*.

Elevation   In architectural drawing, the projection of a building on a plane perpendicular to the horizon.

Entablature   A horizontal structure in classical architecture supported by columns and consisting in the *cornice*, *frieze*, and *architrave*.

Etching   A technique for engraving metal. A copper or zinc plate is coated with a greasy, acid-resistant ground. A metal point is used to scratch the motif on the coating. The plate is then placed into a mordent (diluted nitric acid) that eats away the exposed metal. The coating is then removed; the plate is inked and wiped clean, so that the ink only remains in the grooves created by the point and acid. The print is made by running the plate and the previously-moistened paper through a press.

F

Façade   The front of a building; the face (side, rear) of a building that is given special architectural treatment.

Fauvism   The young painters of bright, aggressively colored works at the 1905 *Salon d'Automne* in Paris were ironically dubbed *fauves*, i.e. wild beasts, by the critics. This movement, one of the main trends through which European expressionism was manifested, is characterized by the recovery of emotion that influences the use of color in an anti-naturalistic manner, applied pure and without shadings or nuances. Matisse was the outstanding member of this compact group that included Derain, Vlaminck, Camoin and Dufy.

Foreshortening   A perspective method or device that distorts or foreshortens a figure or body that is not parallel to the plane of the image in order to create a three-dimensional effect.

Forum   During Roman times, often the main square, where citizens met to do business, administer justice, hold markets. According to the importance of the city, the forum was embellished with lavish structures for various purposes: *basilicas*, *arches*, *loggias*, and *temples*.

Frame   In painting or sculpture it is the painted, sculpted, stone, metal or wooden piece that encloses the object.

Fresco   Wall painting technique. Pigments dissolved in water are quickly applied to still-wet *plaster* so that they are absorbed as it dries and become one with the wall; they can only be touched up with tempera.

Frieze   An ornamental painted or sculpted band. In a classical building, the portion of the *entablature* between the *architrave* and *cornice*. The *Doric* frieze consists of alternating *triglyphs* and *metopes* while the *Ionic* frieze is generally decorated with a continuous carved relief.

G

Gallery   A covered passageway, corridor or *loggia* with one side that is windowed and the other decorated with artwork; used as the room to receive visitors and for social occasions in patrician homes. Subsequently, the term began to be used for art exhibitions. In churches it is an elevated passageway supported by the lateral *naves* or situated above the spans of the central nave, below the wall illuminated by the windows.

Genre Painting   A painted work that portrays daily life or anecdotal scenes, distinguished by liveliness and a wealth of detail.

Glazed Bricks   Generally porous bricks that are coated and waterproofed by colored paint.

Gothic   A style that originated in northern France in around the second half of the thirteenth century. In Italy it was the expression of the culture of the communal period, while in France it represented the artistic language of the royal courts. The Gothic style (named thusly during the Renaissance, with reference to the cultures beyond the Alps that brought it to Italy) is dominated by "linear" effects that suggest tension and upward soaring motion; sometimes it develops in undulations to emphasize delicate structures. A main feature of this style is the pointed or *ogee* arch and the gradual lightening of the parts between *pillars*.

Gutta   Also *campana, drop, treenail*, a decorative motif on Doric *entablatures*, consisting in a small, truncated cone situated below the *triglyph*.

H

Haruspicy   The ancient Etruscan art of divination by interpreting natural phenomena, such as the flight of birds, or examining animal entrails. The Romans adopted the practice and entrusted it to priests known as *augurs*.

Hieroglyphic   An ideographic form of writing used by the ancient Egyptians, Hittites, and other eastern peoples.

I

Iconoclasm   A radical and violent condemnation of the worship and representation of devotional images.

Iconography   In the broad sense, the discipline that studies the meaning of images from the historical, cultural, allegorical, mythological and religious points of view. A distinction has been drawn between *iconography* and *iconology*. The first is dedicated to the recognition and identification of the subject; the second, to the "cultural" interpretation of the artistic form—a search for the intrinsic meaning in the artwork.

Ideogram   A method of writing consisting in symbols that represent an image or idea rather than a single phonetic value or sound.

Illumination   Also miniating, a painting technique that originated in the Far East on parchment, paper, or ivory. The term derives from *minium* (a reddish-orange pigment used by scribes to draw the rubrics, i.e. the first letters of a chapter or page of a manuscript); it also applied to each illustration in a *codex*.

Impressionism   A painting movement that developed in France between 1867 and 1880. The group, which originally consisted in Monet, Pissarro, Guillaumin, and Cézanne, would meet at the Académie Suisse in Paris. They shared a common interest in anti-academic painting, and turned towards naturalism and the individual's impression of the subject—no matter what it was. The first real results came about between 1867 and 1869 when Monet began painting the beaches of Normandy outdoors and, along with Renoir and Pissarro, he tried to reproduce the effects of light on water on canvas. The Franco-Prussian War (1870) broke up the group. The painters went their different ways and each developed his own individual style. Salient features of Impressionist painting are: a commitment to painting from life, the use of complementary colors, the elimination of *chiaroscuro*, and the "devaluation" of the subject.

Incrustation   Decoration of a masonry surface using materials of different color and consistency.

K

Kore In Greek the word means *girl*. In archaeology, the archaic figure of a standing young female wearing a long dress.

Kouros In Greek the word means *boy* or *youth*. In archaeology, an archaic statue depicting a standing, naked, young male figure. It is the male counterpart of the *kore*.

Krater Large, wide-mouthed vase used at banquets in ancient times to mix and serve water and wine.

L

Lacquer A varnish obtained from the sap of the *Rhus vernicifera*, used in the Far East, especially in China and Japan, to decorate wood and metal artistic objects.

Lamassu Assyrian-Babylonian divinity portrayed as a winged bull with a human head; figures of Lamassu were placed at the entrances of buildings.

Leaf Each of the two lateral panels (also known as *doors*) that close and protect an altarpiece.

Lithography A print-making technique developed at the end of the eighteenth century and still used today for fine prints. A design is drawn on a special type of stone using a wax pencil. The pencil marks retain the ink, while the stone, which is treated with acid, repels it. The inked design is transferred onto moistened paper by a press.

Loggia A structure that is open to the outside at least on one side, with columns, *pillars* or *balustrades*, often used as a meeting or gathering place.

M

Madrash A Muslim religious school where the Koran and law are taught.

Majolica A porous ceramic with glazed enamel finish. The word comes from the Spanish city *Majorca*, an important manufacturing center of these wares.

Manner A word generally used in sixteenth-century art literature, meaning style with either positive or negative connotations.

Mannerism Rather than a true painting movement, the term refers to specific aspects of sixteenth-century visual arts, and extends to a style that was no longer based on imitations of Nature but on the styles of masters such as Leonardo da Vinci, Raphael, and Michelangelo. Current criticism tends to re-evaluate the accusations (of artificiality, bizarreness as an end unto itself and the lack of naturalism) that were launched against Mannerism in seventeenth-century art criticism and never brought forth until 1920. The anti-classical trends are now interpreted as symptomatic or symbolic of the turbulent historical background and atmosphere of spiritual unrest during the period. A typical feature of Mannerist works is the almost obsessive formal elegance, a quest for variety and complexity of composition, the "spiral" shapes, unusual colors and color combinations and the haunted facial expressions

Martyrium A church or chapel with a central plan and dome built over the tomb of a martyr. The *martyrium* is typical of Byzantine art.

Mastaba Ancient Egyptian burial structure consisting of a square brick or stone covered tumulus above the underground burial chamber, and connected to the top of the tumulus via a shaft. Inside the mastaba was the room for ritual offerings and a *cubiculum* (a secret room that contained the statue or sarcophagus of the deceased). The mastabas built for the pharaohs reached considerable size, starting from the First Dynasty, and were so richly decorated on the outside that they resembled royal palaces. During the Third Dynasty they began to be built as step pyramids, the most famous of which is the pyramid of the pharaoh Gioser at Saqqarah (ca. 2600 B.C.E.) and constructed on a traditional mastaba.

Mausoleum The word comes from Mausolus, ruler of Caria (died 350 B.C.E.), who was commemorated by a lavish tomb at Halicarnassus, considered one of the wonders of the ancient world. The term is now used for a magnificent tomb for one or more famous figures.

Metallurgy The processing and refining of metals.

Metope A square space, usually decorated with carvings, between two *triglyphs* on Doric *friezes*.

Mihrab In mosques, the niche indicating the *qibla*, which is in the direction of Mecca. Muslims turn in this direction when they pray.

Minaret The balconied tower of the *mosque* from which the *muezzin* calls the faithful to prayer.

Missorium A lavish precious metal, glass or ceramic plate used in the late Roman era.

Molding In architecture and the applied arts each long, narrow, and strip element that protrudes from the surface of a structure; it may be flat, curved or otherwise contoured. Essentially a decorative element, it can be made of various materials and created to enhance an architectural structure.

Mortar A mixture consisting of binder (lime, cement, or gypsum plaster) mixed with water, and sometimes sand; used in masonry or plastering.

Mosaic A technique of arranging small pieces of colored stone, marble or glass paste known as *tesserae* to create a pattern. The technique was born in the East and if the Chaldeans made limited use of it, the Egyptians used it very skillfully. The Greeks used mosaic widely for floor decorations; it was very popular among the Romans and was known as *opus sectile* if made with rectangular bits of stone, and *opus tessellatum* if the pieces were cubic. Wall mosaics made with glass paste tiles date from the Alexandrian era and were the typical art form used by the Byzantines. The small, brightly colored tiles that were sometimes arranged in undulating rows (*opus vermiculatum*) were rendered particularly brilliant by the clever use of *gold leaf* (metallic tiles) and the careful arrangement that used a variable slant with respect to the base surface.

Mosque A building used for Muslim public religious worship and teaching. In early times it also had a civic purpose: the place for political discussions, administration of justice, meetings, bargaining and shelter.

N

Nave The longitudinal space in a church, divided by rows of single or multiple columns or *pillars*. The nave going down the middle is known as the central nave; the others are called lateral naves.

Necropolis In Greek the word means *city of the dead*. It is a group of ancient tombs, an important cemetery. Originally, *necropolis* was the name of a suburb of Alexandria, Egypt that was specifically built for burying the dead.

Neo-Impressionism An artistic movement that developed in France in around 1886 to highlight and restore the meanings of the *Impressionists'* theories to rigorous criteria.

Neolithic A stone age period that is distinguished from the Paleolithic because it replaced chipped stone tools with polished, ground implements. Neolithic man lived in constructed dwellings, grew crops, and domesticated animals.

O

Obelisk A very elongated, monolithic, truncated, pyramid-shaped pillar often inscribed with hieroglyphics. Of Eastern origin and typical of Egyptian art, obelisks were raised on square bases for commemorative or decorative purposes.

Opus alexandrinum Decorative pavement mosaic work, using tiny pieces of colored stone and glass paste to create geometric patterns.

Orders Systems of architecture deriving from the deliberate application of certain rules concerning the shape and proportions of columns in Greek and Roman art. Within the context of these orders the artist could work with total creative freedom. Essential factors for classifying buildings in a given architectural order are the column, specifically the *capital*, and the *entablature*. The Greek orders were *Doric, Ionic* and *Corinthian;* to these two Roman orders were added: *Tuscan* (of Etruscan origin) and *Composite*. During the Renaissance and the Baroque era, the treatise writers also distinguished the *gigantic* or *colossal* order (occupying the entire façade of a building), the *rustic*, and the *figured*.

P

Palette A tool used by painters to prepare and mix oil, tempera or water paints; usually a simple board of wood, enameled metal or porcelain. The palette has a hole for the thumb, while its weight is supported by the forearm. By extension, the word is used to describe the color range that distinguishes a given artist.

Panel A flat element of a structure that is usually set within a frame, having a structural or, more frequently, decorative purpose. In the latter case it is painted or sculpted. The term is also used for each of the sections or tablets of a polyptych.

Pantheon Originally the word meant a temple dedicated to all the gods and goddesses. Later it became synonymous with the monumental building raised to commemorate the memory of illustrious figures. The word also means all the divinities comprising a polytheistic religion.

Peripteral Temple A temple having a row of columns on all sides.

Peristyle (Peristyilium) The colonnade surrounding a building or court; or an open space surrounded by a colonnade.

Perspective A field of descriptive geometry concerned with the depiction of three-dimensional bodies in plane from a specific viewpoint. In art, the term is generally used to describe the rendering of space typical of specific artists or periods. Thus, there are as many types of perspective as there are concepts of space in various eras and cultures.

Pi Chinese term for a jade disc with a gilded center, symbolizing heaven and perhaps imperial power.

Pilaster Strips An upright architectural member, built against and only slightly projecting from a wall; used to break up the monotony of a *façade*. Having only an ornamental, non-structural function, it is decorated identically to the load-bearing columns and *pillars*.

Pillar A generally quadrangular architectural-structural element with a polygonal or composite base; it serves the same purpose as the column and can be plain or decorated, with or without base and *capital*; it may stand alone, at a corner or against a wall. The Gothic pillar, known as the *bundle* or *clustered* pillar, consists in co-penetrating columns and pilaster strips that stand against each other. A *trumeau* is the central pillar supporting the *tympanum* of a large doorway, as in a Gothic cathedral.

Plan A horizontal representation of a building, part of a building or architectural element. The Greek cross-plan has four equal arms. The Latin cross-plan has a short cross arm traversing the longer arm above the middle. The radial is typical of Romanesque churches and is characterized by a series of small *apses* arranged as rays around the central apse that are reached via an aisle known as the *ambulatory*.

Plaster A smooth and level layer of mortar used to prepare walls for painting.

Pointillism From the French verb *pointiller* (to dot). Painting technique that consists in applying pure color in tiny, separate dots. Also known as *Divisionism*.

Polis The Ancient Greek city-state that developed during the Classical period.

Polychrome With many colors, generally with a pleasing decorative effect.

Portal The monumental entrance to civic and religious buildings, where elaborate *reliefs* or architectural compositions flank and crown the opening.

Post-Impressionism Artistic movement that developed in France in around 1880–1890. Specifically, it refers to the works of a group of artists (Cézanne, Seurat, Van Gogh, Gauguin, Toulouse-Lautrec, etc.) who, after their Impressionist periods, went off in several directions with the aim of going beyond the achievements of Manet, Degas, Renoir, and Monet.

Propylaea Monumental entrance, on the west side, to the Acropolis in Athens; by extension, the vestibule or doors to a holy area or a series of religious buildings (singular: *propylaeum*).

Psalter Book of Psalms; specifically the one hundred fifty psalms especially arranged for liturgical use according to the Divine Office of the Roman Catholic Church.

Pulpit Elevated, usually enclosed platform used in preaching or conducting religious services; also known as *tribune*.

Pyramid Typical architectural structure of Ancient Egypt and Pre-Columbian Mexico. As opposed to the Egyptian model, the Central American pyramid is terraced and truncated at the top, where a temple usually stands on a platform. Furthermore, the Central American pyramid was used primarily for worship as opposed to the Egyptian structure, which was built to house tombs. The only exception is the Palenque Temple of the Inscriptions, which contains the sarcophagus of the king, Pacál.

Q

Qibla   The wall in each *mosque* that faces Mecca.

Quadratura   Also known as perspective wall painting on *vaults*, *cupolas*, walls, and ceilings in the seventeenth and eighteenth centuries that created faux architectural scenes. The artists who did this type of work were known as *quadraturists*.

Quoin   Any of the large stones, bricks, or wooden parts forming the exterior corner joining two walls that differ from the walls in material, texture, color, size or projection. Also the keystone of an arch.

R

Relief   Technique of sculpting or carving figures that protrude from the base to varying extents: *high relief*, *bas-relief*, and *stiacciato*.

Renaissance   The term is commonly used to designate a specific period in European art and culture spanning the fourteenth through sixteenth centuries (the chronology is still the subject of debate). The name derives from *rebirth* of the ancient ideals and the return to classical antiquity (in the sense of reconsideration and revival of the Greco-Roman heritage).

Rib   The curved, protruding cordon that supports a *vault* both transversally and at the intersection of two vaults; in this case the ribs divide the vault, called a *cross vault*, into segments that are called *vaulting cells*. In Gothic architecture the very prominent rib is mainly ornamental.

Rococo   Architectural and decorative style that originated in eighteenth-century France. The word itself was a lighthearted reference to the overuse of *rocaille* (artificial grottoes, garden pavilions, fountains, etc., made of extravagantly carved and placed rocks). Although it dominated the European scene

from 1715 to 1760 it did not influence official or religious architecture to any significant extent, since they remained linked to the classic, late-Baroque style. Instead it was prominent in aristocratic homes: *bagatelles*, *sans-soucis*, and *ermitages*.

Roman Painting   The pictorial evidence of Ancient Rome has come down to us primarily in the form of the wall paintings of Pompeii and Herculaneum. They are divided into four styles documented up to 79 C.E., the year the cities were destroyed:
- *First Style*: (from 200 to 80-30 B.C.E.), **incrustation** imitating marble baseboards and horizontal stripes, created with stucco;
- *Second Style*: (from 98-80 B.C.E. to the end of the first century B.C.E.), *architectural* depicting of landscapes and buildings, it is a Roman interpretation of Hellenistic art;
- *Third Style*: (from the end of the first century B.C.E. to the middle of the first century C.E.): *ornamental*, characterized by great use of color and finely executed details.
- *Fourth Style*: (from 35-45 C.E. to the final decades of the first century C.E.): *fantastic*, a development of the previous style, extending the use of imaginary motifs and plays of perspective; portrayals of nude figures and erotic themes are frequent.

Romanesque   Artistic style that developed and spread through Europe starting in the eleventh century; the name is related to the concomitant development of the Romance languages because of the ideal desire to reconnect with the forms of Ancient Roman civilization and art.

Rood-Screen   A thin wooden or masonry wall in Medieval churches that separated the clergy from the faithful.

Rose Window   A large, circular window with splayed and radiating sections, serving a primarily decorative purpose on the *façade* of a church. Usually over the *portal* or sometimes at the end of the *transept*. It is typical of Romanesque and Gothic cathedrals; when it includes small bars arranged in spokes it is called a *wheel window*.

Rusticated   A word to describe the outer facing of the external walls of a building, made with stone blocks that are textured, hewn into patterns or otherwise accented or with emphasized joints.

S

Sacristy   Room adjacent to a church in which church ornaments and vestments are stored in special (often carved or inlaid) cabinets.

Sarcophagus   Ancient stone or marble coffin. The word comes from the Greek *sarkophagos* (flesh-eating [stone]—a type of limestone that hastened the disintegration of the body put in it).

Sardonyx   Literally, *onxy from Sardi* (Lydia). It is a brown and white streaked agate.

Scarification   A body ornamentation technique in use among peoples of Africa and Oceania. They make cuts in the skin and then fill the wound with various substances that retard healing and increase the thickness of the scars.

Scribe   In the ancient world a person who wrote, translated, or copied documents.

Scriptorium   In the Middle Ages, the room or *cell* in a monastery used for copying ancient texts; usually part of an *abbey*. There were also *scriptoria* connected to *chapters*, *cathedrals* and bishops' schools.

Scroll   Ancient manuscripts on strips of papyrus rolled around a small wooden or bone cylinder. This term is also used to describe Medieval documents that are rolled, such as *liturgical scrolls* used in southern Italy from the tenth to fourteenth centuries with prayers and *illuminations*.

Sfumato   A term used to describe a technique similar to *chiaroscuro* based on definition of shapes through delicate gradations from light to shadow, with specific reference to the works of Leonardo da Vinci and his pupils.

Shell   A building without any accessories, decorations or partitions.

Sikhara   A complex, often very tall pyramidal structure with rounded corners often culminating in a more or less flattened cushion over the *cella*– a sanctuary in medieval Hindu temples.

Sketch   A quickly executed drawing or painting that captures the essential features of an idea, or a preparation for a subsequent project.

Span   Each element in a sequence of *arches* or *vaults*.

Splay Oblique flaring of a wall around windows or doors to control light. It was typical of the Romanesque and Gothic styles and could go either inwards or outwards and was often decorated with elongated motifs or figures.

Stele A commemorative stone slab or *pillar*, with carved figures or inscriptions erected over a holy or otherwise significant site, frequently over tombs. In use since the time of the Ancient Greeks, they were also erected by the Etruscans and Romans and returned to fashion during the Neoclassical period.

Stiacciato Renaissance artists used this term to describe a type of low *relief* that created a sensation of deep atmospheric space. This illusion of planes was achieved by the clever use of *perspective*.

Stucco A slow-hardening modeling material made of lime, cooked gypsum, *pozzolana*, clay, and marble powder used mainly indoors for relief decoration of walls and ceilings. Stucco work may be colored or gilded.

Stupa Originally, a simple burial mound that in India was placed over the remains of a chief. Later, the stupa became the typical Buddhist monument: built with a circular *plan*, it is lavishly decorated and sometimes completely covered with statuary and bas-relief work. It is generally encircled by a balustrade (*vedika*) with one to four monumental portals (*torana*) facing the cardinal directions. The stupa conserves relics of the Buddha or the ashes of eminent religious figures.

Stylobate The high pavement on which classical architectural columns stand.

Sumptuary Laws Laws that limited excesses in luxury; were passed several times during the Middle Ages.

Symbolism An artistic movement that originated in literature and then developed in France after 1885. In painting it is characterized by a predilection for exoticism and the primarily decorative use of color.

T

Tabularium Archive. One of the most famous was built on the Capitoline Hill in Rome by Lutatius Catulus in 78 B.C.E.

to house the State documents (*tabulae*); this building was connected to the *forum* by a grand staircase.

Tapering Gradual decrease in the diameter of a column that may begin at the base or from the top of the lower third.

Tapestry Hand-woven fabric in which the weft threads are arranged to create a pattern; used as a lavish wall decoration.

Tarsia Creation of designs or patterns using different color and quality woods, as well as metal, mother-of-pearl or ivory on an underlying support surface. Since the Middle Ages the synonym *inlay* has been used.

Temple A building consecrated to the worship of a divinity. Often considered the home of the god whose image was housed therein. The word, from the Latin *templum* which in turn came from the Greek *témenos* meaning *holy enclosure*, was for Ancient Romans the part of the sky used by the augurs to predict the future. The idea of the temple as the home of the god led to its being built as a palace proper in the Assyrian, Babylonian, and Egyptian civilizations as well as in Ancient Greece and Rome. The temples consisted essentially of the *cella* (the room containing the idol that only the priests could enter) and a porch. Often, a second porch was built behind the *cella* to make the structure symmetrical. In the most important temples the central part was surrounded by a colonnade, known as the *peristyle*.

Tesserae Small pieces of stone or glass paste used in making *mosaics*.

Theater In Ancient Greece an outdoor structure where the great tragedies and comedies were performed. Originally the theater was a place of worship: the performances were linked to the Dionysian rites. The *orchestra* was the area where the actors moved about and where the altar of the god stood. The spectators sat on tiered seats built into the natural slope of the land. The *scene* was opposite the seats and it was completed with a row of columns.

Tholos A sacred, round, domed Mycenaean structure with protruding rectangular stones carved into rock. The *tholos* is accessed via a narrow corridor known as the *dromos*.

Ting A quadrangular or round Chinese ritual bronze vessel with handles and

cylindrical feet for preparing food. *Ting* is also a type of white paste pottery decorated with simple, incised lines typical of the Sung period.

Tomb Burial site, often built with deliberate monumental intentions. After the Neolithic monuments, the Egyptian *pyramids* are the grandiose example of burial architecture. *Mastabas* and underground tombs, *hypogea*, were added to the pyramids. Mycenaean tombs were circular *tholos*. The Ancient Greeks would mark graves with *stele*. The Etruscans, like the later Romans, built *tumuli* and terracotta or stone *sarcophagi*.

Tondo A round painting or bas-relief sculpture highly favored by Renaissance artists.

Transept The transverse *nave* in Latin cross-plan churches.

Triforium Gallery above the lateral *naves* in Romanesque and Gothic cathedrals that opens onto the central nave with triple-lighted windows separating the narrow pillars or columns.

Triglyphs Tablets with vertical channels between *metopes* on *friezes* of Doric temples.

Trompe-l'oeil In French the expression literally means "to fool the eye." A style of painting of accentuated naturalism that uses perspective and compositional and technical devices to obtain illusionist effects that create surprisingly real-looking images and spaces.

Trumeau The central *pillar* in the entrance door of a Gothic cathedral.

Ts'un A large, flared, bronze Chinese ritual vessel for containing beverages. The term also applies to a group of variously shaped ritual vessels that cannot be otherwise classified.

Ts'ung A jade object used in ancient China decorated with a series of complex notches. It symbolized the Earth and the Empress. It could also have had astronomical uses.

Tumbaga An alloy consisting of gold and copper in varying proportions used in pre-Columbian jewelry.

Tympanum A smooth or carved architectural element between the *entablature* and the oblique *cornices* of the *pediment*.

V

Vault The curved ceiling of a building comprising stone *arches* on imposts that support each other. The designations vary according to the styles and features: the *round vault* describes a semi-circle; the *barrel vault* is semi-cylindrical; the *cross vault* is obtained from the perpendicular intersection of two barrel vaults; the *Gothic cross vault* consists in two load-bearing arches or ribs that distribute the weight of the entire arch on the four corner pillars of the *span*.

Vihara A Buddhist monastery with *cells* for the monks, refectories, and large common rooms. The simple, linear *plan* is always the same, though the size varies according to the number of stories.

W

Wall Painting Also known as *murals* these are paintings that are done directly on the wall of a building.

Watercolor Painting technique using colored pigments mixed with gum arabic diluted in water and applied to paper or silk with a brush. Watercolor painting does not permit *pentimento*, or touch-ups. Colors are lightened by diluting the paint against the background rather than by blending with white paint.

Wing Lateral part of a building.

Z

Ziggurat Stepped towers typical of Mesopotamian religious architecture. At the top of these gigantic structures stood a temple where the priests made sacrifices and offerings to the gods.

INDEX OF NAMES AND PLACES

Page numbers in boldface refer to pages in this volume.

G

L

PHOTOGRAPHIC
ACKNOWLEDGMENTS

All the photographs are from Scala Archives, Florence, except the following:

Ancient Art and Architectural Collection, London: 24 fig. 7; 35 fig. 1; 37 fig. 5; 38 fig. 9; 117 fig. 10; 149 fig. 7; 156 fig. 2–3; 157 fig. 5; 167 fig. 12; 193 fig. 8; 194 fig. 13; 295 fig. 6; 296 fig. 9; 298 fig. 16, 18; 315 fig. 14; 317 fig. 18; 382 fig. 13; 386 fig. 3; 411 fig. 6–8.
Architectural Association, London: 437 fig. 5–6; 438 fig. 10–11; 441 fig. 16; 450 fig. 20; 457 fig. 7; 463 fig. 25; 464 fig. 28; 465 fig. 31–32; 469 fig. 5; 475 fig. 22; 476 fig. 23, 24, 26.
Archiv für Kunst und Geschichte, Berlin: 109 fig. 8–9; 407 fig. 19.
Art Resource, New York: 392 fig. 17; 408 fig. 23.
G. Barone, Florence: 103 fig. 23, 25; 160 fig. 15; 173 fig. 5; 182 fig. 8.
Borromeo, Milan: 39 fig. 12; 133 fig. 8.
Bridgeman Art Library, London: 167 fig. 11; 292 fig. 23; 318 fig. 20; 378 fig. 3–4; 379 fig. 5–6; 383 fig. 14; 384 fig. 16; 409 fig. 1; 412 fig. 11.
British Library, London: 153 fig. 19.
British Museum, London: 31 fig. 14; 105 fig. 1; 108 fig. 6; 140 fig. 4; 296 fig. 10; 384 fig. 17; 397 fig. 12; 416 fig. 21.
L. Caraffini, Rome: 328 fig. 26–27.
E. Ciol, Casarsa: 160 fig. 14.
Colotheque, Bruxelles: 339 fig. 5.
C. Costa, Milan: 211 fig. 19.
Daitokuji, Kyoto: 142 fig. 10.
De Antonis, Rome: 83 fig. 29; 100 fig. 15; 260 fig. 30.

R. De Meo, Florence: 326 fig. 20; 327 fig. 23.
D. R.: 121 fig. 1; 122 fig. 2–4; 123 fig. 5–7; 124 fig. 8–10; 125 fig. 11–13; 126 fig. 14–16; 127 fig. 17–18; 128 fig. 19–21; 129 fig. 22, 25; 130 fig. 26–27; 319 fig. 1; 320 fig. 2–3; 321 fig. 5; 322 fig. 8–9; 323 fig. 10–12; 324 fig. 13; 326 fig. 17–18; 328 fig. 24–25; 378 fig. 2; 390 fig. 12–14; 391 fig. 15–16; 398 fig. 14–15; 399 fig. 17; 450 fig. 21–22; 454 fig. 32–34; 464 fig. 30.
FMR, Milan/ Massimo Listri, Florence: 408 fig. 22.
Giraudon, Paris: 30 fig. 11; 39 fig. 11; 40 fig. 18; 41 fig. 20; 50 fig.15; 82 fig. 25; 109 fig. 10; 115 fig. 4; 117 fig. 9; 151 fig. 14–15; 153 fig. 20; 244 fig. 2; 284 fig. 3; 285 fig. 5; 310 fig. 5; 312 fig. 9; 387 fig. 4; 402 fig. 4; 403 fig. 6.
N. Grifoni, Florence: 44 fig. 28; 68 fig. 12; 297 fig. 11.
Guggenheim Museum, Venice: 458 fig. 9–11; 459 fig. 14; 460 fig. 18.
Robert Harding, London: 30 fig. 12; 34 fig. 19; 106 fig. 2; 120 fig.17; 292 fig. 24; 362 fig. 3–4; 296 fig. 8; 297 fig. 12–14; 298 fig. 17; 392 fig. 18; 410 fig. 5; 412 fig. 10; 436 fig. 4; 449 fig. 18–19.
Index, Barcelona: 148 fig. 4; 149 fig. 6.
Katsura, Imperial Villa: 367 fig. 16.
Kunsthistorisches Museum, Wien: 84 fig. 30.
National Gallery, London: 269 fig. 23; 369 fig. 9.
National Maritime Museum, London: 381 fig. 12.
National Museum, Tokyo: 142 fig. 9; 366 fig. 14; 367 fig. 15.
National Portrait Gallery, London: 316 fig. 17; 413 fig. 14.

Naturhistorisches Museum, Wien: 22 fig. 3.
Nelson Art Gallery, Atkins Museum, Kansas City: 141 fig. 7; 144 fig. 14.
Orion Press, Tokyo: 365 fig. 11–12; 366 fig. 13.
Oroñoz, Madrid: 466 fig 34.
Photoservice Fabbri, Milan: 110 fig. 13; 196 fig. 19; 268 fig. 20.
Publiaerfoto, Milan: 173 fig. 8; 272 fig. 30.
Rijksmuseum, Amsterdam: 136 fig. 15; 345 fig. 19; 388 fig. 1.
C. Savona: 469 fig. 6; 470 fig. 7; 476 fig. 25.
A. Schwarz, Milan: 457 fig. 6.
Sef, Turin: 71 fig. 17.
L. Serra, Florence: 117 fig. 11; 294 fig. 3.
Smithsonian Institution, Freer Gallery of Art, Washington: 142 fig. 9, 11: 143 fig. 12–13; 144 fig. 15; 299 fig. 20; 363 fig. 6.
Staatliche Museen, Berlin: 69 fig. 14.
Studio Pizzi, Milan: 263 fig. 5; 407 fig. 20.
Summerfield, Florence: 45 fig. 1; 46 fig. 2–3; 47 fig. 4–7; 49 fig. 9–12; 50 fig. 13–14; 51 fig. 16–19; 141 fig. 8; 360 fig. 2.
Tate Gallery, London: 377 fig. 1; 397 fig. 11; 412 fig. 12; 472 fig. 14; 473 fig. 15–17; 474 fig. 18.
Victoria and Albert Museum, London: 295 fig. 5; 361 fig. 1; 363 fig. 5, 7; 364 fig. 8–9; 365 fig. 10; 368 fig. 18; 410 fig. 4; 438 fig. 9; 439 fig. 13.
Windsor, Royal Collection: 273 fig. 1; 370 fig. 1; 383 fig. 15.
Yale University Art Gallery: 392 fig. 19.

© S.I.A.E.: 434 fig. 30–32; 444 fig. 1; 445 fig. 4, 6; 446 fig. 8–11; 447 fig. 12–14; 448 fig. 16–17; 451 fig. 26; 452 fig. 28–29; 453 fig. 30; 456 fig. 1–3; 457 fig. 5–6; 458 fig. 10–11; 459 fig. 12–14; 460 fig. 15–18; 461 fig. 19–21; 462 fig. 24; 466 fig. 34; 468 fig. 2; 471 fig. 11, 13; 473 fig. 15, 17; 474 fig. 18–20.